PENGUIN CLASSICS

THE COMPLETE POEMS AND TRANSLATIONS
OF CHRISTOPHER MARLOWE

CHRISTOPHER MARLOWE (b. 1564) was the eldest son of Canterbury shoemaker John Marlowe, and his wife, Katherine. He was elected to the King's School Canterbury at the age of fourteen, and within two years had secured a scholarship that took him to Corpus Christi College, Cambridge, where he was supposedly destined for a career in the Anglican Church. He successfully completed his BA examinations in 1584, and continued his studies as a candidate for the MA. During this period his absences from Cambridge stirred rumors that he was about to flee to the Catholic seminary at Rheims in France. In 1587 the Privy Council took the unusual step of persuading the University authorities to grant Marlowe his MA since he had been employed "in matters touching the benefit of his country"; this has fuelled speculation that he was working as a government agent.

Marlowe probably began his writing career at Cambridge, composing translations of Ovid's *Amores*, and Lucan's *Pharsalia*, as well as producing *Dido Queen of Carthage* for the Children of the Chapel in 1586 (possibly cowritten with Thomas Nashe). In 1587–88 he acquired his reputation as one of the leading new talents on the London stage with *Tamburlaine the Great*. This was followed by *The Jew of Malta* (c. 1590), *Edward the Second,* and *The Massacre at Paris* (both c. 1592). His best known play, *Doctor Faustus*, was written in 1592. The erotic epyllion *Hero and Leander* was probably written in 1592–93 when the plague forced the theaters to close.

Throughout this period, Marlowe was frequently in trouble with the authorities, though for his actions and not his playwriting. He and the poet Thomas Watson were briefly imprisoned in September 1589 for their involvement in the death of William Bradley; in 1592 Marlowe was deported from Flushing, Holland, having been implicated in a counterfeiting scheme. He acquired a dangerous reputation as an atheist, and the following year he was summoned to appear before the Privy Council on charges of blasphemy, arising from evidence provided by Thomas Kyd, the author of the hugely popular play *The Spanish Tragedy*.

Several days later, on May 30, 1593, Christopher Marlowe was fatally stabbed in Deptford.

STEPHEN ORGEL is the Jackson Eli Reynolds Professor in Humanities at Stanford and general editor of the Cambridge Studies in Renaissance Literature and Culture. The most recent of his many books are *Imagining Shakespeare* (2003) and *The Authentic Shakespeare* (2002). He has edited editions of Shakespeare's plays for Oxford, as well as works by Jonson, Marlowe, Milton, Trollope, and Edith Wharton. He is the general editor of the Pelican Shakespeare series and edited the individual Pelican editions of *King Lear, The Taming of the Shrew, Pericles, Macbeth,* and *The Sonnets.*

CHRISTOPHER MARLOWE

The Complete Poems and Translations

Edited with an Introduction by
STEPHEN ORGEL

PENGUIN BOOKS

PENGUIN BOOKS

Published by the Penguin Group

Penguin Group (USA) Inc., 375 Hudson Street,
New York, New York 10014, U.S.A.

Penguin Group (Canada), 90 Eglinton Avenue East, Suite 700, Toronto, Ontario, Canada M4P 2Y3
(a division of Pearson Penguin Canada Inc.)

Penguin Books Ltd, 80 Strand, London WC2R 0RL, England

Penguin Ireland, 25 St Stephen's Green, Dublin 2, Ireland
(a division of Penguin Books Ltd)

Penguin Group (Australia), 250 Camberwell Road, Camberwell, Victoria 3124, Australia
(a division of Pearson Australia Group Pty Ltd)

Penguin Books India Pvt Ltd, 11 Community Centre,
Panchsheel Park, New Delhi – 110 017, India

Penguin Group (NZ), 67 Apollo Drive, Rosedale, North Shore 0745,
Auckland, New Zealand (a division of Pearson New Zealand Ltd.)

Penguin Books (South Africa) (Pty) Ltd, 24 Sturdee Avenue,
Rosebank, Johannesburg 2196, South Africa

Penguin Books Ltd, Registered Offices:
80 Strand, London WC2R 0RL, England

First published in Penguin Books (U.K.) 1971
Published in Penguin Books (U.S.A.) 1980
This edition with a new introduction and notes by Stephen Orgel published 2007

Introduction copyright © Stephen Orgel, 2007
Notes copyright © Penguin Group (USA) Inc., 2007
All rights reserved

ISBN 978-0-14-310495-7
CIP data available

Printed in the United States of America
Set in Adobe Sabon

146122990

Contents

Introduction

Christopher Marlowe was christened in the church of St. George the Martyr in Canterbury on February 26, 1564. He was the son of a shoemaker in the town. We know nothing of his childhood, but at the age of fourteen he was granted a scholarship to the King's School in Canterbury. His education there would have been heavily classical, and he clearly emerged as a superlative Latinist—since his tenure at the school was little over a year, he must already have been very proficient when he entered. In 1581 he obtained a scholarship to Corpus Christi College, Cambridge, where he remained for seven years, earning a BA in 1584 and an MA in 1587. During this time he apparently had other employment, as an agent of the Privy Council—a government spy, providing intelligence about recusants and expatriate Roman Catholics. The conferral of his own degree was delayed because of suspicions about his loyalty and was only awarded after an assurance was obtained from the Council that he had done good service to the crown.

After his college years, we know little about his life until the end of it. He was killed in a tavern brawl—or perhaps assassinated in what was represented as a tavern brawl—in 1593, when he was not yet thirty years old. In those six years, whatever else he was doing, Marlowe revolutionized English drama and gave a new voice to Elizabethan poetry. Most of what we must use to construct a biography is gossip or invective, for the most part posthumous. In 1588 he was accused by Robert Greene of atheism, or at least of promoting atheism in *Tamburlaine*. After his death Thomas Kyd, who had shared lodgings with Marlowe, testified to his "rashness in attempting sudden privy injuries to men"—Marlowe had in fact been charged in connection with a street brawl in 1589 in which a man was killed. Kyd also pursued the theme of atheism, recalling his companion's "vile heretical conceits denying the divinity of Jesus." William Baines, a paid informer, provided much more detailed and lurid testimony to Marlowe's dangerous opinions. Among these, according to Baines, were that Moses was a juggler and that Thomas Harriot, Sir Walter Ralegh's servant, "can do more than he"—this has always been taken as an invidious comparison between Harriot and Moses, but it may include something even more subversive, a claim that Ralegh's servant was a better man than Ralegh, too. Marlowe also believed, Baines said, that "the first beginning of religion was only to keep men in awe," that Christ was a bastard, his mother a whore, his father a carpenter, and the crucifixion justified; that Catholicism was a good religion and "all Protestants are hypocritical asses"; that the woman of Samaria and her sister were whores and Christ knew them "dishonestly"; that Christ was the "bedfellow" of John the Evangelist and "used him as the sinners of Sodom"; that all those who love not tobacco and boys were fools, and that he had as much right to issue currency as the queen of England, and intended "to coin French crowns, pistolets, and English shillings."[1] This looks like a jumble, and is certainly rife with contradictory assumptions; but in its historical context the charges have a basic consistency, defining a world in which heresy, scurrility, love, sodomy, counterfeiting, and most of all social mobility and the drive toward success are all aspects of the same dangerous set of desires.

Since Baines was being paid to provide damaging testimony, it would have been in his interest to make Marlowe seem as disreputable as possible. Still, there is much in the poetry and drama to support the picture of Marlowe as a seductively persuasive radical. Did this result in the proscription of his work? Not, certainly, of his drama: both during his lifetime and long after, his plays were among the most popular in the repertory. As for the poems, his Ovid translations were called in, banned, and burned by episcopal order, six years after his death; but it is not clear in this case that the proscription was aimed at Marlowe. The book

was a collection of satirical epigrams by John Davies followed
by ten of Marlowe's translations from the *Amores*—"Davyes
Epigrams, with Marlowes Elegys" is the way the order puts it.
The offensive material may well have been Davies's, and the of-
fense thus libel, not incitement to lechery. As the book is con-
stituted, Marlowe is at most guilty by association: all six early
editions of the Ovid translations include Davies's epigrams,
though those with the complete elegies put Marlowe first, and
all are published either abroad, at Middleburgh, in Holland, or
surreptiously in Scotland with a false Middleburgh imprint. If
Davies was the problem, why not publish Marlowe's Ovid by
itself? Or was it the scurrilous Davies that sold the erotic Mar-
lowe? Would a Marlowe untainted by libel not have been mar-
ketable?

ALL OVID'S ELEGIES

Marlowe's translation of the *Amores, All Ovids Elegies,* was
unpublished during Marlowe's lifetime. After his death, the
manuscript would have recommended itself to publishers not
merely as the work of Marlowe the erotic classicist, cashing in
on the success of *Hero and Leander* (also unpublished but cir-
culated in manuscript), but equally as the first translation of the
Amores not only into English but into any modern language.
The *Amores* was the least well known of Ovid's works in the
Renaissance, untouched by the allegorizing and moralizing
commentaries that had safely contextualized Ovid's other work
for Christian readers. Marlowe's interest in these poems would
have been as much in their urbanity of tone as in their world of
erotic possibilities—the social Ovid is fully complementary to
the mythological Ovid of the *Metamorphoses* and the *Fasti*. But
Marlowe's Ovidian elegies are more than translations. They un-
dertake, with remarkable energy and ingenuity, the adaptation
of a quintessentially classical mode to the uses of English po-
etry. In a sense, this is Marlowe's sonnet sequence, the psychic
drama of a poet-lover whose love is both his creation and his ul-
timate monomania, frustration, and despair. The excitement

Marlowe brought to these poems is obvious, as much in the vividness and wit of the language as in the evident haste and occasional carelessness of the composition. The six early editions, and the heavy hand of the ecclesiastical censor, testify to the excitement readers got out of the work. But licentiousness is not the *Elegies'* primary claim on our attention—indeed, by current standards they are barely warm. Their rhetoric, however, brings a new tone and a new range of possibilities into English verse. Donne's elegies are full of a sense of Marlowe's language, which looks forward, too, to Carew and Marvell, and even to Pope.

Nevertheless, *All Ovid's Elegies* is a strange book. It reads like a promising first draft, occasionally felicitous but often routine, with moments of real brilliance and also moments of striking ineptitude. Time after time, the only way to understand Marlowe's English is to use the Latin as a crib. "So, chaste Minerva, did Cassandra fall/Deflowered except, within thy temple wall" (1.7)—the Latin says that the only chastity left to Cassandra was the fact that she was raped in Minerva's temple; it's difficult to see how one would get this out of the English. "Hector to arms went from his wife's embraces,/And on Andromache his helmet laces" (1.9)—only the Latin will reveal that it is Andromache who is lacing the helmet on Hector, not the other way around. "Object thou then what she may well excuse,/To stain in faith all truth, by all crimes use" (2.2)—the Latin says "accuse her only of what she can explain away; a false charge undermines the credibility of a true one": is there any way of eliciting this from Marlowe? "Wilt thou her fault learn, she may make thee tremble;/Fear to be guilty, then thou mayst dissemble" (2.2)—even the Latin will not help to explain this. Often the gibberish is undeniably beautiful, the work of a poet with a superb ear working too fast for meaning: "What day was that which, all sad haps to bring/White birds to lovers did not always sing" (3.11)—Ovid says, this is the day when, as a permanent bad omen, love birds stopped singing; but Marlowe's version is all connotation with no denotation.

Nevertheless, the translation is an impressive achievement, especially if, as appears to be the case, it is the work of Marlowe's undergraduate years; and its completeness is not the least of its virtues. It remained unique in English until an anonymous translation appeared in 1683, followed by Dryden. As for its occasional impenetrability, the Elizabethans had a higher tolerance for obscurity than we have, and though there is evidence that Ben Jonson was involved in the preparation of at least one of the early surreptitious editions, his concern was obviously not with revision or clarification. What Marlowe undertook was the domestication of the erotic Ovid in the wake of the many previous generations' mythographic Ovid. And after Marlowe's sensational death, the combination of Ovid, Marlowe, and English would probably have been sufficient to warrant publication surreptitiously, even if John Davies's scurrilous epigrams had not been included. But since the erotic Marlowe looms so large in the modern construction of the poet, it is worth pausing over the sexuality of *All Ovid's Elegies*. How erotically transgressive is it?

Transgressive enough, certainly: it is a chronicle not merely of lechery, but of adultery, pandering, promiscuity, faithlessness, irreverence. It is even, on occasion, explicit and smutty where Ovid is merely metonymic: "The whore stands to be bought for each man's money,/And seeks vile wealth by selling of her coney" (1.10.21–2), where the Latin specifies only "corpore," her body. Ovid's urbane cynicism in English, moreover, translates directly into Marlowe's alleged atheism: "God is a name, no substance, feared in vain,/And doth the world in fond belief detain" (3.3.23–4). Reason enough to publish the book surreptitiously. Still, it is the nature of the eroticism we should pause over. Since Marlowe's homosexual interests figure so significantly in both Baines's and Kyd's charges against him, and are certainly manifest in *Edward II*, the openings of *Dido Queen of Carthage* and *Hero and Leander*, and are especially prominent in the construction of the modern Marlowe, it is worth observing that the erotics of *All Ovid's Elegies* are exclusively heterosexual—not even Cupid in Elegy 1.10 (15–17), a beautiful naked youth selling himself, without so much as a pocket to put his money in, raises Marlowe's rhetorical eyebrow. Ovid himself observes that his sexual interests are primarily in women: he says in the *Ars*

Amatoria that the sex he likes is the kind that gives equal plea-
sure to both partners, and therefore sex with boys doesn't inter-
est him much (2.683–4)—the "therefore" made sense to Roman
readers because the boy, as the passive partner in the buggery,
was supposed not to enjoy the sex, a prophylactic fiction de-
signed to license the practice of pederasty while simultaneously
preserving the youth of the realm from any suspicion of real de-
pravity.[2] If Marlowe's erotic imagination was essentially homo-
sexual, and sex was the point, Catullus, Martial, Horace, or even
the Virgil of the *Eclogues* would surely have been more likely
texts for domestication. Was it then something other than the sex
that attracted him to the *Amores?*

Perhaps so: a case can be made for the young Marlowe's
translation of the *Amores* as part of a grand design, the first
step in the creation of a poetic career consciously modeled on
Ovid, an anti-Virgilian, and anti-Spenserian, model.[3] This may
be correct; nevertheless, the sex may well have been a factor
after all: perhaps the whole question is anachronistic, the issue
construed too narrowly. Perhaps, in short, homosexuality is our
problem, not Marlowe's. The first published account of the
murder, Thomas Beard's in *The Theatre of God's Iudgments,*
1597, cites only "epicurism" and atheism as Marlowe's mortal
sins. In the next year, Francis Meres cites Beard, and adds
the information, derived from no known source, that Mar-
lowe "was stabbed to death by a bawdy serving man, a rival of
his in his lewd love"[4]—is this perhaps merely an expansion of
the implications of "epicurism"? Recently Charles Nicholl has
elaborated the account still further by suggesting that "this
serving-man was, like Marlowe, a homosexual, and that the
cause of the fight, the object of their 'lewd love,' was another
man."[5] Marlowe's sexual preferences are not really in question,
but this surely confuses the issue. To begin with, there is no rea-
son to assume that Meres has a love triangle in mind; "rival"
can mean simply "partner" (as Bernardo calls Horatio and
Marcellus "the rivals of my watch" at the opening of *Hamlet*),
and if we want Marlowe's "lewd love" to be homosexual, its
object may simply be the bawdy serving man. But it is surely to

the point that the object is unspecified, the crime "epicurism," the pursuit of pleasure. The sin is precisely the subject of the *Amores,* "lewd love," illicit sexuality, of whatever kind—if homosexuality had been a worse kind of "lewd love," Marlowe would have been guilty of it. A century later Antony à Wood elaborated Meres's account for his age as revealingly as Nicholl has done for ours: "For so it fell out that he being deeply in love with a certain woman . . . had for his rival a bawdy serving-man, one rather fit to be a pimp than an ingenious amoretto as Marlowe conceived himself to be."[6]

In fact, homosexuality in the charges against Marlowe is primarily an aspect of his blasphemy and atheism—Baines and Kyd do not assert that Marlowe was a sodomite, but that he said Christ and St. John were: this is apparently worse than being a sodomite oneself. The link between the love of boys and the love of tobacco is an intriguing one, but it is not part of a claim that Marlowe systematically debauched the youth of London, as it might well have been. Though his own works could easily have been used as evidence against him, the charge of sodomy appears almost marginal. Commentators have undertaken to connect tobacco to the charge of atheism, noting its source in the pagan New World, but this seems to me misguided. The point is the same one Jonson makes when, in *Every Man Out of His Humour,* the rustic would-be gentleman Sogliardo is discovered at a London tavern with "his villainous Ganymede . . . droning a tobacco pipe there ever since yesterday noon" (4.3.83–5). Sogliardo here is certainly assumed to be guilty of the abominable crime against nature, but this is not the issue. Pederasty and smoking are generic vices, not specific ones: Sogliardo practices them because they are the marks of the London sophisticate. His lust is, like Marlowe's, all for upward mobility, for class. The more intriguing conjunction in Baines's document is that of tobacco and Thomas Harriot. It leads us to Sir Walter Ralegh, Harriot's patron and employer, the major advocate of tobacco in Elizabethan England, investigated in 1594 on a charge of freethinking; imprisoned, however, not for atheism but for impregnating and secretly marrying, probably in that order, one of Elizabeth's maids of honor—for sexual offenses that were construed as treasonable. Thomas Kyd's charges against Marlowe explicitly associate him with the Ralegh circle, which included not only Harriot but also John Dee and Henry Percy, the "Wizard Earl" of Northumberland (of whom the *DNB* says he was "passionately addicted to tobacco smoking"). With Ralegh we are back to atheism and sex, but with Harriot, Dee, and Northumberland we have arrived at conjuring and science, the world of Marlowe's most famous play, *Doctor Faustus.*

HERO AND LEANDER

Marlowe's greatest achievement as a poet is certainly *Hero and Leander,* a passionate, tragic, comic fragment of an erotic epic. The poem is an adaptation of a late classical work by Musaeus; and its divided life is exemplified in its scholarly history. The earliest printed edition came from the press of Aldus Manutius, in Venice, in 1494, which included the Greek text with a Latin translation—its printed history begins mediated through translation. The manuscript Aldus was working from identified the poem simply as the work of Musaeus, and Aldus therefore ascribed it to the legendary poet of that name, a pupil of Orpheus, and assumed it to be the most ancient classical poetry to survive—poetry, thus, in its purest, original form. And though throughout the next century there were many doubters concerning its antiquity, it was widely praised and often translated, again into Latin, and into various vernaculars (though not English). Julius Caesar Scaliger, in his early sixteenth-century *Poetics,* notoriously preferred it to Homer, and maintained that if Musaeus had written the *Iliad* and *Odyssey,* they would have been better poems. But after the great scholar Isaac Casaubon, late in the century, demonstrated that stylistically the poem could not, in fact, be early, but was clearly a work of the fifth century A.D. (its poet is appropriately called, in a number of other early manuscripts, not Musaeus but Musaeus the Grammarian) interest in it gradually subsided. The character of the poem thus went from radical innocence to oversophistication in a very few decades.

It is customary to praise Marlowe's scholarly achievement in *Hero and Leander* by observing how accurately it captures the high rhetorical flashiness of Musaeus's style, though the style of the original is far more artificial and literary. There is no match in Musaeus for Marlowe's enthusiasm. Marlowe's excitement may be the expression of his sense of the adolescence of poetry itself; but clearly this is a classic he is having a great deal of fun with, and there surely cannot have been many other young poets in Elizabethan England to whom Greek was this much fun. Certainly when, after Marlowe's death, George Chapman undertook to complete Marlowe's fragment, it became much more serious.

Hero and Leander is very daring, in many of the ways that *Doctor Faustus* is. Like *Faustus,* it tempts the Renaissance reader with his deepest desires—the reader is in this case surely assumed to be male. If *Faustus* condemns blasphemy, the play nevertheless realizes or embodies it, represents blasphemy on the stage. *Hero and Leander* is a secular version of that Faustian presumptuousness, and all the blasphemy is sexual. The hero and heroine are incredibly, miraculously, outrageously beautiful, constantly being compared to the most perfect things imaginable: gods and goddesses; jewels; works of art; and coming out ahead. The god Apollo courted Hero ("for her hair"); Cupid himself pined for her, and mistook her for Venus; Leander was more beautiful than Endymion or Ganymede, his hair was more wonderful than the Golden Fleece, and so forth. A whole world of allusion and poetic elaboration is invoked just to adorn these two; the poem, the style, the rhetoric impose on the lovers a dangerous case of hubris; and none of this comes from Musaeus.

One of the most striking aspects of the poem is its overt sexuality. There are Italian poems like this, but almost none in English until the seventeenth century; it is emotionally very daring. It is also very open about its sexual interests—the tradition that says that Marlowe was gay gets a good deal of support from *Hero and Leander.* Both lovers are described as infinitely desirable; but the praise of Leander is much more frankly sexual

than that of Hero, and specifically homosexual. Gods and men
pine away for Hero, but the measure of Leander's beauty is not
that women desire him, but that men do: "Jove might have sipped
out nectar from his hand"—he is as desirable as Ganymede; had
Hippolytus seen him he would have abandoned his chastity;
"The barbarous Thracian soldier, moved with naught,/Was
moved with him, and for his favor sought"—rough trade solicits
him. Again, none of this comes from Musaeus, where Leander is
not described—Hero is beautiful; Leander is all desire, the vali-
dation of her beauty.

Marlowe is certainly daring, though less so in a Renaissance
context than he seems now—for adult men to be attracted to
good-looking youths was quite conventional. Still, there is no
way of arguing that it's *merely* conventional, that Marlowe
doesn't really mean it, or doesn't mean it the way it sounds. The
first sestiad includes a teasing description of how beautiful
Leander's body is—

> I could tell ye
> How smooth his breast was, and how white his belly,
> And whose immortal fingers did imprint
> That heavenly path, with many a curious dint,
> That runs along his back . . .

and the second sestiad has an extraordinary passage about
Neptune making passes at Leander as he swims the Helle-
spont.

> He clapped his plump cheeks, with his tresses played,
> And smiling wantonly, his love bewrayed.
> He watched his arms, and as they opened wide
> At every stroke, betwixt them would he slide
> And steal a kiss, and then run out and dance,
> And as he turned, cast many a lustful glance,
> And threw him gaudy toys to please his eye,
> And dive into the water, and there pry
> Upon his breast, his thighs, and every limb,
> And up again, and close beside him swim,
> And talk of love.

There is no indication that Marlowe feels, or expects his readers to feel, any anxiety over the enthusiastic depiction of a man making love to another man. Marlowe gets away with this partly because the subject is classical—"Greek" love—but partly, too, because sexuality in the period is simply much more undifferentiated than it is now. Neptune's lust for Leander in this context is neither abnormal nor shocking, though it is certainly comic. Leander's reaction—"You are deceived, I am no woman, I"—is an indication of his sexual naivete, not of his straightness.

Marlowe's poem is the best expression of the Ovidian world view in English. It is hyperbolic in much the same way Renaissance tragedy is; its heroes are braver or more beautiful than we are, and they are capable of more suffering; more is lost when they die, and indeed, they provide us with the exemplary instances of passion against which ours are to be measured. The other side of the enthusiasm and overt sexuality is the sense of foreboding that also fills the poem, a sense that these heroes are too good for their world, that the gods are jealous, that nothing this beautiful is ever allowed to get away with it. The undercurrent of tragedy is always there, but Marlowe handles the moral issues in a characteristically subversive way. The tragedy we know is coming never qualifies the sensuality—the point is not that Hero and Leander ought not to be behaving this way. Quite the contrary: the point is that our world is simply not good enough for its heroes. Marlowe deals with the necessary tragic conclusion by omitting it, not finishing the poem. This is a work designed to be a fragment—another thing about it that is "classical."

CHAPMAN'S CONTINUATION

The most subversive of Marlowe's subjects is how you get away with pleasure, and omitting the conclusion, the punishment for the lovers'—and the readers'—extraordinary enjoyment is a neat way of cheating the moralists. Ironically, but also significantly, the poem was completed by the most moral and moralistic of

Marlowe's contemporaries, George Chapman: two editions of *Hero and Leander* appeared in 1598, the second of which included Chapman's continuation. Chapman was an immensely learned and philosophical poet; but the kinship he felt with Marlowe was not based only on the fact that they were both classicists. In Chapman's continuation, the lovers are perfect, but their love is unsanctified because they are unmarried; the goddess Juno, patron of marriage, has been neglected. They rectify the omission by sacrificing to Juno and formally marrying, but Venus is their true patron, not Juno, and the fates hate Venus and are jealous of the lovers' beauty and perfection, and this time Leander crossing the Hellespont drowns, and Hero dies of grief. Chapman's style is quite different from Marlowe's, but his admiration for Marlowe is clear, and he has his own kind of power and pathos. At the conclusion of the poem, the lovers are metamorphosed into goldfinches:

> Neptune for pity in his arms did take them,
> Flung them into the air, and did awake them
> Like two sweet birds . . .
> And so most beautiful their colors show,
> As none (so little) like them: her sad brow
> A sable velvet feather covers quite,
> Even like the forehead-cloths that in the night,
> Or when they sorrow, ladies use to wear;
> Their wings, blue, red, and yellow, mixed appear;
> Colors that, as we construe colors, paint
> Their states to life; the yellow shows their saint,
> The devil Venus, left them; blue, their truth;
> The red and black, ensigns of death and ruth.
> And this true honor from their love-deaths sprung,
> They were the first that ever poet sung.

"Their saint / The devil Venus" is a good indication of how divided Chapman's moral imagination is here. The point is not, obviously, to blame the lovers for falling in love; it is that the distinction between saint and devil is discernable only in hindsight.

When he subsequently revised the poem, Chapman had second thoughts about even this, and "the devil Venus" became "the dainty Venus"—both delicately beautiful and fastidious or reluctant; but no longer damnable. The most extraordinary thing about Chapman's continuation is that this moralist wants to be associated with the work of Marlowe at all: when he was murdered in 1593, Marlowe was under investigation for atheism, blasphemy, counterfeiting (all that is missing is sodomy, and the charges hover dangerously close to that, too)—in short, universal subversion. But Chapman saw a different Marlowe, his life, like the poem, passionate and tragically incomplete. Similarly, when Shakespeare quotes Marlowe in *As You Like It*—"Dead shepherd, now I feel thy saw of might,/Whoever loved that loved not at first sight?" (III.5.81–2; compare *Hero and Leander* I.176)—it is as the model of the innocent wisdom of love. Chapman's and Shakespeare's Marlowe is the fictitious Musaeus, the primal poet. Chapman's continuation appears to the modern reader very different in character from Marlowe's fragment. The seventeenth-century reader would have found the differences less striking, and there is no evidence that Chapman's addition was ever considered either inappropriate or unworthy. Indeed, it immediately established itself as an integral part of the poem, and was invariably, until well into the twentieth century, reprinted with it.

PETOWE'S CONTINUATION

Henry Petowe (1575/6–1636?) was a London scrivener (a profession combining the functions of scribe, accountant, and legal adviser) and published a good deal of poetry. His continuation of *Hero and Leander*, was, as he says in his preface, his first work, and appeared, like Chapman's, in 1598; though unlike Chapman's, it has not entered the literary histories. It is unquestionably inept and silly, with a distinctly unearned happy ending, and has surely deserved its almost complete neglect. But it represents the alternative Elizabethan view of Marlowe's poem, as high romance rather than philosophical tragedy, and is worth reading as a relevant cultural document.

LUCAN'S FIRST BOOK

Marlowe's translation of Lucan is the first in English; it was published in only a single edition, in 1600—clearly it represented the bottom of the Marlowe barrel, the last bit of unpublished work of the most successful classicist of the age. The work is undeniably less engaging than *All Ovid's Elegies* or *Hero and Leander*. The project, however, would not have been a mere academic exercise. Ben Jonson said of Lucan's *Pharsalia,* or *Civil War,* that it was "written with an admirable height," and that he was "never weary to transcribe" its "admirable verses." Modern opinion has been less enthusiastic. The general critical attitude is expressed by the *Oxford Classical Dictionary*: "Lucan shows an excessive fondness for the purple patch. There is much exaggeration, often absurd; bizarre effects and farfetched paradoxes abound." Tastes change. To the Renaissance poet, farfetched paradoxes were a virtue, and restraint in the use of hyperbole—as *Hero and Leander* amply demonstrates—was not. Style is not the least of Lucan's attractions for Marlowe, as for Jonson.

But to the Elizabethans, this classic study of the horrors of civil war had a special relevance. The drama had inaugurated Elizabeth's reign with a play in the Senecan style on the same theme, *Gorboduc*—Lucan's concerns were the substance of modern history for anyone who had lived through the reign of Mary Tudor. The Queen of Scots, Catholic claimant to Elizabeth's throne, was not executed until 1587, and the question of Elizabeth's successor was not positively settled until the end of the reign. Lucan was regarded as a classic model for the treatment of recent events (evident, for example, in Drayton's *Barons' Wars* and Daniel's *Civil Wars*), not merely as a literary monument to be domesticated through translation.

THE PASSIONATE SHEPHERD
TO HIS LOVE

The most famous of Marlowe's poems, the lyric "The Passionate Shepherd to His Love," was in existence by 1589, when it was paraphrased in Robert Greene's *Menaphon*. It was first printed anonymously in the collection *The Passionate Pilgrim* in 1599, where it is untitled, and again in a version with two additional stanzas in *England's Helicon* in 1600, where it is ascribed to Marlowe and given the title by which it is now known—there is no reason to assume the title is Marlowe's. The poem is parodied in *The Jew of Malta* (IV.4.95–105), and Sir Hugh Evans sings a garbled version of one stanza in *The Merry Wives of Windsor* (III.1.17–26). Versions of the poem, sometimes with additions, appear in a number of early commonplace books, and Isaac Walton included yet another version in the second edition of *The Compleat Angler* (1655), where it is titled "The Milk Maid's Song." A musical setting appears in William Corkine's *Second Book of Airs* (1612). The poem was endlessly imitated, parodied, and answered, well into the seventeenth century; some examples are included in this edition. An account of the poem's history can be found in R. S. Forsythe, "*The Passionate Shepherd* and English Poetry," *PMLA* 40 (September 1925), pp. 692–742.

ELEGY FOR MANWOOD

Marlowe's only Latin poem is the elegy for Sir Roger Manwood (1525–92), an important jurist who had dealt leniently with Marlowe when he and Thomas Watson were brought up before him on a murder charge stemming from a street brawl in 1589 (they were acquitted on the grounds of self-defense). It is not known what other connection, if any, Marlowe had with Manwood.

NOTES

1. A facsimile and transcription are in A. D. Wraight, *In Search of Christopher Marlowe* (New York: Vanguard Press, 1965), pp. 308–9. The best biography is that of David Riggs, *The World of Christopher Marlowe* (New York: Henry Holt, 2005).
2. See David Halperin, *One Hundred Years of Homosexuality* (New York: Routledge, 1990), p. 134.
3. See Patrick Cheney, *Marlowe's Counterfeit Profession* (Toronto: University of Toronto Press, 1997).
4. Cited in Tucker Brooke, *The Works of Christopher Marlowe* (Oxford: Clarendon Press, 1910), p. 114.
5. *The Reckoning* (London: Jonathan Cape, 1992), p. 68.
6. Cited in Brooke, *Marlowe*, p. 114.

A Note on the Text,
and on Emendation, Modernization,
and Annotation

The major twentieth-century editions of Marlowe's poems and translations are those of C. F. Tucker Brooke (Oxford, 1910), L. C. Martin (London, 1931), Millar McClure (London, 1968), Fredson Bowers (Cambridge, 1974), and Roma Gill (Oxford, 1987). Though Gill's edition is now generally considered the standard one, in fact it is textually less reliable than those of McClure and Bowers. Martin's and McClure's editions have modernized spelling; all the editions adjust punctuation to some degree. Modernization is an undeniable advantage for the modern reader, who should be urged, however, to bear in mind that sixteenth-century English was far more ambiguous than the language is today, and updating spelling and punctuation is a form of translation. Many of the ambiguities get lost in the process. To give only a single example, the line in *Hero and Leander* that in a modernized text reads "Ay, and she wished, albeit not from her heart," (2.37) is in the original, "I, and shee wisht, albeit not from her hart"—for the sixteenth-century reader, Hero's wish was seconding Marlowe's.

There is a major emendation in *Hero and Leander* that has been incorporated into most modern editions, including the present one. Though the emendation is almost certainly correct, the original reading is so striking that it is worth pausing over. In II.279–300, Marlowe describes the lovers' first sexual intercourse. Hero, having allowed the half-frozen Leander into her bed, resists his initial attempts to penetrate "the ivory mount." Through "gentle parley" Leander obtains a "truce," and then his kisses and caresses enable him to enter "the orchard of th' Hesperides"; at which Hero "wished this night were never done." In

the original version, however, the first twelve lines *follow* the last
ten; so that Leander's sweet talk and caresses take place after the
initial penetration—it is this, as much as the physical entry into
her body, that makes Hero wish the night to last forever. A prob-
lem with the passage only started to be noticed in the mid-
nineteenth century, and the revision, which first appeared in
Tucker Brooke's edition of 1910, was justified on the grounds of
common sense. But Vincenzo Pasquarella, a young Italian scholar
working on the textual history of the poem, has questioned the
emendation in a forthcoming article, and it is certainly true that
the original not only makes sense, but makes a more interesting
sense psychologically than the revision.

Perhaps the fact that no problem was noticed in the passage
for two and a half centuries reflects not the inattentiveness of
readers and editors but a change in the psychology of sex. What
persuades me, however, that the emendation is correct is the
progression of Marlowe's metaphors. At line 278, "gentle par-
ley did the truce obtain," and the truce metaphor continues
into the transposed passage, where it is completed: "And every
kiss to her was as a charm /And to Leander as a fresh alarm,/So
that the truce was broke, and she alas /(Poor silly maiden) at his
mercy was." Leander cannot be free to enter "the orchard of
th'Hesperides" until after this. I regret the loss of the garbled
original; and Pasquarella seems to me a very good reader. Com-
mon sense is not always the bottom line in editorial protocols.

The greatest single problem in annotating Marlowe for the
modern reader is the persistent and complex use of classical al-
lusions. It is not feasible to give a complete account of every
classical name every time it appears; but allusions have always
been glossed in the Notes in sufficient detail to explain their use
in their immediate context. Readers' requirements differ, how-
ever, and for the reader who is concerned as well with the larger
contexts of classical myth and history, and Renaissance atti-
tudes toward them, a complete dictionary of classical names
has been provided. Thus, in order to understand the point of
Marlowe's reference to Hippolytus in *Hero and Leander* I.77,
it is, strictly speaking, only necessary to know that Hippolytus
rejected love. But readers might reasonably wish to have a

broader sense of such an allusion, and for this they may turn to the dictionary. Again, the significance of the series of classical names in Ovid's *Elegies,* III.v is, for the context, sufficiently elucidated by the fact that they are all the names of river gods and their loves. For the reader who wishes to have a more detailed understanding of the allusions the dictionary provides brief accounts of the individual stories. The inevitable duplication in this method of annotation has seemed preferable either to deleting classical names from the notes entirely, and thereby requiring the reader to use the glossary and notes simultaneously merely in order to understand the sense of the text or, alternatively, to filling the notes with a great deal of detail, which many readers will find superfluous.

Table of Dates

1564 *February 6* Christopher Marlowe born, son of John Marlowe, shoemaker of Canterbury.

1579 Scholarship to King's School, Canterbury.

1581 Scholarship to Corpus Christi College, Cambridge.

1584 BA.

***c.* 1586** Employed, probably unofficially, by the Privy Council as a foreign intelligence agent.

1587 MA. All Marlowe's poems and translations are traditionally assigned to his Cambridge years, though there is in fact no evidence to support this view.
The First Part of Tamburlaine the Great produced (?).

1588 *The Second Part of Tamburlaine the Great* produced (?). Accused of atheism in Robert Greene's *Perimedes*.

1589 *The Jew of Malta* produced (?). Attacked in Greene's *Menaphon*.

1591 Shares lodgings with Thomas Kyd.

1592 *Edward II* produced (?).
Doctor Faustus produced (?).
Tamburlaine published.
Attacked in Greene's *Groatsworth of Wit*.

before 1593 *Dido, Queen of Carthage*, written in collaboration with Thomas Nashe, produced.

1593 *The Massacre at Paris* produced.
May 18 Arrested at the house of Sir Thomas Walsingham and summoned to the Privy Council to answer charges of blasphemy arising from evidence given by Kyd.

June 1   Murdered by Ingram Friser in a tavern in Dept-
ford, and buried there.

September 28   Hero and Leander and *Lucan's First
Book* entered in the Stationer's Register.

1594   *Dido, Edward II,* and (probably) *The Massacre at Paris*
published.

1598   *Hero and Leander* published by Edward Blount, and
again by Paul Linley with Chapman's continuation. Petowe's
continuation published.

1599   *The Passionate Shepherd to His Love* published in *The
Passionate Pilgrim*, a poetical miscellany ascribed on the title-
page to Shakespeare. *Epigrams and Elegies* by Sir John Davies
and Christopher Marlowe, containing ten of Marlowe's Ovid
translations, having been surreptitiously published sometime
earlier, banned and burned by episcopal order.

c. **1600**   Two complete editions of the *Elegies* published "at
Middlebourgh" (Holland).

1600   *Lucan's First Book* published. *The Passionate Shepherd*
appears in *England's Helicon*, followed by *The Nymph's Re-
ply*, probably by Ralegh, and by an anonymous imitation.

1604   *Doctor Faustus* published.

1633   *The Jew of Malta* published.

The Complete Poems
and Translations

HERO AND LEANDER

Sir: we think not ourselves discharged of the duty we owe to our friend when we have brought the breathless body to the earth; for albeit the eye there taketh his ever farewell of that beloved object, yet the impression of the man that hath been dear unto us, living an after life in our memory, there putteth us in mind of farther obsequies due unto the deceased. And namely, of the performance of whatsoever we may judge shall make to his living credit, and to the effecting of his determinations prevented by the stroke of death. By these meditations (as by an intellectual will) I suppose myself executor to the unhappily deceased author of this poem, upon whom knowing that in his lifetime you bestowed many kind favors, entertaining the parts of reckoning and worth which you found in him, with good countenance and liberal affection: I cannot but see so far into the will of him dead, that whatsoever issue of his brain should chance to come abroad, that the first breath it should take might be the gentle air of your liking; for since his self had been accustomed thereunto, it would prove more agreeable and thriving to his right children than any other foster countenance whatsoever. At this time seeing that this unfinished tragedy happens under my hands to be imprinted, of a double duty, the one to yourself, the

10

20

3

other to the deceased, I present the same to your most favorable allowance, offering my utmost self now and ever to be ready, at your worship's disposing.

EDWARD BLOUNT

THE ARGUMENT OF THE FIRST SESTIAD

Hero's description and her love's;
The fane of Venus, where he moves
His worthy love-suit, and attains;
Whose bliss the wrath of Fates restrains
For Cupid's grace to Mercury:
Which tale the author doth imply.

On Hellespont, guilty of true love's blood,
In view and opposite two cities stood,
Sea-borderers, disjoined by Neptune's might:
The one Abydos, the other Sestos hight.
At Sestos Hero dwelt; Hero the fair,
Whom young Apollo courted for her hair,
And offered as a dower his burning throne,
Where she should sit for men to gaze upon.
The outside of her garments were of lawn,
The lining purple silk, with gilt stars drawn;   10
Her wide sleeves green, and bordered with a grove,
Where Venus in her naked glory strove
To please the careless and disdainful eyes
Of proud Adonis that before her lies.
Her kirtle blue, whereon was many a stain,
Made with the blood of wretched lovers slain.
Upon her head she ware a myrtle wreath,
From whence her veil reached to the ground beneath.
Her veil was artificial flowers and leaves,

20 Whose workmanship both man and beast deceives.
Many would praise the sweet smell as she passed,
When 'twas the odor which her breath forth cast;
And there for honey bees have sought in vain,
And beat from thence, have lighted there again.
About her neck hung chains of pebble-stone,
Which lightened by her neck, like diamonds shone.
She ware no gloves, for neither sun nor wind
Would burn or parch her hands, but to her mind,
Or warm or cool them, for they took delight
30 To play upon those hands, they were so white.
Buskins of shells all silvered usèd she,
And branched with blushing coral to the knee,
Where sparrows perched, of hollow pearl and gold,
Such as the world would wonder to behold:
Those with sweet water oft her handmaid fills,
Which as she went would chirrup through the bills.
Some say for her the fairest Cupid pined,
And looking in her face, was strooken blind.
But this is true, so like was one the other,
40 As he imagined Hero was his mother;
And oftentimes into her bosom flew,
About her naked neck his bare arms threw;
And laid his childish head upon her breast,
And with still panting rocked, there took his rest.
So lovely fair was Hero, Venus' nun,
As Nature wept, thinking she was undone,
Because she took more from her than she left,
And of such wondrous beauty her bereft:
Therefore, in sign her treasure suffered wrack,
50 Since Hero's time hath half the world been black.
Amorous Leander, beautiful and young
(Whose tragedy divine Musaeus sung)
Dwelt at Abydos; since him dwelt there none
For whom succeeding times make greater moan.
His dangling tresses that were never shorn,
Had they been cut, and unto Colchos borne,
Would have allured the vent'rous youth of Greece

To hazard more than for the Golden Fleece.
Fair Cynthia wished his arms might be her sphere;
Grief makes her pale because she moves not there.   60
His body was as straight as Circe's wand;
Jove might have sipped out nectar from his hand.
Even as delicious meat is to the taste,
So was his neck in touching, and surpassed
The white of Pelops' shoulder; I could tell ye
How smooth his breast was, and how white his belly,
And whose immortal fingers did imprint
That heavenly path with many a curious dint
That runs along his back, but my rude pen
Can hardly blazon forth the loves of men,   70
Much less of powerful gods: let it suffice
That my slack muse sings of Leander's eyes,
Those orient cheeks and lips, exceeding his
That leapt into the water for a kiss
Of his own shadow, and despising many,
Died ere he could enjoy the love of any.
Had wild Hippolytus Leander seen,
Enamored of his beauty had he been;
His presence made the rudest peasant melt,
That in the vast uplandish country dwelt;   80
The barbarous Thracian soldier, moved with nought,
Was moved with him, and for his favor sought.
Some swore he was a maid in man's attire,
For in his looks were all that men desire,
A pleasant smiling cheek, a speaking eye,
A brow for love to banquet royally;
And such as knew he was a man would say,
"Leander, thou art made for amorous play:
Why art thou not in love, and loved of all?
Though thou be fair, yet be not thine own thrall."   90

The men of wealthy Sestos, every year
(For his sake whom their goddess held so dear,
Rose-cheeked Adonis), kept a solemn feast.
Thither resorted many a wand'ring guest

To meet their loves; such as had none at all
Came lovers home from this great festival.
For every street like to a firmament
Glistered with breathing stars, who where they went
Frighted the melancholy earth, which deemed
100 Eternal heaven to burn, for so it seemed,
As if another Phaëthon had got
The guidance of the sun's rich chariot.
But far above the loveliest Hero shined,
And stole away th' enchanted gazer's mind;
For like sea-nymphs' inveigling harmony,
So was her beauty to the standers by.
Nor that night-wand'ring, pale and watery star
(When yawning dragons draw her thirling car
From Latmus' mount up to the gloomy sky,
110 Where crowned with blazing light and majesty,
She proudly sits), more overrules the flood
Than she the hearts of those that near her stood.
Even as, when gaudy nymphs pursue the chase,
Wretched Ixion's shaggy-footed race,
Incensed with savage heat, gallop amain
From steep pine-bearing mountains to the plain:
So ran the people forth to gaze upon her,
And all that viewed her were enamored on her.
And as in fury of a dreadful fight,
120 Their fellows being slain or put to flight,
Poor soldiers stand with fear of death dead-strooken,
So at her presence all surprised and tooken
Await the sentence of her scornful eyes:
He whom she favors lives, the other dies.
There might you see one sigh, another rage,
And some (their violent passions to assuage)
Compile sharp satires, but alas too late,
For faithful love will never turn to hate.
And many seeing great princes were denied,
130 Pined as they went, and thinking on her died.
On this feast day, O cursèd day and hour,
Went Hero thorough Sestos, from her tower

To Venus' temple, where unhappily,
As after chanced, they did each other spy.
So fair a church as this had Venus none:
The walls were of discolored jasper stone,
Wherein was Proteus carvèd, and o'erhead
A lively vine of green sea agate spread;
Where by one hand light-headed Bacchus hung,
And with the other wine from grapes outwrung.   140
Of crystal shining fair the pavement was;
The town of Sestos called it Venus' glass;
There might you see the gods in sundry shapes,
Committing heady riots, incest, rapes:
For know that underneath this radiant floor
Was Danae's statue in a brazen tower,
Jove slyly stealing from his sister's bed,
To dally with Idalian Ganymede,
And for his love Europa bellowing loud,
And tumbling with the Rainbow in a cloud;   150
Blood-quaffing Mars, heaving the iron net
Which limping Vulcan and his Cyclops set;
Love kindling fire, to burn such towns as Troy;
Sylvanus weeping for the lovely boy
That now is turned into a cypress tree,
Under whose shade the wood-gods love to be.
And in the midst a silver altar stood;
There Hero sacrificing turtles' blood,
Vailed to the ground, vailing her eyelids close,
And modestly they opened as she rose: 160
Thence flew Love's arrow with the golden head,
And thus Leander was enamorèd.
Stone still he stood, and evermore he gazèd,
Till with the fire that from his count'nance blazèd
Relenting Hero's gentle heart was strook:
Such force and virtue hath an amorous look.

It lies not in our power to love or hate,
For will in us is overruled by fate.
When two are stripped, long ere the course begin

170   We wish that one should lose, the other win;
And one especially do we affect
Of two gold ingots like in each respect.
The reason no man knows: let it suffice,
What we behold is censured by our eyes.
Where both deliberate, the love is slight;
Who ever loved, that loved not at first sight?

He kneeled, but unto her devoutly prayed;
Chaste Hero to herself thus softly said:
"Were I the saint he worships, I would hear him,"
180   And as she spake those words, came somewhat
        near him.
He started up, she blushed as one ashamed;
Wherewith Leander much more was inflamed.
He touched her hand, in touching it she trembled:
Love deeply grounded hardly is dissembled.
These lovers parlèd by the touch of hands;
True love is mute, and oft amazèd stands.
Thus while dumb signs their yielding hearts entangled,
The air with sparks of living fire was spangled,
And Night, deep-drenched in misty Acheron,   *A periphrasis*
190   Heaved up her head, and half the world upon   *of Night*
Breathed darkness forth (dark night is Cupid's day).
And now begins Leander to display
Love's holy fire, with words, with sighs and tears,
Which like sweet music entered Hero's ears,
And yet at every word she turned aside,
And always cut him off as he replied.
At last, like to a bold sharp sophister,
With cheerful hope thus he accosted her.

"Fair creature, let me speak without offense,
200   I would my rude words had the influence
To lead thy thoughts, as thy fair looks do mine,
Then shouldst thou be his prisoner, who is thine.
Be not unkind and fair; misshapen stuff
Are of behavior boisterous and rough.

O shun me not, but hear me ere you go,
God knows I cannot force love, as you do.
My words shall be as spotless as my youth,
Full of simplicity and naked truth.
This sacrifice (whose sweet perfume descending
From Venus' altar to your footsteps bending)   210
Doth testify that you exceed her far,
To whom you offer, and whose nun you are.
Why should you worship her? her you surpass
As much as sparkling diamonds flaring glass.
A diamond set in lead his worth retains;
A heavenly nymph, beloved of human swains,
Receives no blemish, but oft-times more grace,
Which makes me hope, although I am but base,
Base in respect of thee, divine and pure,
Dutiful service may thy love procure;   220
And I in duty will excel all other,
As thou in beauty dost exceed Love's mother.
Nor heaven, nor thou, were made to gaze upon;
As heaven preserves all things, so save thou one.
A stately builded ship, well-rigged and tall,
The ocean maketh more majestical:
Why vowest thou then to live in Sestos here,
Who on Love's seas more glorious wouldst appear?
Like untuned golden strings all women are,
Which long time lie untouched will harshly jar.   230
Vessels of brass oft handled brightly shine;
What difference betwixt the richest mine
And basest mold but use? for both, not used,
Are of like worth. Then treasure is abused
When misers keep it; being put to loan,
In time it will return us two for one.
Rich robes themselves and others do adorn;
Neither themselves nor others, if not worn.
Who builds a palace and rams up the gate,
Shall see it ruinous and desolate.   240
Ah simple Hero, learn thyself to cherish;
Lone women like to empty houses perish.

Less sins the poor rich man that starves himself
In heaping up a mass of drossy pelf,
Than such as you: his golden earth remains,
Which, after his decease, some other gains;
But this fair gem, sweet in the loss alone,
When you fleet hence, can be bequeathed to none.
Or if it could, down from th' enameled sky
250 All heaven would come to claim this legacy,
And with intestine broils the world destroy,
And quite confound nature's sweet harmony.
Well therefore by the gods decreed it is,
We human creatures should enjoy that bliss.
One is no number; maids are nothing then,
Without the sweet society of men.
Wilt thou live single still? one shalt thou be,
Though never-singling Hymen couple thee.
Wild savages, that drink of running springs,
260 Think water far excels all earthly things:
But they that daily taste neat wine, despise it.
Virginity, albeit some highly prize it,
Compared with marriage, had you tried them both,
Differs as much as wine and water doth.
Base bullion for the stamp's sake we allow,
Even so for men's impression do we you.
By which alone, our reverend fathers say,
Women receive perfection every way.
This idol which you term virginity
270 Is neither essence subject to the eye,
No, nor to any one exterior sense,
Nor hath it any place of residence,
Nor is 't of earth or mold celestial,
Or capable of any form at all.
Of that which hath no being, do not boast;
Things that are not at all, are never lost.
Men foolishly do call it virtuous:
What virtue is it that is born with us?
Much less can honor be ascribed thereto,
280 Honor is purchased by the deeds we do.

Believe me, Hero, honor is not won,
Until some honorable deed be done.
Seek you for chastity, immortal fame,
And know that some have wronged Diana's name?
Whose name is it, if she be false or not,
So she be fair, but some vile tongues will blot?
But you are fair (aye me) so wondrous fair,
So young, so gentle, and so debonair,
As Greece will think, if thus you live alone,
Some one or other keeps you as his own.   290
Then, Hero, hate me not, nor from me fly,
To follow swiftly blasting infamy.
Perhaps thy sacred priesthood makes thee loth,
Tell me, to whom mad'st thou that heedless oath?"

"To Venus," answered she, and as she spake,
Forth from those two tralucent cisterns brake
A stream of liquid pearl, which down her face
Made milk-white paths, whereon the gods might trace
To Jove's high court. He thus replied: "The rites
In which love's beauteous empress most delights,   300
Are banquets, Doric music, midnight revel,
Plays, masques, and all that stern age counteth evil.
Thee as a holy idiot doth she scorn,
For thou in vowing chastity hast sworn
To rob her name and honor, and thereby
Commit'st a sin far worse than perjury,
Even sacrilege against her deity,
Through regular and formal purity.
To expiate which sin, kiss and shake hands,
Such sacrifice as this Venus demands."   310

Thereat she smiled, and did deny him so,
As put thereby, yet might he hope for mo.
Which makes him quickly reinforce his speech,
And her in humble manner thus beseech:

"Though neither gods nor men may thee deserve,
Yet for her sake whom you have vowed to serve,

Abandon fruitless cold virginity,
The gentle queen of love's sole enemy.
Then shall you most resemble Venus' nun,
320   When Venus' sweet rites are performed and done.
Flint-breasted Pallas joys in single life,
But Pallas and your mistress are at strife.
Love, Hero, then, and be not tyrannous,
But heal the heart that thou hast wounded thus,
Nor stain thy youthful years with avarice;
Fair fools delight to be accounted nice.
The richest corn dies if it be not reaped;
Beauty alone is lost, too warily kept."
These arguments he used, and many more,
330   Wherewith she yielded, that was won before.
Hero's looks yielded, but her words made war;
Women are won when they begin to jar.
Thus having swallowed Cupid's golden hook,
The more she strived, the deeper was she strook.
Yet evilly feigning anger, strove she still,
And would be thought to grant against her will.
So having paused a while, at last she said:
"Who taught thee rhetoric to deceive a maid?
Aye me, such words as these should I abhor,
340   And yet I like them for the orator."

With that, Leander stooped, to have embraced her,
But from his spreading arms away she cast her,
And thus bespake him: "Gentle youth, forbear
To touch the sacred garments which I wear.
Upon a rock, and underneath a hill,
Far from the town (where all is whist and still,
Save that the sea, playing on yellow sand,
Sends forth a rattling murmur to the land,
Whose sound allures the golden Morpheus
350   In silence of the night to visit us)
My turret stands, and there God knows I play
With Venus' swans and sparrows all the day.
A dwarfish beldam bears me company,

That hops about the chamber where I lie,
And spends the night (that might be better spent)
In vain discourse and apish merriment.
Come thither." As she spake this, her tongue tripped,
For unawares "Come thither" from her slipped,
And suddenly her former color changed,
And here and there her eyes through anger ranged.   360
And like a planet, moving several ways
At one self instant, she poor soul assays,
Loving, not to love at all, and every part
Strove to resist the motions of her heart.
And hands so pure, so innocent, nay such
As might have made heaven stoop to have a touch,
Did she uphold to Venus, and again
Vowed spotless chastity, but all in vain.
Cupid beats down her prayers with his wings,
Her vows above the empty air he flings;   370
All deep enraged, his sinewy bow he bent,
And shot a shaft that burning from him went,
Wherewith she strooken looked so dolefully,
As made Love sigh to see his tyranny.
And as she wept, her tears to pearl he turned,
And wound them on his arm, and for her mourned.
Then towards the palace of the Destinies
Laden with languishment and grief he flies,
And to those stern nymphs humbly made request
Both might enjoy each other, and be blest.   380
But with a ghastly dreadful countenance,
Threat'ning a thousand deaths at every glance,
They answered Love, nor would vouchsafe so much
As one poor word, their hate to him was such.
Hearken awhile, and I will tell you why.

Heaven's wingèd herald, Jove-born Mercury,
The self-same day that he asleep had laid
Enchanted Argus, spied a country maid,
Whose careless hair, instead of pearl t' adorn it,
Glistered with dew, as one that seemed to scorn it.   390

Her breath as fragrant as the morning rose,
Her mind pure, and her tongue untaught to glose,
Yet proud she was (for lofty Pride that dwells
In towered courts is oft in shepherds' cells),
And too too well the fair vermilion knew,
And silver tincture of her cheeks, that drew
The love of every swain. On her this god
Enamored was, and with his snaky rod
Did charm her nimble feet, and made her stay,
400   The while upon a hillock down he lay,
And sweetly on his pipe began to play,
And with smooth speech her fancy to assay,
Till in his twining arms he locked her fast,
And then he wooed with kisses, and at last,
As shepherds do, her on the ground he laid,
And tumbling in the grass, he often strayed
Beyond the bounds of shame, in being bold
To eye those parts which no eye should behold.
And like an insolent commanding lover,
410   Boasting his parentage, would needs discover
The way to new Elysium; but she,
Whose only dower was her chastity,
Having striv'n in vain, was now about to cry,
And crave the help of shepherds that were nigh.
Herewith he stayed his fury, and began
To give her leave to rise; away she ran,
After went Mercury, who used such cunning,
As she, to hear his tale, left off her running.
Maids are not won by brutish force and might,
420   But speeches full of pleasure and delight.
And, knowing Hermes courted her, was glad
That she such loveliness and beauty had
As could provoke his liking, yet was mute,
And neither would deny nor grant his suit.
Still vowed he love; she, wanting no excuse
To feed him with delays, as women use,
Or thirsting after immortality—
All women are ambitious naturally—

Imposed upon her lover such a task
As he ought not perform, nor yet she ask.   430
A draught of flowing nectar she requested,
Wherewith the king of gods and men is feasted.
He ready to accomplish what she willed,
Stole some from Hebe (Hebe Jove's cup filled)
And gave it to his simple rustic love;
Which being known (as what is hid from Jove?)
He inly stormed, and waxed more furious
Than for the fire filched by Prometheus,
And thrusts him down from heaven; he wand'ring here,
In mournful terms, with sad and heavy cheer,   440
Complained to Cupid. Cupid for his sake,
To be revenged on Jove did undertake,
And those on whom heaven, earth, and hell relies,
I mean the adamantine Destinies,
He wounds with love, and forced them equally
To dote upon deceitful Mercury.
They offered him the deadly fatal knife
That shears the slender threads of human life;
At his fair feathered feet the engines laid,
Which th' earth from ugly Chaos' den upweighed.   450
These he regarded not, but did entreat
That Jove, usurper of his father's seat,
Might presently be banished into hell,
And agèd Saturn in Olympus dwell.
They granted what he craved, and once again
Saturn and Ops began their golden reign.
Murder, rape, war, lust and treachery
Were with Jove closed in Stygian empery.
But long this blessèd time continued not:
As soon as he his wishèd purpose got,   460
He reckless of his promise did despise
The love of th' everlasting Destinies.
They seeing it, both Love and him abhorred,
And Jupiter unto his place restored.
And but that Learning, in despite of Fate,
Will mount aloft, and enter heaven gate,

And to the seat of Jove itself advance,
Hermes had slept in hell with Ignorance.
Yet as a punishment they added this,
470   That he and Poverty should always kiss.
And to this day is every scholar poor;
Gross gold from them runs headlong to the boor.
Likewise the angry sisters, thus deluded,
To venge themselves on Hermes, have concluded
That Midas' brood shall sit in honor's chair,
To which the Muses' sons are only heir:
And fruitful wits that inaspiring are
Shall discontent run into regions far.
And few great lords in virtuous deeds shall joy,
480   But be surprised with every garish toy,
And still enrich the lofty servile clown,
Who with encroaching guile keeps learning down.
Then muse not Cupid's suit no better sped,
Seeing in their loves the Fates were injurèd.

The end of the first Sestiad

THE ARGUMENT OF THE
SECOND SESTIAD

Hero of love takes deeper sense,
And doth her love more recompense;
Their first night's meeting, where sweet kisses
Are th' only crowns of both their blisses;
He swims t' Abydos, and returns;
Cold Neptune with his beauty burns,
Whose suit he shuns, and doth aspire
Hero's fair tow'r and his desire.

By this, sad Hero, with love unacquainted,
Viewing Leander's face, fell down and fainted.
He kissed her, and breathed life into her lips,

Wherewith, as one displeased, away she trips.
Yet as she went, full often looked behind,
And many poor excuses did she find
To linger by the way, and once she stayed,
And would have turned again, but was afraid,
In offering parley, to be counted light.
So on she goes, and in her idle flight,   10
Her painted fan of curlèd plumes let fall,
Thinking to train Leander therewithal.
He being a novice, knew not what she meant,
But stayed, and after her a letter sent,
Which joyful Hero answered in such sort,
As he had hope to scale the beauteous fort
Wherein the liberal Graces locked their wealth,
And therefore to her tower he got by stealth.
Wide open stood the door, he need not climb,
And she herself before the pointed time   20
Had spread the board, with roses strewed the room,
And oft looked out, and mused he did not come.
At last he came; O who can tell the greeting
These greedy lovers had at their first meeting?
He asked, she gave, and nothing was denied;
Both to each other quickly were affied.
Look how their hands, so were their hearts united,
And what he did she willingly requited.
(Sweet are the kisses, the embracements sweet,
When like desires and affections meet,   30
For from the earth to heaven is Cupid raised,
Where fancy is in equal balance peised.)
Yet she this rashness suddenly repented,
And turned aside, and to herself lamented,
As if her name and honor had been wronged
By being possessed of him for whom she longed;
Ay, and she wished, albeit not from her heart,
That he would leave her turret and depart.
The mirthful god of amorous pleasure smiled
To see how he this captive nymph beguiled;   40
For hitherto he did but fan the fire,

And kept it down that it might mount the higher.
Now waxed she jealous, lest his love abated,
Fearing her own thoughts made her to be hated.
Therefore unto him hastily she goes,
And, like light Salmacis, her body throws
Upon his bosom, where with yielding eyes
She offers up herself a sacrifice,
To slake his anger, if he were displeased.
50   O what god would not therewith be appeased?
Like Aesop's cock, this jewel he enjoyèd,
And as a brother with his sister toyèd,
Supposing nothing else was to be done,
Now he her favor and good will had won.
But know you not that creatures wanting sense
By nature have a mutual appetence,
And wanting organs to advance a step,
Moved by love's force, unto each other leap?
Much more in subjects having intellect
60   Some hidden influence breeds like effect.
Albeit Leander, rude in love, and raw,
Long dallying with Hero, nothing saw
That might delight him more, yet he suspected
Some amorous rites or other were neglected.
Therefore unto his body hers he clung;
She, fearing on the rushes to be flung,
Strived with redoubled strength; the more she strivèd,
The more a gentle pleasing heat revivèd,
Which taught him all that elder lovers know,
70   And now the same 'gan so to scorch and glow,
As in plain terms (yet cunningly) he craved it;
Love always makes those eloquent that have it.
She, with a kind of granting, put him by it,
And ever as he thought himself most nigh it,
Like to the tree of Tantalus she fled,
And, seeming lavish, saved her maidenhead.
Ne'er king more sought to keep his diadem,
Than Hero this inestimable gem.
Above our life we love a steadfast friend,

Yet when a token of great worth we send,   80
We often kiss it, often look thereon,
And stay the messenger that would be gone:
No marvel, then, though Hero would not yield
So soon to part from that she dearly held.
Jewels being lost are found again, this never;
'Tis lost but once, and once lost, lost forever.

Now had the Morn espied her lover's steeds,
Whereat she starts, puts on her purple weeds,
And red for anger that he stayed so long,
All headlong throws herself the clouds among,   90
And now Leander, fearing to be missed,
Embraced her suddenly, took leave, and kissed.
Long was he taking leave, and loth to go,
And kissed again, as lovers use to do.
Sad Hero wrung him by the hand, and wept,
Saying, "Let your vows and promises be kept."
Then standing at the door, she turned about,
As loth to see Leander going out.
And now the sun, that through th' horizon peeps,
As pitying these lovers, downward creeps,   100
So that in silence of the cloudy night,
Though it was morning, did he take his flight.
But what the secret trusty night concealed,
Leander's amorous habit soon revealed:
With Cupid's myrtle was his bonnet crowned,
About his arms the purple riband wound
Wherewith she wreathed her largely spreading hair;
Nor could the youth abstain, but he must wear
The sacred ring wherewith she was endowed
When first religious chastity she vowed;   110
Which made his love through Sestos to be known,
And thence unto Abydos sooner blown
Than he could sail; for incorporeal Fame,
Whose weight consists in nothing but her name,
Is swifter than the wind, whose tardy plumes
Are reeking water, and dull earthly fumes.

Home when he came, he seemed not to be there,
But like exilèd air thrust from his sphere,
Set in a foreign place; and straight from thence,
120   Alcides-like, by mighty violence,
He would have chased away the swelling main,
That him from her unjustly did detain.
Like as the sun in a diameter
Fires and inflames objects removèd far
And heateth kindly, shining lat'rally,
So beauty sweetly quickens when 'tis nigh,
But being separated and removèd,
Burns where it cherished, murders where it lovèd.
Therefore even as an index to a book,
130   So to his mind was young Leander's look.
O none but gods have power their love to hide,
Affection by the count'nance is descried.
The light of hidden fire itself discovers,
And love that is concealed betrays poor lovers.
His secret flame apparently was seen,
Leander's father knew where he had been,
And for the same mildly rebuked his son,
Thinking to quench the sparkles new begun.
But love resisted once grows passionate,
140   And nothing more than counsel lovers hate.
For as a hot proud horse highly disdains
To have his head controlled, but breaks the reins,
Spits forth the ringled bit, and with his hooves
Checks the submissive ground: so he that loves,
The more he is restrained, the worse he fares.
What is it now, but mad Leander dares?
"O Hero, Hero!" thus he cried full oft,
And then he got him to a rock aloft,
Where having spied her tower, long stared he on't,
150   And prayed the narrow toiling Hellespont
To part in twain, that he might come and go,
But still the rising billows answered no.
With that he stripped him to the ivory skin,
And crying, "Love, I come," leapt lively in.

Whereat the sapphire-visaged god grew proud,
And made his capering Triton sound aloud,
Imagining that Ganymede, displeased,
Had left the heavens; therefore on him he seized.
Leander strived, the waves about him wound,
And pulled him to the bottom, where the ground   160
Was strewed with pearl, and in low coral groves
Sweet singing mermaids sported with their loves
On heaps of heavy gold, and took great pleasure
To spurn in careless sort the shipwrack treasure.
For here the stately azure palace stood
Where kingly Neptune and his train abode.
The lusty god embraced him, called him love,
And swore he never should return to Jove.
But when he knew it was not Ganymede,
For under water he was almost dead,   170
He heaved him up, and looking on his face,
Beat down the bold waves with his triple mace,
Which mounted up, intending to have kissed him,
And fell in drops like tears because they missed him.
Leander being up, began to swim,
And, looking back, saw Neptune follow him;
Whereat aghast, the poor soul 'gan to cry,
"O let me visit Hero ere I die."
The god put Helle's bracelet on his arm,
And swore the sea should never do him harm.   180
He clapped his plump cheeks, with his tresses played,
And smiling wantonly, his love bewrayed.
He watched his arms, and as they opened wide
At every stroke, betwixt them would he slide
And steal a kiss, and then run out and dance,
And as he turned, cast many a lustful glance,
And threw him gaudy toys to please his eye,
And dive into the water, and there pry
Upon his breast, his thighs, and every limb,
And up again, and close beside him swim,   190
And talk of love. Leander made reply,
"You are deceived, I am no woman, I."

Thereat smiled Neptune, and then told a tale,
How that a shepherd, sitting in a vale,
Played with a boy so fair and kind,
As for his love both earth and heaven pined;
That of the cooling river durst not drink,
Lest water-nymphs should pull him from the brink;
And when he sported in the fragrant lawns,
200   Goat-footed satyrs and up-staring fauns
Would steal him thence. Ere half this tale was done,
"Aye me," Leander cried, "th' enamored sun,
That now should shine on Thetis' glassy bower,
Descends upon my radiant Hero's tower.
O that these tardy arms of mine were wings!"
And as he spake, upon the waves he springs.
Neptune was angry that he gave no ear,
And in his heart revenging malice bare:
He flung at him his mace, but as it went,
210   He called it in, for love made him repent.
The mace returning back, his own hand hit,
As meaning to be venged for darting it.
When this fresh bleeding wound Leander viewed,
His color went and came, as if he rued
The grief which Neptune felt. In gentle breasts
Relenting thoughts, remorse and pity rests.
And who have hard hearts and obdurate minds,
But vicious, harebrained, and illit'rate hinds?
The god, seeing him with pity to be movèd,
220   Thereon concluded that he was belovèd.
(Love is too full of faith, too credulous,
With folly and false hope deluding us.)
Wherefore Leander's fancy to surprise,
To the rich Ocean for gifts he flies.
'Tis wisdom to give much, a gift prevails
When deep persuading oratory fails.

By this, Leander being near the land,
Cast down his weary feet, and felt the sand.
Breathless albeit he were, he rested not

Till to the solitary tower he got,   230
And knocked, and called, at which celestial noise
The longing heart of Hero much more joys
Than nymphs and shepherds when the timbrel rings,
Or crooked dolphin when the sailor sings;
She stayed not for her robes, but straight arose,
And drunk with gladness to the door she goes,
Where seeing a naked man, she screeched for fear;
Such sights as this to tender maids are rare;
And ran into the dark herself to hide.
Rich jewels in the dark are soonest spied.   240
Unto her was he led, or rather drawn,
By those white limbs, which sparkled through the lawn.
The nearer that he came, the more she fled,
And seeking refuge, slipped into her bed.
Whereon Leander sitting thus began,
Through numbing cold, all feeble, faint and wan:
"If not for love, yet, love, for pity sake,
Me in thy bed and maiden bosom take;
At least vouchsafe these arms some little room,
Who, hoping to embrace thee, cheerly swum.   250
This head was beat with many a churlish billow,
And therefore let it rest upon thy pillow."
Herewith affrighted Hero shrunk away,
And in her lukewarm place Leander lay,
Whose lively heat, like fire from heaven fet,
Would animate gross clay, and higher set
The drooping thoughts of base declining souls
Than dreary Mars carousing nectar bowls.
His hands he cast upon her like a snare;
She, overcome with shame and sallow fear,   260
Like chaste Diana when Actaeon spied her,
Being suddenly betrayed, dived down to hide her.
And as her silver body downward went,
With both her hands she made the bed a tent,
And in her own mind thought herself secure,
O'ercast with dim and darksome coverture.
And now she lets him whisper in her ear,

Flatter, entreat, promise, protest and swear,
Yet ever as he greedily assayed
270   To touch those dainties, she the harpy played,
And every limb did as a soldier stout
Defend the fort, and keep the foeman out.
For though the rising ivory mount he scaled,
Which is with azure circling lines empaled,
Much like a globe (a globe may I term this,
By which love sails to regions full of bliss),
Yet there with Sisyphus he toiled in vain,
Till gentle parley did the truce obtain.
Wherein Leander on her quivering breast
280   Breathless spoke something, and sighed out the rest;
Which so prevailed, as he with small ado
Enclosed her in his arms and kissed her too.
And every kiss to her was as a charm,
And to Leander as a fresh alarm,
So that the truce was broke, and she alas
(Poor silly maiden) at his mercy was.
Love is not full of pity (as men say)
But deaf and cruel where he means to prey.
Even as a bird, which in our hands we wring,
290   Forth plungeth, and oft flutters with her wing,
She trembling strove; this strife of hers (like that
Which made the world) another world begat
Of unknown joy. Treason was in her thought,
And cunningly to yield herself she sought.
Seeming not won, yet won she was at length,
In such wars women use but half their strength.
Leander now, like Theban Hercules,
Entered the orchard of th' Hesperides,
Whose fruit none rightly can describe but he
300   That pulls or shakes it from the golden tree.
And now she wished this night were never done,
And sighed to think upon th' approaching sun,
For much it grieved her that the bright daylight
Should know the pleasure of this blessèd night,
And them like Mars and Erycine displayed,

Both in each other's arms chained as they laid.
Again she knew not how to frame her look,
Or speak to him who in a moment took
That which so long so charily she kept,
And fain by stealth away she would have crept,   310
And to some corner secretly have gone,
Leaving Leander in the bed alone.
But as her naked feet were whipping out,
He on the sudden clinged her so about
That mermaid-like unto the floor she slid;
One half appeared, the other half was hid.
Thus near the bed she blushing stood upright,
And from her countenance behold ye might
A kind of twilight break, which through the hair,
As from an orient cloud, glimpse here and there.   320
And round about the chamber this false morn
Brought forth the day before the day was born.
So Hero's ruddy cheek Hero betrayed,
And her all naked to his sight displayed,
Whence his admiring eyes more pleasure took
Than Dis on heaps of gold fixing his look.
By this Apollo's golden harp began
To sound forth music to the Ocean,
Which watchful Hesperus no sooner heard,
But he the day's bright-bearing car prepared,   330
And ran before, as harbinger of light,
And with his flaring beams mocked ugly Night,
Till she, o'ercome with anguish, shame and rage,
Danged down to hell her loathsome carriage.

Desunt nonnulla

GEORGE CHAPMAN

Continuation of Hero and Leander

TO MY BEST ESTEEMED AND

WORTHILY HONORED LADY,

THE LADY WALSINGHAM, ONE OF THE

LADIES OF HER MAJESTY'S BEDCHAMBER.

I present your ladyship with the last affections of the first
two lovers that ever muse shrined in the temple of memory;
being drawn by strange instigation to employ some of my
serious time in so trifling a subject, which yet made the first
author, divine Musaeus, eternal. And were it not that we
must subject our accounts of these common received con-
ceits to servile custom, it goes much against my hand to
sign that for a trifling subject, on which more worthiness of
soul hath been showed, and weight of divine wit, than can
vouchsafe residence in the leaden gravity of any money-   10
monger, in whose profession all serious subjects are con-
cluded. But he that shuns trifles must shun the world; out of
whose reverend heaps of substance and austerity I can, and
will ere long, single or tumble out as brainless and passion-
ate fooleries as ever panted in the bosom of the most ridicu-
lous lover. Accept it therefore, good madam, though as a
trifle, yet as a serious argument of my affection: for to be
thought thankful for all free and honorable favors is a great
sum of that riches my whole thrift intendeth.

Such uncourtly and silly dispositions as mine, whose   20
contentment hath other objects than profit or glory, are as

glad, simply for the naked merit of virtue, to honor such as advance her, as others that are hired to commend with deepliest politic bounty.

It hath therefore adjoined much contentment to my desire of your true honor to hear men of desert in court add to mine own knowledge of your noble disposition how gladly you do your best to prefer their desires, and have as absolute respect to their mere good parts, as if they came
30 perfumed and charmed with golden incitements. And this most sweet inclination, that flows from the truth and eternity of noblesse, assure your ladyship, doth more suit your other ornaments, and makes more to the advancement of your name, and happiness of your proceedings, than if (like others) you displayed ensigns of state and sourness in your forehead, made smooth with nothing but sensuality and presents.

This poor dedication (in figure of the other unity betwixt Sir Thomas and yourself) hath rejoined you with him, my
40 honored best friend, whose continuance of ancient kindness to my still-obscured estate, though it cannot increase my love to him, which hath ever been entirely circular, yet shall it encourage my deserts to their utmost requital, and make my hearty gratitude speak; to which the unhappiness of my life hath hitherto been uncomfortable and painful dumbness.

By your ladyship's vowed in most wished service:

GEORGE CHAPMAN

THE ARGUMENT OF THE
THIRD SESTIAD

Leander to the envious light
Resigns his night-sports with the night,
And swims the Hellespont again;
Thesme, the deity sovereign
Of customs and religious rites,
Appears, improving his delights
Since nuptial honors he neglected,
Which straight he vows shall be effected.
Fair Hero, left devirginate,
Weighs, and with fury wails her state;   10
But with her love and woman's wit
She argues, and approveth it.

New light gives new directions, fortunes new,
To fashion our endeavors that ensue;
More harsh (at least more hard) more grave and high
Our subject runs, and our stern muse must fly;
Love's edge is taken off, and that light flame,
Those thoughts, joys, longings, that before became
High unexperienced blood, and maids' sharp plights,
Must now grow staid, and censure the delights,
That being enjoyed ask judgment; now we praise,
As having parted: evenings crown the days.   10

And now ye wanton loves and young desires,
Pied vanity, the mint of strange attires,
Ye lisping flatteries and obsequious glances,
Relentful musics and attractive dances,
And you detested charms constraining love,
Shun love's stol'n sports by that these lovers prove.

By this the sovereign of heaven's golden fires,
And young Leander, lord of his desires,
Together from their lovers' arms arose:
20 Leander into Hellespontus throws
His Hero-handled body, whose delight
Made him disdain each other epithet.
And as amidst th' enamored waves he swims,
The god of gold of purpose gilt his limbs,   *He calls Phoebus*
That this word gilt including double sense,   *the God of Gold*
The double guilt of his incontinence   *since the virtue of*
                                                     his beams creates it
Might be expressed, that had no stay t' employ
The treasure which the love-god let him joy
In his dear Hero, with such sacred thrift
30 As had beseemed so sanctified a gift;
But like a greedy vulgar prodigal
Would on the stock dispend, and rudely fall
Before his time, to that unblessèd blessing,
Which for lust's plague doth perish with possessing.
Joy graven in sense, like snow in water, wastes;
Without preserve of virtue nothing lasts.
What man is he that with a wealthy eye
Enjoys a beauty richer than the sky,
Through whose white skin, softer than soundest sleep,
40 With damask eyes the ruby blood doth peep,
And runs in branches through her azure veins,
Whose mixture and first fire his love attains;
Whose both hands limit both love's deities,
And sweeten human thoughts like paradise;
Whose disposition silken is and kind,
Directed with an earth-exempted mind—
Who thinks not heaven with such a love is given?

And who like earth would spend that dower of heaven,
With rank desire to joy it all at first?
What simply kills our hunger, quencheth thirst,   50
Clothes but our nakedness, and makes us live,
Praise doth not any of her favors give:
But what doth plentifully minister
Beauteous apparel and delicious cheer,
So ordered that it still excites desire,
And still gives pleasure freeness to aspire,
The palm of bounty ever moist preserving:
To love's sweet life this is the courtly carving.
Thus Time, and all-states-ordering Ceremony
Had banished all offense: Time's golden thigh   60
Upholds the flowery body of the earth
In sacred harmony, and every birth
Of men and actions makes legitimate,
Being used aright. *The use of time is Fate.*

Yet did the gentle flood transfer once more
This prize of love home to his father's shore,
Where he unlades himself of that false wealth
That makes few rich, treasures composed by stealth;
And to his sister, kind Hermione
(Who on the shore kneeled, praying to the sea   70
For his return), he all love's goods did show,
In Hero seised for him, in him for Hero.
His most kind sister all his secrets knew,
And to her singing like a shower he flew,
Sprinkling the earth, that to their tombs took in
Streams dead for love to leave his ivory skin,
Which yet a snowy foam did leave above,
As soul to the dead water that did love;
And from thence did the first white roses spring
(For love is sweet and fair in every thing)   80
And all the sweetened shore as he did go,
Was crowned with od'rous roses white as snow.
Love-blest Leander was with love so fillèd,
That love to all that touched him he instillèd.

And as the colors of all things we see
To our sight's powers communicated be,
So to all objects that in compass came
Of any sense he had, his senses' flame
Flowed from his parts with force so virtual,
90   It fired with sense things mere insensual.

Now (with warm baths and odors comforted)
When he lay down he kindly kissed his bed,
As consecrating it to Hero's right,
And vowed thereafter that whatever sight
Put him in mind of Hero, or her bliss,
Should be her altar to prefer a kiss.

Then laid he forth his late enrichèd arms,
In whose white circle Love writ all his charms,
And made his characters sweet Hero's limbs,
100   When on his breast's warm sea she sidling swims.
And as those arms (held up in circle) met,
He said: "See, sister, Hero's carcanet,
Which she had rather wear about her neck,
Than all the jewels that doth Juno deck."

But as he shook with passionate desire
To put in flame his other secret fire,
A music so divine did pierce his ear,
As never yet his ravished sense did hear:
When suddenly a light of twenty hues
110   Brake through the roof, and like the rainbow views
Amazed Leander; in whose beams came down
The goddess Ceremony, with a crown
Of all the stars, and heaven with her descended;
Her flaming hair to her bright feet extended,
By which hung all the bench of deities,
And in a chain, compact of ears and eyes,
She led Religion. All her body was
Clear and transparent as the purest glass:
For she was all presented to the sense;

Devotion, Order, State, and Reverence   120
Her shadows were; Society, Memory;
All which her sight made live, her absence die.
A rich disparent pentacle she wears,
Drawn full of circles and strange characters;
Her face was changeable to every eye,
One way looked ill, another graciously;
Which while men viewed, they cheerful were and holy,
But looking off, vicious and melancholy.
The snaky paths to each observèd law
Did Policy in her broad bosom draw;   130
One hand a mathematic crystal sways,
Which gathering in one line a thousand rays
From her bright eyes, Confusion burns to death,
And all estates of men distinguisheth.
By it Morality and Comeliness
Themselves in all their sightly figures dress.
Her other hand a laurel rod applies,
To beat back Barbarism and Avarice
That followed, eating earth and excrement
And human limbs, and would make proud ascent   140
To seats of gods, were Ceremony slain.
The Hours and Graces bore her glorious train,
And all the sweets of our society
Were sphered and treasured in her bounteous eye.
Thus she appeared, and sharply did reprove
Leander's bluntness in his violent love;
Told him how poor was substance without rites,
Like bills unsigned, desires without delights;
Like meats unseasoned; like rank corn that grows
On cottages, that none or reaps or sows;   150
Not being with civil forms confirmed and bounded,
For human dignities and comforts founded,
But loose and secret, all their glories hide;
Fear fills the chamber, darkness decks the bride.

She vanished, leaving pierced Leander's heart
With sense of his unceremonious part,

In which with plain neglect of nuptial rites,
He close and flatly fell to his delights;
And instantly he vowed to celebrate
160 All rites pertaining to his married state.
So up he gets, and to his father goes,
To whose glad ears he doth his vows disclose.
The nuptials are resolved with utmost power,
And he at night would swim to Hero's tower,
From whence he meant to Sestos' forkèd bay
To bring her covertly, where ships must stay,
Sent by his father, throughly rigged and manned,
To waft her safely to Abydos' strand.
There leave we him, and with fresh wing pursue
170 Astonished Hero, whose most wishèd view
I thus long have forborne, because I left her
So out of count'nance, and her spirits bereft her.
To look on one abashed is impudence,
When of slight faults he hath too deep a sense.
Her blushing het her chamber; she looked out,
And all the air she purpled round about;
And after it a foul black day befell,
Which ever since a red morn doth foretell,
And still renews our woes for Hero's woe.
180 And foul it proved, because it figured so
The next night's horror, which prepare to hear:
I fail, if it profane your daintiest ear.

Then thou most strangely-intellectual fire,
That proper to my soul hast power t' inspire
Her burning faculties, and with the wings
Of thy unspherèd flame visit'st the springs
Of spirits immortal; now (as swift as Time
Doth follow Motion) find th' eternal clime
Of his free soul, whose living subject stood
190 Up to the chin in the Pierian flood,
And drunk to me half this Musaean story,
Inscribing it to deathless memory:

Confer with it, and make my pledge as deep,
That neither's draught be consecrate to sleep.
Tell it how much his late desires I tender
(If yet it know not), and to light surrender
My soul's dark offspring, willing it should die
To loves, to passions, and society.

Sweet Hero left upon her bed alone,
Her maidenhead, her vows, Leander gone,   200
And nothing with her but a violent crew
Of new come thoughts that yet she never knew,
Even to herself a stranger, was much like
Th' Iberian city that war's hand did strike
By English force in princely Essex' guide,
When peace assured her tow'rs had fortified,
And golden-fingered India had bestowed
Such wealth on her, that strength and empire flowed
Into her turrets, and her virgin waist
The wealthy girdle of the sea embraced;   210
Till our Leander, that made Mars his Cupid,
For soft love-suits, with iron thunders chid,
Swum to her towers, dissolved her virgin zone,
Led in his power, and made Confusion
Run through her streets amazed, that she supposed
She had not been in her own walls enclosed,
But rapt by wonder to some foreign state,
Seeing all her issue so disconsolate,
And all her peaceful mansions possessed
With war's just spoil, and many a foreign guest   220
From every corner driving an enjoyer,
Supplying it with power of a destroyer.
So fared fair Hero in th' expugnèd fort
Of her chaste bosom, and of every sort
Strange thoughts possessed her, ransacking her breast
For that that was not there, her wonted rest.
She was a mother straight, and bore with pain
Thoughts that spake straight, and wished their mother slain;

        She hates their lives, and they their own and hers:
230   Such strife still grows where sin the race prefers.
        Love is a golden bubble full of dreams,
        That waking breaks, and fills us with extremes.
        She mused how she could look upon her sire,
        And not show that without, that was intire.
        For as a glass is an inanimate eye,
        And outward forms embraceth inwardly,
        So is the eye an animate glass that shows
        In-forms without us. And as Phoebus throws
        His beams abroad though he in clouds be closed,
240   Still glancing by them till he find opposed
        A loose and rorid vapor that is fit
        T' event his searching beams, and useth it
        To form a tender twenty-colored eye,
        Cast in a circle round about the sky:
        So when our fiery soul, our body's star
        (That ever is in motion circular),
        Conceives a form, in seeking to display it
        Through all our cloudy parts, it doth convey it
        Forth at the eye, as the most pregnant place,
250   And that reflects it round about the face.
        And this event uncourtly Hero thought
        Her inward guilt would in her looks have wrought;
        For yet the world's stale cunning she resisted,
        To bear foul thoughts, yet forge what looks she listed,
        And held it for a very silly sleight,
        To make a perfect metal counterfeit:
        Glad to disclaim herself proud of an art
        That makes the face a pander to the heart.
        Those be the painted moons, whose lights profane
260   Beauty's true heaven, at full still in their wane.
        Those be the lapwing faces that still cry,
        "Here 'tis," when that they vow is nothing nigh.
        Base fools, when every moorish fowl can teach
        That which men think the height of human reach.
        But custom that the apoplexy is
        Of bedrid nature and lives led amiss,

And takes away all feeling of offense,
Yet brazed not Hero's brow with impudence;
And this she thought most hard to bring to pass,
To seem in count'nance other than she was,   270
As if she had two souls, one for the face,
One for the heart, and that they shifted place
As either list to utter or conceal
What they conceived; or as one soul did deal
With both affairs at once, keeps and ejects
Both at an instant contrary effects;
Retention and ejection in her powers
Being acts alike; for this one vice of ours,
That forms the thought, and sways the countenance,
Rules both our motion and our utterance.   280

These and more grave conceits toiled Hero's spirits;
For though the light of her discursive wits
Perhaps might find some little hole to pass
Through all these worldly cinctures, yet (alas)
There was a heavenly flame encompassed her,
Her goddess, in whose fane she did prefer
Her virgin vows; from whose impulsive sight
She knew the black shield of the darkest night
Could not defend her, nor wit's subtlest art:
This was the point pierced Hero to the heart.   290
Who heavy to the death, with a deep sigh
And hand that languished, took a robe was nigh,
Exceeding large, and of black cypress made,
In which she sat, hid from the day in shade,
Even over head and face down to her feet;
Her left hand made it at her bosom meet;
Her right hand leaned on her heart-bowing knee,
Wrapped in unshapeful folds 'twas death to see;
Her knee stayed that, and that her falling face,
Each limb helped other to put on disgrace.   300
No form was seen, where form held all her sight;
But like an embryon that saw never light,
Or like a scorchèd statue made a coal

With three-winged lightning, or a wretched soul
Muffled with endless darkness she did sit:
The night had never such a heavy spirit.
Yet might an imitating eye well see
How fast her clear tears melted on her knee
Through her black veil, and turned as black as it,
310   Mourning to be her tears. Then wrought her wit
With her broke vow, her goddess' wrath, her fame,
All tools that enginous despair could frame;
Which made her strew the floor with her torn hair,
And spread her mantle piecemeal in the air.
Like Jove's son's club, strong passion strook her
      down,
And with a piteous shriek enforced her swoon.
Her shriek made with another shriek ascend
The frighted matron that on her did tend;
And as with her own cry her sense was slain,
320   So with the other it was called again.
She rose, and to her bed made forcèd way,
And laid her down even where Leander lay;
And all this while the red sea of her blood
Ebbed with Leander; but now turned the flood,
And all her fleet of sprites came swelling in,
With child of sail, and did hot fight begin
With those severe conceits she too much marked,
And here Leander's beauties were embarked.
He came in swimming painted all with joys,
330   Such as might sweeten hell; his thought destroys
All her destroying thoughts; she thought she felt
His heart in hers with her contentions melt,
And chid her soul that it could so much err,
To check the true joys he deserved in her.
Her fresh heat blood cast figures in her eyes,
And she supposed she saw in Neptune's skies
How her star wandered, washed in smarting brine
For her love's sake, that with immortal wine
Should be embathed, and swim in more heart's-ease
340   Than there was water in the Sestian seas.

Then said her Cupid-prompted spirit: "Shall I
Sing moans to such delightsome harmony?
Shall slick-tongued Fame, patched up with voices rude,
The drunken bastard of the multitude
(Begot when father Judgment is away,
And, gossip-like, says because others say,
Takes news as if it were too hot to eat,
And spits it slavering forth for dog-fees meat),
Make me, for forging a fantastic vow,
Presume to bear what makes grave matrons bow?   350
Good vows are never broken with good deeds,
For then good deeds were bad; vows are but seeds,
And good deeds fruits; even those good deeds that grow
From other stocks than from th' observèd vow.
That is a good deed that prevents a bad:
Had I not yielded, slain myself I had.
Hero Leander is, Leander Hero:
Such virtue love hath to make one of two.
If then Leander did my maidenhead get,
Leander being myself I still retain it.   360
We break chaste vows when we live loosely ever;
But bound as we are, we live loosely never.
Two constant lovers being joined in one,
Yielding to one another, yield to none.
We know not how to vow, till love unblind us,
And vows made ignorantly never bind us.
Too true it is that when 'tis gone men hate
The joys as vain they took in love's estate;
But that's since they have lost the heavenly light
Should show them way to judge of all things right.   370
When life is gone, death must implant his terror;
As death is foe to life, so love to error.
Before we love, how range we through this sphere,
Searching the sundry fancies hunted here:
Now with desire of wealth transported quite
Beyond our free humanity's delight;
Now with ambition climbing falling towers,
Whose hope to scale our fear to fall devours;

Now rapt with pastimes, pomp, all joys impure:
In things without us no delight is sure.
But love, with all joys crowned, within doth sit:
O goddess, pity love, and pardon it!"

This spake she weeping, but her goddess' ear
Burned with too stern a heat, and would not hear.
Aye me, hath heaven's strait fingers no more graces
For such as Hero, than for homeliest faces?
Yet she hoped well, and in her sweet conceit
Weighing her arguments, she thought them weight,
And that the logic of Leander's beauty,
And them together, would bring proofs of duty.
And if her soul, that was a skillful glance
Of heaven's great essence, found such imperance
In her love's beauties, she had confidence
Jove loved him too, and pardoned her offense.
Beauty in heaven and earth this grace doth win,
It supples rigor, and it lessens sin.
Thus her sharp wit, her love, her secrecy,
Trooping together, made her wonder why
She should not leave her bed, and to the temple.
Her health said she must live; her sex, dissemble.
She viewed Leander's place, and wished he were
Turned to his place, so his place were Leander.
"Aye me," said she, "that love's sweet life and sense
Should do it harm! my love had not gone hence
Had he been like his place. O blessèd place,
Image of constancy! Thus my love's grace
Parts nowhere, but it leaves something behind
Worth observation: he renowns his kind.
His motion is like heaven's, orbicular,
For where he once is, he is ever there.
This place was mine; Leander, now 'tis thine;
Thou being myself, then it is double mine,
Mine, and Leander's mine, Leander's mine.
O see what wealth it yields me, nay yields him!
For I am in it, he for me doth swim.

Rich, fruitful love, that, doubling self-estates,
Elixir-like contracts, though separates.
Dear place, I kiss thee, and do welcome thee,
As from Leander ever sent to me."

The end of the third Sestiad

THE ARGUMENT OF THE
FOURTH SESTIAD

Hero, in sacred habit decked,
Doth private sacrifice effect;
Her scarf's description, wrought by Fate;
Ostents that threaten her estate;
The strange, yet physical events,
Leander's counterfeit presents;
In thunder Cyprides descends,
Presaging both the lovers' ends.
Ecte the goddess of remorse
With vocal and articulate force   10
Inspires Leucote, Venus' swan,
T'excuse the beauteous Sestian;
Venus, to wreak her rites' abuses,
Creates the monster Eronusis,   Eronusis, Dissimulation
Inflaming Hero's sacrifice
With lightning darted from her eyes;
And thereof springs the painted beast,
That ever since taints every breast.

Now from Leander's place she rose, and found
Her hair and rent robe scattered on the ground;
Which taking up, she every piece did lay
Upon an altar, where in youth of day
She used t' exhibit private sacrifice.
Those would she offer to the deities
Of her fair goddess and her powerful son,

As relics of her late-felt passion;
And in that holy sort she vowed to end them,
In hope her violent fancies that did rend them
Would as quite fade in her love's holy fire,
As they should in the flames she meant t' inspire.
Then put she on all her religious weeds,
That decked her in her secret sacred deeds:
A crown of icicles, that sun nor fire
Could ever melt, and figured chaste desire;
A golden star shined in her naked breast,
In honor of the queen-light of the east;
In her right hand she held a silver wand,
On whose bright top Peristera did stand,
Who was a nymph, but now transformed a dove,
And in her life was dear in Venus' love;
And for her sake she ever since that time
Choosed doves to draw her coach through heaven's
    blue clime.
Her plenteous hair in curlèd billows swims
On her bright shoulder; her harmonious limbs
Sustained no more but a most subtle veil
That hung on them, as it durst not assail
Their different concord; for the weakest air
Could raise it swelling from her beauties fair;
Nor did it cover, but adumbrate only
Her most heart-piercing parts, that a blest eye
Might see (as it did shadow) fearfully
All that all-love-deserving paradise.
It was as blue as the most freezing skies,
Near the sea's hue, for thence her goddess came.
On it a scarf she wore of wondrous frame,
In midst whereof she wrought a virgin's face,
From whose each cheek a fiery blush did chase
Two crimson flames, that did two ways extend,
Spreading the ample scarf to either end,
Which figured the division of her mind,
Whiles yet she rested bashfully inclined,
And stood not resolute to wed Leander.

This served her white neck for a purple sphere,
And cast itself at full breadth down her back.
There (since the first breath that begun the wrack
Of her free quiet from Leander's lips)
She wrought a sea in one flame full of ships;
But that one ship where all her wealth did pass   50
(Like simple merchants' goods) Leander was;
For in that sea she naked figured him;
Her diving needle taught him how to swim,
And to each thread did such resemblance give,
For joy to be so like him it did live.
Things senseless live by art, and rational die
By rude contempt of art and industry.
Scarce could she work but in her strength of thought
She feared she pricked Leander as she wrought,
And oft would shriek so, that her guardian, frighted,   60
Would staring haste, as with some mischief cited.
They double life that dead things' griefs sustain;
They kill that feel not their friends' living pain.
Sometimes she feared he sought her infamy,
And then as she was working of his eye,
She thought to prick it out to quench her ill;
But as she pricked, it grew more perfect still.
Trifling attempts no serious acts advance;
The fire of love is blown by dalliance.
In working his fair neck she did so grace it,   70
She still was working her own arms t' embrace it;
That, and his shoulders, and his hands were seen
Above the stream, and with a pure sea green
She did so quaintly shadow every limb,
All might be seen beneath the waves to swim.

In this conceited scarf she wrought beside
A moon in change, and shooting stars did glide
In number after her with bloody beams,
Which figured her affects in their extremes,
Pursuing Nature in her Cynthian body,   80
And did her thoughts running on change imply;

For maids take more delights when they prepare
And think of wives' states, than when wives they are.
Beneath all these she wrought a fisherman,
Drawing his nets from forth that ocean,
Who drew so hard, ye might discover well
The toughened sinews in his neck did swell;
His inward strains drave out his bloodshot eyes,
And springs of sweat did in his forehead rise;
90   Yet was of nought but of a serpent sped,
That in his bosom flew and stung him dead.
And this by fate into her mind was sent,
Not wrought by mere instinct of her intent.
At the scarf's other end her hand did frame,
Near the forked point of the divided flame,
A country virgin keeping of a vine,
Who did of hollow bulrushes combine
Snares for the stubble-loving grasshopper,
And by her lay her scrip that nourished her.
100 Within a myrtle shade she sat and sung,
And tufts of waving reeds about her sprung,
Where lurked two foxes, that while she applied
Her trifling snares, their thieveries did divide:
One to the vine, another to her scrip,
That she did negligently overslip;
By which her fruitful vine and wholesome fare
She suffered spoiled, to make a childish snare.
These ominous fancies did her soul express,
And every finger made a prophetess,
110 To show what death was hid in love's disguise,
And make her judgment conquer destinies.
O what sweet forms fair ladies' souls do shroud,
Were they made seen and forcèd through their blood;
If through their beauties, like rich work through lawn,
They would set forth their minds with virtues drawn,
In letting graces from their fingers fly,
To still their eyas thoughts with industry;
That their plied wits in numbered silks might sing
Passion's huge conquest, and their needles leading

Affection prisoner through their own-built cities,   120
Pinioned with stories and Arachnean ditties.

Proceed we now with Hero's sacrifice:
She odors burned, and from their smoke did rise
Unsavory fumes, that air with plagues inspired,
And then the consecrated sticks she fired,
On whose pale flame an angry spirit flew,
And beat it down still as it upward grew.
The virgin tapers that on th' altar stood,
When she inflamed them burned as red as blood:
All sad ostents of that too-near success,   130
That made such moving beauties motionless.
Then Hero wept; but her affrighted eyes
She quickly wrested from the sacrifice,
Shut them, and inwards for Leander looked,
Searched her soft bosom, and from thence she plucked
His lovely picture, which when she had viewed,
Her beauties were with all love's joys renewed.
The odors sweetened, and the fires burned clear,
Leander's form left no ill object there.
Such was his beauty that the force of light,   140
Whose knowledge teacheth wonders infinite,
The strength of number and proportion,
Nature had placed in it to make it known
Art was her daughter, and what human wits
For study lost, entombed in drossy spirits.
After this accident (which for her glory
Hero could not but make a history)
Th' inhabitants of Sestos and Abydos
Did every year with feasts propitious
To fair Leander's picture sacrifice;   150
And they were persons of especial prize
That were allowed it, as an ornament
T' enrich their houses, for the continent
Of the strange virtues all approved it held;
For even the very look of it repelled
All blastings, witchcrafts, and the strifes of nature

In those diseases that no herbs could cure.
The wolfy sting of Avarice it would pull,
And make the rankest miser bountiful.
160   It killed the fear of thunder and of death;
The discords that conceits engendereth
'Twixt man and wife it for the time would cease;
The flames of love it quenched, and would increase;
Held in a prince's hand it would put out
The dreadful'st comet; it would ease all doubt
Of threatened mischiefs; it would bring asleep
Such as were mad; it would enforce to weep
Most barbarous eyes; and many more effects
This picture wrought, and sprung Leandrian sects,
170   Of which was Hero first, for he whose form
(Held in her hand) cleared such a fatal storm,
From hell she thought his person would defend her,
Which night and Hellespont would quickly send her.
With this confirmed, she vowed to banish quite
All thought of any check to her delight;
And in contempt of silly bashfulness,
She would the faith of her desires profess:
Where her religion should be policy,
To follow love with zeal her piety;
180   Her chamber her cathedral church should be,
And her Leander her chief deity.
For in her love these did the gods forego;
And though her knowledge did not teach her so,
Yet did it teach her this, that what her heart
Did greatest hold in her self greatest part,
That she did make her god; and 'twas less naught
To leave gods in profession and in thought,
Than in her love and life; for therein lies
Most of her duties and their dignities;
190   And rail the brain-bald world at what it will,
That's the grand atheism that reigns in it still.
Yet singularity she would use no more,
For she was singular too much before:
But she would please the world with fair pretext;

Love would not leave her conscience perplexed.
Great men that will have less do for them, still
Must bear them out, though th' acts be ne'er so ill;
Meanness must pander be to excellence;
Pleasure atones falsehood and conscience.
Dissembling was the worst (thought Hero then)   200
And that was best, now she must live with men.
O virtuous love, that taught her to do best
When she did worst, and when she thought it least.
Thus would she still proceed in works divine,
And in her sacred state of priesthood shine,
Handling the holy rites with hands as bold
As if therein she did Jove's thunder hold,
And need not fear those menaces of error,
Which she at others threw with greatest terror.
O lovely Hero, nothing is thy sin,   210
Weighed with those foul faults other priests are in,
That having neither faiths, nor works, nor beauties,
T' engender any scuse for slubbered duties,
With as much count'nance fill their holy chairs,
And sweat denouncements 'gainst profane affairs,
As if their lives were cut out by their places,
And they the only fathers of the Graces.

Now as with settled mind she did repair
Her thoughts to sacrifice her ravished hair
And her torn robe, which on the altar lay,   220
And only for religion's fire did stay,
She heard a thunder by the Cyclops beaten,
In such a volley as the world did threaten,
Given Venus as she parted th' airy sphere,
Descending now to chide with Hero here.
When suddenly the goddess' waggoners,
The swans and turtles that in coupled feres
Through all worlds' bosoms draw her influence,
Lighted in Hero's window, and from thence
To her fair shoulders flew the gentle doves,   230
Graceful Aedone that sweet pleasure loves,

And ruff-foot Chreste with the tufted crown;
Both which did kiss her, though their goddess frown.
The swans did in the solid flood, her glass,
Proin their fair plumes; of which the fairest was
Jove-loved Leucote, that pure brightness is,
The other bounty-loving Dapsilis.
All were in heaven, now they with Hero were,
But Venus' looks brought wrath, and urgèd fear.
240 Her robe was scarlet, black her head's attire,
And through her naked breast shined streams of fire,
As when the rarefièd air is driven
In flashing streams, and opes the darkened heaven.
In her white hand a wreath of yew she bore,
And breaking th' icy wreath sweet Hero wore,
She forced about her brows her wreath of yew,
And said, "Now, minion, to thy fate be true,
Though not to me; endure what this portends;
Begin where lightness will, in shame it ends.
250 Love makes thee cunning; thou art current now
By being counterfeit: thy broken vow
Deceit with her pied garters must rejoin,
And with her stamp thou count'nances must coin:
Coyness, and pure deceits, for purities,
And still a maid wilt seem in cozened eyes,
And have an antic face to laugh within,
While thy smooth looks make men digest thy sin.
But since thy lips (lest thought forsworn) forswore,
Be never virgin's vow worth trusting more."

260 When Beauty's dearest did her goddess hear
Breathe such rebukes 'gainst that she could not
     clear,
Dumb sorrow spake aloud in tears and blood
That from her grief-burst veins in piteous flood
From the sweet conduits of her favor fell.
The gentle turtles did with moans make swell
Their shining gorges; the white black-eyed swans
Did sing as woeful epicedians,

As they would straightways die: when pity's queen,
The goddess Ecte, that had ever been
Hid in a wat'ry cloud near Hero's cries,   270
Since the first instant of her broken eyes,
Gave bright Leucote voice, and made her speak
To ease her anguish, whose swol'n breast did break
With anger at her goddess, that did touch
Hero so near for that she used so much.
And thrusting her white neck at Venus, said:
"Why may not amorous Hero seem a maid,
Though she be none, as well as you suppress
In modest cheeks your inward wantonness?
How often have we drawn you from above,   280
T' exchange with mortals rites for rites in love?
Why in your priest then call you that offense
That shines in you, and is your influence?"
With this the Furies stopped Leucote's lips,
Enjoined by Venus, who with rosy whips
Beat the kind bird. Fierce lightning from her eyes
Did set on fire fair Hero's sacrifice,
Which was her torn robe, and enforcèd hair;
And the bright flame became a maid most fair
For her aspect: her tresses were of wire,   *Description*   290
Knit like a net, where hearts all set on fire *and creation of*
Struggled in pants and could not get released; *Dissimulation*
Her arms were all with golden pincers drest,
And twenty-fashioned knots, pulleys, and brakes,
And all her body girdled with painted snakes.
Her down parts in a scorpion's tail combined,
Freckled with twenty colors; pied wings shined
Out of her shoulders; cloth had never dye,
Nor sweeter colors never viewèd eye,
In scorching Turkey, Cares, Tartary,   300
Than shined about this spirit notorious;
Nor was Arachne's web so glorious.
Of lightning and of shreds she was begot;
More hold in base dissemblers is there not.
Her name was Eronusis. Venus flew

From Hero's sight, and at her chariot drew
This wondrous creature to so steep a height
That all the world she might command with sleight
Of her gay wings; and then she bade her haste,
310   Since Hero had dissembled, and disgraced
Her rites so much, and every breast infect
With her deceits; she made her architect
Of all dissimulation, and since then
Never was any trust in maids nor men.

O it spited
Fair Venus' heart to see her most delighted,
And one she choosed, for temper of her mind,
To be the only ruler of her kind,
So soon to let her virgin race be ended;
320   Not simply for the fault a whit offended,
But that in strife for chasteness with the moon,
Spiteful Diana bade her show but one
That was her servant vowed, and lived a maid.
And now she thought to answer that upbraid,
Hero had lost her answer; who knows not
Venus would seem as far from any spot
Of light demeanor as the very skin
'Twixt Cynthia's brows? Sin is ashamed of sin.
Up Venus flew, and scarce durst up for fear
330   Of Phoebe's laughter, when she passed her sphere;
And so most ugly clouded was the light,
That day was hid in day, night came ere night,
And Venus could not through the thick air pierce,
Till the day's king, god of undaunted verse,
Because she was so plentiful a theme
To such as wore his laurel anademe,
Like to a fiery bullet made descent,
And from her passage those fat vapors rent,
That being not throughly rarefied to rain,
340   Melted like pitch as blue as any vein;
And scalding tempests made the earth to shrink
Under their fervor, and the world did think

In every drop a torturing spirit flew,
It pierced so deeply, and it burned so blue.

Betwixt all this and Hero, Hero held
Leander's picture, as a Persean shield;
And she was free from fear of worst success.
The more ill threats us, we suspect the less;
As we grow hapless, violence subtle grows,
Dumb, deaf, and blind, and comes when no man   350
    knows.

The end of the fourth Sestiad

THE ARGUMENT OF THE
FIFTH SESTIAD

Day doubles her accustomed date,
As loth the night, incensed by Fate,
Should wrack our lovers; Hero's plight
Longs for Leander and the night;
Which ere her thirsty wish recovers,
She sends for two betrothèd lovers,
And marries them, that (with their crew,
Their sports and ceremonies due)
She covertly might celebrate
With secret joy her own estate;   10
She makes a feast, at which appears
The wild nymph Teras, that still bears
An ivory lute, tells ominous tales,
And sings at solemn festivals.

Now was bright Hero weary of the day,
Thought an Olympiad in Leander's stay.
Sol and the soft-foot Hours hung on his arms,
And would not let him swim, foreseeing his harms:
That day Aurora double grace obtained

Of her love Phoebus; she his horses reined,
Set on his golden knee, and as she list
She pulled him back; and as she pulled, she kissed,
To have him turn to bed; he loved her more,
10   To see the love Leander Hero bore.
Examples profit much; ten times in one,
In persons full of note, good deeds are done.

Day was so long, men walking fell asleep;
The heavy humors that their eyes did steep
Made them fear mischiefs. The hard streets were beds
For covetous churls, and for ambitious heads,
That spite of nature would their business ply.
All thought they had the falling epilepsy,
Men groveled so upon the smothered ground,
20   And pity did the heart of heaven confound.
The gods, the Graces, and the Muses came
Down to the Destinies, to stay the frame
Of the true lovers' deaths, and all world's tears:
But Death before had stopped their cruel ears.
All the celestials parted mourning then,
Pierced with our human miseries more than men.
Ah, nothing doth the world with mischief fill,
But want of feeling one another's ill.

With their descent the day grew something fair,
30   And cast a brighter robe upon the air.
Hero, to shorten time with merriment,
For young Alcmane and bright Mya sent,
Two lovers that had long craved marriage dues
At Hero's hands; but she did still refuse,
For lovely Mya was her consort vowed
In her maid's state, and therefore not allowed
To amorous nuptials, yet fair Hero now
Intended to dispense with her cold vow,
Since hers was broken, and to marry her.
40   The rites would pleasing matter minister
To her conceits, and shorten tedious day.

They came; sweet Music ushered th' odorous way,
And wanton Air in twenty sweet forms danced
After her fingers; Beauty and Love advanced
Their ensigns in the downless rosy faces
Of youths and maids, led after by the Graces.
For all these Hero made a friendly feast,
Welcomed them kindly, did much love protest,
Winning their hearts with all the means she might,
That when her fault should chance t' abide the
     light,   50
Their loves might cover or extenuate it,
And high in her worst fate make pity sit.

She married them, and in the banquet came,
Borne by the virgins; Hero strived to frame
Her thoughts to mirth. Aye me, but hard it is
To imitate a false and forcèd bliss.
Ill may a sad mind forge a merry face,
Nor hath constrainèd laughter any grace.
Then laid she wine on cares to make them sink;
Who fears the threats of Fortune, let him drink.   60

To these quick nuptials entered suddenly
Admired Teras with the ebon thigh,
A nymph that haunted the green Sestian groves,
And would consort soft virgins in their loves,
At gaysome triumphs and on solemn days,
Singing prophetic elegies and lays,
And fing'ring of a silver lute she tied
With black and purple scarfs by her left side.
Apollo gave it, and her skill withal,
And she was termed his dwarf, she was so small.   70
Yet great in virtue, for his beams enclosed
His virtues in her; never was proposed
Riddle to her, or augury, strange or new,
But she resolved it; never slight tale flew
From her charmed lips without important sense,
Shown in some grave succeeding consequence.

This little sylvan with her songs and tales
Gave such estate to feasts and nuptials,
That though oft times she forewent tragedies,
80   Yet for her strangeness still she pleased their eyes,
And for her smallness they admired her so,
They thought her perfect born, and could not grow.

All eyes were on her: Hero did command
An altar decked with sacred state should stand
At the feast's upper end, close by the bride,
On which the pretty nymph might sit espied.
Then all were silent; everyone so hears,
As all their senses climbed into their ears;
And first this amorous tale that fitted well
90   Fair Hero and the nuptials she did tell.

The Tale of Teras
Hymen, that now is god of nuptial rites,
And crowns with honor love and his delights,
Of Athens was a youth so sweet of face,
That many thought him of the female race;
Such quick'ning brightness did his clear eyes dart,
Warm went their beams to his beholder's heart.
In such pure leagues his beauties were combined,
That there your nuptial contracts first were signed.
For as proportion, white and crimson, meet
100 In beauty's mixture, all right clear and sweet,
The eye responsible, the golden hair,
And none is held without the other fair,
All spring together, all together fade:
Such intermixed affections should invade
Two perfect lovers, which being yet unseen,
Their virtues and their comforts copied been
In beauty's concord, subject to the eye;
And that, in Hymen, pleased so matchlessly,
That lovers were esteemed in their full grace
110 Like form and color mixed in Hymen's face;
And such sweet concord was thought worthy then

Of torches, music, feasts, and greatest men.
So Hymen looked, that even the chastest mind
He moved to join in joys of sacred kind;
For only now his chin's first down consorted
His head's rich fleece, in golden curls contorted;
And as he was so loved, he loved so too,
So should best beauties, bound by nuptials, do.

Bright Eucharis, who was by all men said
The noblest, fairest, and the richest maid   120
Of all th' Athenian damsels, Hymen loved
With such transmission, that his heart removed
From his white breast to hers, but her estate
In passing his was so interminate
For wealth and honor, that his love durst feed
On nought but sight and hearing, nor could breed
Hope of requital, the grand prize of love;
Nor could he hear or see, but he must prove
How his rare beauty's music would agree
With maids in consort; therefore robbèd he   130
His chin of those same few first fruits it bore,
And, clad in such attire as virgins wore,
He kept them company, and might right well,
For he did all but Eucharis excel
In all the fair of beauty; yet he wanted
Virtue to make his own desires implanted
In his dear Eucharis, for women never
Love beauty in their sex, but envy ever.
His judgment yet (that durst not suit address,
Nor past due means presume of due success)   140
Reason gat Fortune in the end to speed
To his best prayers: but strange it seemed indeed
That Fortune should a chaste affection bless;
Preferment seldom graceth bashfulness.
Nor graced it Hymen yet; but many a dart
And many an amorous thought enthralled his heart
Ere he obtained her; and he sick became,
Forced to abstain her sight, and then the flame

Raged in his bosom. O what grief did fill him:
150   Sight made him sick, and want of sight did kill him.
The virgins wondered where Diaetia stayed,
For so did Hymen term himself a maid.
At length with sickly looks he greeted them:
'Tis strange to see 'gainst what an extreme stream
A lover strives; poor Hymen looked so ill,
That as in merit he increasèd still
By suff'ring much, so he in grace decreased.
Women are most won when men merit least:
If merit look not well, love bids stand by;
160   Love's special lesson is to please the eye.
And Hymen soon recovering all he lost,
Deceiving still these maids, but himself most,
His love and he with many virgin dames,
Noble by birth, noble by beauty's flames,
Leaving the town with songs and hallowed lights,
To do great Ceres Eleusina rites
Of zealous sacrifice, were made a prey
To barbarous rovers that in ambush lay,
And with rude hands enforced their shining spoil,
170   Far from the darkened city, tired with toil.
And when the yellow issue of the sky
Came trooping forth, jealous of cruelty
To their bright fellows of this under-heaven,
Into a double night they saw them driven,
A horrid cave, the thieves' black mansion,
Where weary of the journey they had gone,
Their last night's watch, and drunk with their sweet
      gains,
Dull Morpheus entered, laden with silken chains,
Stronger than iron, and bound the swelling veins
180   And tired senses of these lawless swains.
But when the virgin lights thus dimly burned,
O what a hell was heaven in! how they mourned
And wrung their hands, and wound their gentle forms
Into the shapes of sorrow! Golden storms
Fell from their eyes; as when the sun appears,

And yet it rains, so showed their eyes their tears.
And as when funeral dames watch a dead corse,
Weeping about it, telling with remorse
What pains he felt, how long in pain he lay,
How little food he ate, what he would say;   190
And then mix mournful tales of others' deaths,
Smothering themselves in clouds of their own
    breaths;
At length, one cheering other, call for wine,
The golden bowl drinks tears out of their eyne,
As they drink wine from it; and round it goes,
Each helping other to relieve their woes:
So cast these virgins beauty's mutual rays,
One lights another, face the face displays;
Lips by reflection kissed, and hands hands shook,
Even by the whiteness each of other took.   200

But Hymen now used friendly Morpheus' aid,
Slew every thief, and rescued every maid.
And now did his enamored passion take
Heart from his hearty deed, whose worth did make
His hope of bounteous Eucharis more strong;
And now came Love with Proteus, who had long
Ingled the little god with prayers and gifts,
Ran through all shapes, and varied all his shifts,
To win Love's stay with him, and make him love him;
And when he saw no strength of sleight could
    move him   210
To make him love, or stay, he nimbly turned
Into Love's self, he so extremely burned.
And thus came Love with Proteus and his pow'r,
T' encounter Eucharis: first like the flow'r
That Juno's milk did spring, the silver lily,
He fell on Hymen's hand, who straight did spy
The bounteous godhead, and with wondrous joy
Offered it Eucharis. She, wondrous coy,
Drew back her hand: the subtle flow'r did woo it,
And drawing it near, mixed so you could not know it.   220

As two clear tapers mix in one their light,
So did the lily and the hand their white.
She viewed it, and her view the form bestows
Amongst her spirits: for as color flows
From superficies of each thing we see,
Even so with colors forms emitted be,
And where Love's form is, Love is; Love is form.
He entered at the eye, his sacred storm
Rose from the hand, Love's sweetest instrument;
230   It stirred her blood's sea so, that high it went,
And beat in bashful waves 'gainst the white shore
Of her divided cheeks; it raged the more,
Because the tide went 'gainst the haughty wind
Of her estate and birth. And as we find
In fainting ebbs the flow'ry Zephyr hurls
The green-haired Hellespont, broke in silver curls
'Gainst Hero's tower, but in his blast's retreat,
The waves obeying him, they after beat,
Leaving the chalky shore a great way pale,
240   Then moist it freshly with another gale:
So ebbed and flowed the blood in Eucharis' face,
Coyness and Love strived which had greatest grace.
Virginity did fight on Coyness' side,
Fear of her parents' frowns, and female pride
Loathing the lower place more than it loves
The high contents desert and virtue moves.
With Love fought Hymen's beauty and his valor,
Which scarce could so much favor yet allure
To come to strike, but fameless, idle stood:
250   *Action is fiery valor's sovereign good.*
But Love once entered, wished no greater aid
Than he could find within; thought thought betrayed;
The bribed, but incorrupted garrison
Sung "Io Hymen." There those songs begun,
And Love was grown so rich with such a gain,
And wanton with the ease of his free reign,
That he would turn into her roughest frowns
To turn them out; and thus he Hymen crowns

King of his thoughts, man's greatest empery:
This was his first brave step to deity.   260

Home to the mourning city they repair,
With news as wholesome as the morning air
To the sad parents of each savèd maid;
But Hymen and his Eucharis had laid
This plot, to make the flame of their delight
Round as the moon at full, and full as bright.

Because the parents of chaste Eucharis
Exceeding Hymen's so, might cross their bliss,
And as the world rewards deserts, that law
Cannot assist with force, so when they saw   270
Their daughter safe, take vantage of their own,
Praise Hymen's valor much, nothing bestown,
Hymen must leave the virgins in a grove
Far off from Athens, and go first to prove,
If to restore them all with fame and life,
He should enjoy his dearest as his wife.
This told to all the maids, the most agree:
The riper sort, knowing what 'tis to be
The first mouth of a news so far derived,
And that to hear and bear news brave folks lived,   280
As being a carriage special hard to bear
Occurrents, these occurrents being so dear,
They did with grace protest they were content
T' accost their friends with all their complement
For Hymen's good; but to incur their harm,
There he must pardon them. This wit went warm
To Adolesche's brain, a nymph born high,
Made all of voice and fire, that upwards fly:
Her heart and all her forces' nether train
Climbed to her tongue, and thither fell her brain,   290
Since it could go no higher, and it must go;
All powers she had, even her tongue, did so.
In spirit and quickness she much joy did take,
And loved her tongue, only for quickness' sake;

And she would haste and tell. The rest all stay;
Hymen goes one, the nymph another way,
And what became of her I'll tell at last.
Yet take her visage now: moist-lipped, long-faced,
Thin like an iron wedge, so sharp and tart
300   As 'twere of purpose made to cleave Love's heart;
Well were this lovely beauty rid of her.
And Hymen did at Athens now prefer
His welcome suit, which he with joy aspired:
A hundred princely youths with him retired
To fetch the nymphs; chariots and music went,
And home they came: heaven with applauses rent.
The nuptials straight proceed, whiles all the town
Fresh in their joys might do them most renown.
First gold-locked Hymen did to church repair,
310   Like a quick off'ring burned in flames of hair;
And after, with a virgin firmament,
The godhead-proving bride attended went
Before them all; she looked in her command,
As if form-giving Cyprias' silver hand
Gripped all their beauties, and crushed out one flame;
She blushed to see how beauty overcame
The thoughts of all men. Next before her went
Five lovely children decked with ornament
Of her sweet colors, bearing torches by,
320   For light was held a happy augury
Of generation, whose efficient right
Is nothing else but to produce to light.
The odd disparent number they did choose,
To show the union married loves should use,
Since in two equal parts it will not sever,
But the midst holds one to rejoin it ever,
As common to both parts: men therefore deem
That equal number gods do not esteem,
Being authors of sweet peace and unity,
330   But pleasing to th' infernal empery
Under whose ensigns wars and discords fight,
Since an even number you may disunite

In two parts equal, nought in middle left
To reunite each part from other reft;
And five they hold in most especial prize,
Since 'tis the first odd number that doth rise
From the two foremost numbers' unity,
That odd and even are: which are two and three,
For one no number is, but thence doth flow
The powerful race of number. Next did go   340
A noble matron that did spinning bear
A housewife's rock and spindle, and did wear
A wether's skin, with all the snowy fleece,
To intimate that even the daintiest piece
And noblest-born dame should industrious be;
That which does good disgraceth no degree.

And now to Juno's temple they are come,
Where her grave priest stood in the marriage room.
On his right arm did hang a scarlet veil,
And from his shoulders to the ground did trail,   350
On either side, ribbons of white and blue;
With the red veil he hid the bashful hue
Of the chaste bride, to show the modest shame,
In coupling with a man, should grace a dame.
Then took he the disparent silks, and tied
The lovers by the waists, and side to side,
In token that thereafter they must bind
In one self sacred knot each other's mind.
Before them on an altar he presented
Both fire and water, which was first invented,   360
Since to ingenerate every human creature,
And every other birth produced by Nature,
Moisture and heat must mix: so man and wife
For human race must join in nuptial life.
Then one of Juno's birds, the painted jay,
He sacrificed, and took the gall away;
All which he did behind the altar throw,
In sign no bitterness of hate should grow
'Twixt married loves, nor any least disdain.

370 Nothing they spake, for 'twas esteemed too plain
     For the most silken mildness of a maid
     To let a public audience hear it said
     She boldly took the man; and so respected
     Was bashfulness in Athens, it erected
     To chaste Agneia, which is shamefastness,
     A sacred temple, holding her a goddess.
     And now to feasts, masques, and triumphant shows
     The shining troops returned, even till earth's throes
     Brought forth with joy the thickest part of night,
380 When the sweet nuptial song, that used to cite
     All to their rest, was by Phemonoe sung,
     First Delphian prophetess, whose graces sprung
     Out of the Muses' well: she sung before
     The bride into her chamber, at which door
     A matron and a torch-bearer did stand;
     A painted box of comfits in her hand
     The matron held, and so did other some
     That compassed round the honored nuptial room.
     The custom was that every maid did wear,
390 During her maidenhead, a silken sphere
     About her waist, above her inmost weed,
     Knit with Minerva's knot, and that was freed
     By the fair bridegroom on the marriage night,
     With many ceremonies of delight.
     And yet eternized Hymen's tender bride
     To suffer it dissolved so sweetly cried.
     The maids that heard so loved and did adore her,
     They wished with all their hearts to suffer for her.
     So had the matrons, that with comfits stood
400 About the chamber, such affectionate blood,
     And so true feeling of her harmless pains,
     That every one a shower of comfits rains,
     For which the bride-youths scrambling on the
             ground,
     In noise of that sweet hail her cries were drowned.
     And thus blest Hymen joyed his gracious bride,
     And for his joy was after deified.

The saffron mirror by which Phoebus' love,
Green Tellus, decks her, now he held above
The cloudy mountains, and the noble maid,
Sharp-visaged Adolesche, that was strayed   410
Out of her way, in hasting with her news,
Not till this hour th' Athenian turrets views;
And now brought home by guides, she heard by all
That her long kept occurrents would be stale,
And how fair Hymen's honors did excel
For those rare news, which she came short to tell.
To hear her dear tongue robbed of such a joy
Made the well-spoken nymph take such a toy,
That down she sunk; when lightning from above
Shrunk her lean body, and for mere free love,   420
Turned her into the pied-plumed Psittacus,
That now the parrot is surnamed by us,
Who still with counterfeit confusion prates
Nought but news common to the common'st
      mates.
This told, strange Teras touched her lute, and sung
This ditty that the torchy evening sprung.

Epithalamion Teratos
Come, come, dear Night, Love's mart of kisses,
Sweet close of his ambitious line,
The fruitful summer of his blisses,
Love's glory doth in darkness shine.   430
O come, soft rest of cares, come Night,
Come naked Virtue's only tire,
The reapèd harvest of the light,
Bound up in sheaves of sacred fire.
      Love calls to war,
      Sighs his alarms,
      Lips his swords are,
      The field his arms.
Come, Night, and lay thy velvet hand
On glorious Day's outfacing face,   440
And all thy crownèd flames command

For torches to our nuptial grace.
    Love calls to war,
    Sighs his alarms,
    Lips his swords are,
    The field his arms.
No need have we of factious Day,
To cast in envy of thy peace
Her balls of discord in thy way:
450 Here Beauty's day doth never cease;
Day is abstracted here,
And varied in a triple sphere.
Hero, Alcmane, Mya so outshine thee,
Ere thou come here let Thetis thrice refine thee.
    Love calls to war,
    Sighs his alarms,
    Lips his swords are,
    The field his arms.
The evening star I see:
460 Rise, youths, the evening star
Helps Love to summon war;
Both now embracing be.
Rise, youths, Love's right claims more than
    banquets, rise.
Now the bright marigolds that deck the skies,
Phoebus' celestial flowers, that (contrary
To his flowers here) ope when he shuts his eye,
And shut when he doth open, crown your sports.
Now Love in Night, and Night in Love exhorts
Courtship and dances. All your parts employ,
470 And suit Night's rich expansure with your joy.
Love paints his longings in sweet virgins' eyes:
Rise, youths, Love's right claims more than
    banquets, rise.
Rise, virgins, let fair nuptial loves enfold
Your fruitless breasts: the maidenheads ye hold
Are not your own alone, but parted are;
Part in disposing them your parents share,
And that a third part is, so must ye save

Your loves a third, and you your thirds must have.
Love paints his longings in sweet virgins' eyes:
Rise, youths, Love's right claims more than   480
    banquets, rise.

Herewith the amorous spirit that was so kind
To Teras' hair, and combed it down with wind,
Still as it comet-like brake from her brain,
Would needs have Teras gone, and did refrain
To blow it down: which staring up dismayed
The timorous feast, and she no longer stayed,
But bowing to the bridegroom and the bride,
Did like a shooting exhalation glide
Out of their sights; the turning of her back
Made them all shriek, it looked so ghastly black.   490
O hapless Hero, that most hapless cloud
Thy soon-succeeding tragedy foreshowed.
Thus all the nuptial crew to joys depart,
But much-wronged Hero stood hell's blackest dart;
Whose wound because I grieve so to display,
I use digressions thus t' increase the day.

The end of the fifth Sestiad

THE ARGUMENT OF THE
SIXTH SESTIAD

Leucote flies to all the winds,
And from the Fates their outrage binds,
That Hero and her love may meet.
Leander (with Love's complete fleet
Manned in himself), puts forth to seas,
When straight the ruthless Destinies
With Ate stir the winds to war
Upon the Hellespont; their jar
Drowns poor Leander; Hero's eyes,

10   *Wet witnesses of his surprise,*
      Her torch blown out, grief casts her down
      Upon her love, and both doth drown;
      In whose just ruth the god of seas
      Transforms them to th' Acanthides.

      No longer could the Day nor Destinies
      Delay the Night, who now did frowning rise
      Into her throne; and at her humorous breasts
      Visions and Dreams lay sucking: all men's rests
      Fell like the mists of death upon their eyes,
      Day's too-long darts so killed their faculties.
      The winds yet, like the flow'rs, to cease began,
      For bright Leucote, Venus' whitest swan,
      That held sweet Hero dear, spread her fair wings,
10   Like to a field of snow, and message brings
      From Venus to the Fates, t' entreat them lay
      Their charge upon the winds their rage to stay,
      That the stern battle of the seas might cease,
      And guard Leander to his love in peace.
      The Fates consent (aye me, dissembling Fates),
      They showed their favors to conceal their hates,
      And draw Leander on, lest seas too high
      Should stay his too obsequious Destiny;
      Who like a fleering slavish parasite,
      In warping profit or a traitorous sleight,   20
      Hoops round his rotten body with devotes,
      And pricks his descant face full of false notes,
      Praising with open throat, and oaths as foul
      As his false heart, the beauty of an owl;
      Kissing his skipping hand with charmèd skips,
      That cannot leave, but leaps upon his lips
      Like a cock-sparrow, or a shameless quean
      Sharp at a red-lipped youth, and nought doth mean
      Of all his antic shows, but doth repair
      More tender fawns, and takes a scattered hair   30
      From his tame subject's shoulder; whips, and calls
      For every thing he lacks; creeps 'gainst the walls

With backward humbless, to give needless way:
Thus his false fate did with Leander play.

First to black Eurus flies the white Leucote,
Born 'mongst the negroes in the Levant sea,
On whose curled head the glowing sun doth rise,
And shows the sovereign will of Destinies,
To have him cease his blasts, and down he lies.
Next, to the fenny Notus course she holds,   40
And found him leaning with his arms in folds
Upon a rock, his white hair full of show'rs,
And him she chargeth by the fatal pow'rs
To hold in his wet cheeks his cloudy voice.
To Zephyr then that doth in flow'rs rejoice;
To snake-foot Boreas next she did remove,
And found him tossing of his ravished love,
To heat his frosty bosom hid in snow,
Who with Leucote's sight did cease to blow.
Thus all were still to Hero's heart's desire,   50
Who with all speed did consecrate a fire
Of flaming gums and comfortable spice,
To light her torch, which in such curious price
She held, being object to Leander's sight,
That nought but fires perfumed must give it light.
She loved it so, she grieved to see it burn,
Since it would waste and soon to ashes turn;
Yet if it burned not, 'twere not worth her eyes,
What made it nothing gave it all the prize.
Sweet torch, true glass of our society: 60
What man does good, but he consumes thereby?
But thou wert loved for good, held high, given show;
Poor virtue loathed for good, obscured, held low.
Do good, be pined; be deedless good, disgraced:
Unless we feed on men, we let them fast.
Yet Hero with these thoughts her torch did spend:
When bees makes wax, Nature doth not intend
It shall be made a torch, but we that know
The proper virtue of it make it so,

70   And when 'tis made we light it; nor did Nature
     Propose one life to maids, but each such creature
     Makes by her soul the best of her free state,
     Which without love is rude, disconsolate,
     And wants love's fire to make it mild and bright,
     Till when, maids are but torches wanting light.
     Thus 'gainst our grief, not cause of grief we fight;
     The right of nought is gleaned, but the delight.
     Up went she, but to tell how she descended,
     Would God she were not dead, or my verse ended!
80   She was the rule of wishes, sum and end,
     For all the parts that did on love depend.
     Yet cast the torch his brightness further forth;
     But what shines nearest best, holds truest worth.
     Leander did not through such tempests swim
     To kiss the torch, although it lighted him;
     But all his pow'rs in her desires awakèd,
     Her love and virtues clothed him richly naked.
     Men kiss but fire that only shows pursue;
     Her torch and Hero figure show and virtue.

90   Now at opposed Abydos nought was heard
     But bleating flocks, and many a bellowing herd
     Slain for the nuptials, cracks of falling woods,
     Blows of broad axes, pourings out of floods.
     The guilty Hellespont was mixed and stained
     With bloody torrents that the shambles rained;
     Not arguments of feast, but shows that bled,
     Foretelling that red night that followèd.
     More blood was spilt, more honors were addressed,
     Than could have gracèd any happy feast.
100 Rich banquets, triumphs, every pomp employs
     His sumptuous hand: no miser's nuptial joys.
     Air felt continual thunder with the noise,
     Made in the general marriage violence;
     And no man knew the cause of this expense,
     But the two hapless lords, Leander's sire,
     And poor Leander, poorest where the fire

Of credulous love made him most rich surmised.
As short was he of that himself he prized
As is an empty gallant full of form,
That thinks each look an act, each drop a storm,   110
That falls from his brave breathings; most brought up
In our metropolis, and hath his cup
Brought after him to feasts; and much palm bears
For his rare judgment in th' attire he wears;
Hath seen the hot Low Countries, not their heat,
Observes their rampires and their buildings yet;
And for your sweet discourse with mouths is heard
Giving instructions with his very beard;
Hath gone with an ambassador, and been
A great man's mate in traveling, even to Rhene;   120
And then puts all his worth in such a face
As he saw brave men make, and strives for grace
To get his news forth. As when you descry
A ship with all her sail contends to fly
Out of the narrow Thames with winds unapt,
Now crosseth here, then there, then this way rapt,
And then hath one point reached; then alters all,
And to another crooked reach doth fall
Of half a bird-bolt's shoot, keeping more coil
Than if she danced upon the ocean's toil: 130
So serious is his trifling company,
In all his swelling ship of vacantry.
And so short of himself in his high thought
Was our Leander in his fortunes brought,
And in his fort of love that he thought won,
But otherwise he scorns comparison.

O sweet Leander, thy large worth I hide
In a short grave; ill-favored storms must chide
Thy sacred favor: I in floods of ink
Must drown thy graces, which white papers drink,   140
Even as thy beauties did the foul black seas.
I must describe the hell of thy dis-ease,
That heaven did merit; yet I needs must see

Our painted fools and cockhorse peasantry
Still, still usurp, with long lives, loves, and lust,
The seats of Virtue, cutting short as dust
Her dear-bought issue. Ill to worse converts,
And tramples in the blood of all deserts.

Night close and silent now goes fast before
150   The captains and their soldiers to the shore,
On whom attended the appointed fleet
At Sestos' bay, that should Leander meet,
Who feigned he in another ship would pass;
Which must not be, for no one mean there was
To get his love home, but the course he took.
Forth did his beauty for his beauty look,
And saw her through her torch, as you behold
Sometimes within the sun a face of gold,
Formed in strong thoughts by that tradition's force
160   That says a god sits there and guides his course.
His sister was with him, to whom he showed
His guide by sea, and said, "Oft have you viewed
In one heaven many stars, but never yet
In one star many heavens till now were met.
See, lovely sister, see, now Hero shines,
No heaven but her appears; each star repines,
And all are clad in clouds, as if they mourned
To be by influence of earth outburned.
Yet doth she shine, and teacheth virtue's train,
170   Still to be constant in hell's blackest reign,
Though even the gods themselves do so entreat them
As they did hate, and Earth as she would eat them."

Off went his silken robe, and in he leapt,
Whom the kind waves so licorously clept,
Thick'ning for haste one in another so,
To kiss his skin, that he might almost go
To Hero's tow'r, had that kind minute lasted.
But now the cruel Fates with Ate hasted

To all the winds, and made them battle fight
Upon the Hellespont, for either's right   180
Pretended to the windy monarchy.
And forth they brake, the seas mixed with the sky,
And tossed distressed Leander, being in hell,
As high as heaven; bliss not in height doth dwell.
The Destinies sat dancing on the waves,
To see the glorious winds with mutual braves
Consume each other: O true glass, to see
How ruinous ambitious statists be
To their own glories! Poor Leander cried
For help to sea-born Venus; she denied;   190
To Boreas, that for his Atthaea's sake,
He would some pity on his Hero take,
And for his own love's sake, on his desires;
But Glory never blows cold Pity's fires.
Then called he Neptune, who through all the noise
Knew with affright his wracked Leander's voice,
And up he rose; for haste his forehead hit
'Gainst heaven's hard crystal; his proud waves he smit
With his forked scepter, that could not obey;
Much greater powers than Neptune's gave them sway.   200
They loved Leander so, in groans they brake
When they came near him; and such space did take
'Twixt one another, loth to issue on,
That in their shallow furrows earth was shown,
And the poor lover took a little breath;
But the curst Fates sat spinning of his death
On every wave, and with the servile winds
Tumbled them on him. And now Hero finds,
By that she felt, her dear Leander's state.
She wept, and prayed for him to every Fate,   210
And every wind that whipped her with her hair
About the face, she kissed and spake it fair,
Kneeled to it, gave it drink out of her eyes
To quench his thirst; but still their cruelties
Even her poor torch envied, and rudely beat

The bating flame from that dear food it eat;
Dear, for it nourished her Leander's life,
Which with her robe she rescued from their strife.
But silk too soft was such hard hearts to break,
220 And she, dear soul, even as her silk, faint, weak,
Could not preserve it; out, O out it went.
Leander still called Neptune, that now rent
His brackish curls, and tore his wrinkled face
Where tears in billows did each other chase,
And (burst with ruth) he hurled his marble mace
At the stern Fates; it wounded Lachesis
That drew Leander's thread, and could not miss
The thread itself, as it her hand did hit,
But smote it full and quite did sunder it.
230 The more kind Neptune raged, the more he rased
His love's life's fort, and killed as he embraced.
Anger doth still his own mishap increase;
If any comfort live, it is in peace.
O thievish Fates, to let blood, flesh, and sense
Build two fair temples for their excellence,
To rob it with a poisoned influence.
Though soul's gifts starve, the body's are held dear
In ugliest things; sense-sport preserves a bear.
But here nought serves our turns: O heaven and earth,
240 How most most wretched is our human birth!
And now did all the tyrannous crew depart,
Knowing there was a storm in Hero's heart
Greater than they could make, and scorned their smart.
She bowed herself so low out of her tow'r,
That wonder 'twas she fell not ere her hour
With searching the lamenting waves for him;
Like a poor snail, her gentle supple limb
Hung on her turret's top so most downright,
As she would dive beneath the darkness quite
250 To find her jewel; jewel—her Leander,
A name of all earth's jewels pleased not her
Like his dear name: "Leander, still my choice,

Come nought but my Leander; O my voice,
Turn to Leander: henceforth be all sounds,
Accents, and phrases that show all grief's wounds,
Analyzed in Leander. O black change!
Trumpets do you with thunder of your clange,
Drive out this change's horror, my voice faints:
Where all joy was, now shriek out all complaints."
Thus cried she, for her mixèd soul could tell   260
Her love was dead. And when the Morning fell
Prostrate upon the weeping Earth for woe,
Blushes that bled out of her cheeks did show
Leander brought by Neptune, bruised and torn
With cities' ruins he to rocks had worn,
To filthy usuring rocks, that would have blood,
Though they could get of him no other good.
She saw him, and the sight was much much more
Than might have served to kill her: should her store
Of giant sorrows speak? Burst, die, bleed,   270
And leave poor plaints to us that shall succeed.
She fell on her love's bosom, hugged it fast,
And with Leander's name she breathed her last.

Neptune for pity in his arms did take them,
Flung them into the air, and did awake them
Like two sweet birds, surnamed th' Acanthides,
Which we call thistle-warps, that near no seas
Dare ever come, but still in couples fly,
And feed on thistle-tops, to testify
The hardness of their first life in their last: 280
The first in thorns of love, and sorrows past;
And so most beautiful their colors show,
As none (so little) like them: her sad brow
A sable velvet feather covers quite,
Even like the forehead-cloths that in the night,
Or when they sorrow, ladies use to wear;
Their wings, blue, red, and yellow mixed appear;
Colors that, as we construe colors, paint

Their states to life; the yellow shows their saint,
290   The devil Venus, left them; blue, their truth;
The red and black, ensigns of death and ruth.
And this true honor from their love-deaths sprung,
They were the first that ever poet sung.

Finis

HENRY PETOWE

The Second Part of Hero and Leander, *Containing their Further Fortunes*

TO THE RIGHT WORSHIPFUL

SIR HENRY GUILFORD, KNIGHT, H. P. WISHETH

ALL INCREASE OF WORSHIP,

AND ENDLESS FELICITY.

Right worshipful: although presumption merit penance in dedicating such rude and unpolished lines to the protection of so worthy a personage, yet I hope your wonted favor and clemency will privilege me from blame, and accept of the giver, as one who would hazard life to move your worship the least jot of content. If it be thought a point of wisdom in that impoverished soul that by taking sanctuary doth free himself from many dangers, then impute no blame unto myself, that seek for safeguard, being round beset with many enemies. No sooner had report made known my harmless muse's first progress, how she intended to make trial of her unfledged plumes, but (myself being present where that babbling dame was prating) I heard injurious Envy reply to this effect:

> Dares she presume to fly that cannot go?
> We'll cut her plumes, said they; it shall be so.

Then with a snarl or two these ever meddling carpers betook them to their cabins. At the next rousing I expect no other favor than Envy's extremest fury, which to withstand,

77

20 if I may purchase your worship's safe protection, no better
guard will my fearful soul desire. To make the cause mani-
fest unto your worthiness why Envy thus barketh at me, I
entreat your wisdom to consider the sequel. This history of
Hero and Leander, penned by that admired poet Marlowe,
but not finished (being prevented by sudden death), and the
same (though not abruptly, yet contrary to all men's expec-
tation) resting like a head separated from the body, with
this harsh sentence, *Desunt nonnulla;* I being enriched by a
gentleman, a friend of mine, with the true Italian discourse
30 of those lovers' further fortunes, have presumed to finish
the history, though not so well as divers riper wits doubtless
would have done: but as it is rude and not praiseworthy, so
neither do I expect praise nor commendations. This there-
fore is the cause of their sudden enmity, that I being but a
fly dare presume to soar with the eagle. But however they
dislike it, may your worthiness but grace this my first labor
with your kind acceptance, my heart shall enjoy the depth
of his desire. And your worship shall continually bind me
in all serviceable duty to rest unto your worship always
40 devoted.

Your worship's most humbly to command,

HENRY PETOWE

TO THE QUICK-SIGHTED READER.

Kind gentlemen, what I would I cannot, but what I could
with that little skill I had, I have presumed to present to
your favorable views: I am not ashamed to beg your kind
favors, because I find myself altogether insufficient to per-
form that which my good will hath taken in hand; yet with
my soul I wish my labors may merit your kind favors: if not
50 for the toil herein taken, which I confess have no way de-
served the least jot of favor, yet for the subject's sake, for
Hero and Leander's sake. If neither of these purchase favor,
the frowning brows of sad discontent will banish my poor
harmless muse into the vast wilderness of eternal oblivion.

I am assured, gentlemen, you will marvel what folly or rather fury enforced me to undertake such a weighty matter, I being but a slender Atlas to uphold or undergo such a massy burden; yet I hope you will rather assist, and further me with the wings of your sweet favors, than to hinder my forward endeavors with your dislikings, esteeming it as the first fruits of an unripe wit, done at certain vacant hours. In which hope I rest captivated till I be freed by your liberal and kind censures.

    Yours still, if mine ever,

HENRY PETOWE

When young Apollo, heaven's sacred beauty,
Gan on his silver harp with reverent duty
To blazon forth the fair of Tellus' wonder,
Whose fair all other fairs brought subject under,
Heaven gan to frown at earth's fragility,
Made proud with such adorèd majesty.
Hero the fair, so do I name this fair,
With whom immortal fairs might not compare,
Such was her beauty framed in heaven's scorn,
10 Her spotless fair caused other fairs to mourn;
Heaven frowned, Earth shamed, that none so fair as she,
Base-born of earth, in heaven might equal be.
Fell moody Venus pale with fretting ire;
"Aye me," quoth she, for want of her desire,
"Earth's basest mold, framed of the baser dust,
Strumpet to filth, bawd to loathèd lust,
Worse than Medea's charms are thy enticements,
Worse than the mermaids' songs are thy allurements,
Worse than the snaky hag Tisiphone
20 To mortal souls is thy inveigling beauty!"
Thus she exclaims 'gainst harmless Hero's fair,
And, would the gods consent, her dangling hair,
Wherewith the busy air doth often play
(As wanton birds upon a sunshine day)
Should be transformed to snakes all ugly black,
To be a means of her eternal wrack.
But wanton Jove, sweet beauty's favorite,
Demands of Beauty beauty's worthy merit:

"If beauty's guerdon merit pain," quoth he,
"Your fair deserves no less as fair as she."   30
Then moody Juno frowning gan reply,
"I'll want my will, but strumpet she shall die!"
"Juno," quoth he, "we ought not tyrannize."
"On such," said she, "as you do wantonize!
But since our continent, the scope of heaven,
Contains her not unless from earth beriven,
I'll make a transformation of her hue,
And force the haughty mother Earth to rue
That her base womb dare yield such bastard fairs
That Jove must seek on earth immortal heirs.   40
I'll cause a second desperate Phaëthon
To rule the fiery chariot of the sun,
That topsy-turvey heaven and earth may turn,
That heaven, earth, sea and hell may endless burn."
"Stay, headstrong goddess," Jove to Juno said,
"Can you do this without your husband's aid?"
With that she gan entreat it might be so,
But Jove would not sweet beauty overthrow;
But this he granted Juno, that Apollo
Should never more extol the fair of Hero.   50
His censure past, the ireful queen doth hie
To set a period to his harmony.
From forth his yielding arms she soon bereaves
Apollo's lute, whom comfortless she leaves,
Making a thousand parts of two gold strings;
Into Oblivion's cell the same she flings.

Quick-sighted spirits, this supposed Apollo,
Conceit no other but th'admired Marlowe;
Marlowe admired, whose honey-flowing vein
No English writer can as yet attain;   60
Whose name in Fame's immortal treasury
Truth shall record to endless memory;
Marlowe late mortal, now framed all divine,
What soul more happy than that soul of thine?
Live still in heaven thy soul, thy fame on earth

(Thou dead) of Marlowe's Hero finds a dearth.
Weep aged Tellus, all earth on earth complain,
Thy chief-born fair hath lost her fair again:
Her fair in this is lost, that Marlowe's want
70 Enforceth Hero's fair be wondrous scant.
O had that king of poets breathèd longer,
Then had fair beauty's fort been much more stronger;
His golden pen had closed her so about,
No bastard eaglet's quill the world throughout
Had been of force to mar what he had made,
For why they were not expert in that trade:
What mortal soul with Marlowe might contend,
That could 'gainst reason force him stoop or bend?
Whose silver charming tongue moved such delight
80 That men would shun their sleep in still dark night
To meditate upon his golden lines,
His rare conceits and sweet according rhymes.
But Marlowe, still admired Marlowe's gone,
To live with Beauty in Elysium,
Immortal Beauty, who desires to hear
His sacred poesies sweet in every ear:
Marlowe must frame to Orpheus' melody
Hymns all divine to make heaven harmony.
There ever live the prince of poetry,
90 Live with the living in eternity!

Apollo's lute bereaved of silver string,
Fond Mercury doth harshly gin to sing,
A counterfeit unto his honey note;
But I do fear he'll chatter it by rote.
Yet if his ill-according voice be such
That, hearing part, you think you hear too much,
Bear with his rashness and he will amend;
His folly blame, but his good will commend.
Yet rather discommend what I entreat;
100 For if you like it, some will storm and fret;
And then insulting eagles soaring high
Will prey upon the silly harmless fly—

Nil refert; for I'll pawn my better part,
Ere sweet-faced Beauty lose her due desert.

Avaunt base steel where shrill-tongued silver rings;
The chatt'ring pie may range when blackbirds sings:
Birds black as jet with sweet according voices,
Like to Elysium's saints with heavenly noises.
Why should harsh Mercury recount again
What sweet Apollo, living, did maintain?   110
Which was of Hero her all-pleasing fair,
Her pretty brows, her lip, her amber hair,
Her roseate cheek, her lily fingers white,
Her sparkling eyes that lend the day his light:
What should I say? Her all in all he praisèd,
Wherewith the spacious world was much amazèd.
Leander's love and lovers' sweetest pleasure
He wrought a full discourse of beauty's treasure,
And left me nothing pleasing to recite,
But of unconstant Chance and Fortune's spite.   120
Then in this glass view beauty's frailty,
Fair Hero and Leander's misery.

The virgin princess of the western isle,
Fair Cambarina of the golden soil—
And yet not fair, but of a swarthy hue,
For by her gold her beauty did renew:
Renew as thus, that having gold to spare,
Men held it duty to protest and swear
Her fair was such as all the world admired it,
Her blushing beauty such, all men desired it.   130
The scornful queen made proud with fainèd praises,
Her black-framed soul to a higher rate she raises,
That men bewitchèd with her gold, not beauty,
A thousand knights as homage proffer duty.
If such a base deformèd lump of clay,
In whom no sweet content had any stay,
No pleasure residence, no sweet delight,
Shelter from heat of day or cold of night;

If such a she so many suitors had,
140 Hero, whose angry frowns made heaven sad,
Hero, whose gaze gracing dark Pluto's cell,
Pluto would deem Phoebus came there to dwell,
Hero, whose eyes heaven's fiery tapers stain,
Hero, whose beauty makes night day again,
How much more love merits so sweet a queen,
Whose like no outworn world hath ever seen.
Of sweet Leander's love to Hero's beauty,
Heaven, Earth, and Hell, and all the world is guilty;
Of Hero's kindness to her trusty fere,
150 By lost Apollo's tale it doth appear,
Recorded in the register of Fame:
The works of Marlowe do express the same.
But ere he gan of fickle Chance to tell,
How bad Chance 'gainst the better did rebel,
When love in love's sweet garden newly planted,
Remorseful Hero to Leander granted
Free liberty to yield the world increase;
Unconstant Fortune, foe to harmless peace,
Played such unruly pranks in love's despite
160 That love was forcèd from his true love's sight.

Duke Archilaüs, cruel, void of pity,
Where Hero dwelt was regent of that city:
Woe worth that town where bloody homicides
And tyrants are elected city's guides;
Woe worth that country where unlawful lust
Sits in a regal throne: of force it must
Down to the low-laid bowels of the earth,
Like to a stillborn child's untimely birth.
Duke Archilaüs loved, but whom loved he?
170 He courted Hero, but it would not be.
Why should he plant where other knights have sown?
The land is his, therefore the fruit his own.
Must it be thus? Alas, it is not so;
Lust may not force true lovers' overthrow.
Lust hath no limits, lust will have his will,

Like to a ravening wolf that's bent to kill,
The duke affecting her that was beloved
(Hero, whose firm-fixed love Leander proved)
Gave onset to the still-resisting fort;
But fearful hate set period to his sport.   180
Lust egged him on to further his desire,
But fell disdain enforced him to retire.
When Archilaüs saw that thundering threats
Could not prevail, he mildly then entreats.
But all in vain; the doe had chose her make,
And whom she took she never would forsake.
The doe's sweet deer this hunter seeks to chase,
Harmless Leander, whose all-smiling face
Graced with unspotted fair to all men's sight
Would force the hounds retire, and not to bite: 190
Which when the duke perceived, another cur
Was forcèd from his den, that made much stir,
And Treason he was named, which held so fast
That fear's swift wings did lend some aid at last.
For force perforce Leander must depart
From Sestos, yet behind he left his heart.
His heart in Hero's breast Leander left;
Leander's absence Hero's joys bereft;
Leander's want the cruel duke thought sure
Some ease to discontent would soon procure.   200
Leander having heard his woeful doom,
Towards his weeping lady he doth come,
Dewing her cheeks with his distilling tears,
Which Hero dryeth with her dangling hairs;
They weeping greet each other with sweet kisses,
Kindly embracing, thus they gan their wishes:
"O that these folding arms might ne'er undo!"
As she desired, so wished Leander too;
Then with her hand she touched his sacred breast,
Where in his bosom she desires to rest.   210
Like to a snake she clung unto him fast,
And wound about him, which, snatched up in haste
By the prince of birds, borne lightly up aloft,

Doth writhe herself about his neck, and oft
About his wings displayèd in the wind;
Or like as ivy on trees cling 'bout the rind;
Or as the crab-fish having caught in seas
His enemies, doth clasp him with his cleas.
So joined in one these two together stood,
220   Even as Hermaphroditus in the flood,
Until the duke did banish him away;
Then gan Leander to his Hero say.
"Let me go where the sun doth parch the green
In temperate heat, where he is felt and seen;
Or where his beams do not dissolve the ice;
In presence pressed of people mad or wise;
Set me in high, or else in low degree,
In clearest sky, or where clouds thickest be,
In longest night, or in the shortest day,
230   In lusty youth, or when my hairs be gray;
Go I to heaven, to earth, or else to hell,
Thrall or at large, alive whereso I dwell,
On hill or dale, or on the foaming flood,
Sick or in health, in evil fame or good,
Thine will I be, and only with this thought:
Content thyself, although my chance be naught."
Thus parted these two lovers full of woes;
She stays behind, on pilgrimage he goes.
Leave we awhile Leander, wandering knight,
240   To Delphos taking all his speedy flight,
That by the oracle of Apollo
His further fortunes he may truly know.

True love quite banished, lust began to plead
To Hero, like a scholar deeply read:
"The flaming sighs that boil within my breast,
Fair love," quoth he, "are cause of my unrest.
Unrest I entertain for thy sweet sake,
And in my tent choose sorrow for my make.
Why dost thou frown?" quoth he, and then she
    turned;

"O cool the fainting soul that flaming, burned,   250
Forced by desire to touch thy matchless beauty,
To whom thy servant vows all reverent duty."
With that her ireful brows clouded with frowns;
His soul already drenched in woe's sea drowns.
But floating on the waves, thus he gan say:
"Flint-hearted lady, canst thou be so coy?
Can pity take no place, is kind remorse
Quite banishèd, quite fled?" Then gan he to be hoarse,
Unable to exclaim against her longer,
Whose woe lament made Hero's heart more stronger,   260
Hero that gave no ear to her commander,
But ever weeps for her exiled Leander;
And weeping sore amongst her liquid tears,
These words she spake, wherewith her sorrow wears:
"The pillar perished is whereto I leant,
To my unhap, for lust away hath sent
Of all my joy the very bark and rind,
The strongest stay of my unquiet mind;
And I alas am forced without consent
Daily to mourn, till death do it relent.   270
O my Leander, he is banishèd,
From his sweet Hero's sight he is exilèd!
O ye just heavens, if that heaven be just,
Rein the unbridled head of haughty lust;
Make him to stoop that forceth others bend,
Bereave his joys that reft me of my friend.
I want myself, for Hero wants her love,
And where Leander is my self doth move.
What can I more but have a woeful heart,
My mind in woe, my body full of smart,   280
And I myself myself always to hate,
Till dreadful death do ease my doleful state."

The angry duke lay listening to her words,
And till she ends no speech at all affords,
Until at length exclaiming 'gainst her kind,
Thus he breathed forth the venom of his mind:

"O timorous taunters that delights in toys,
Jangling jesters, deprivers of sweet joys,
Tumbling cock-boats tottering to and fro,
290   Growned of the graft whence all my grief doth grow;
Sullen serpents environed with despite,
That ill for good at all times doth requite;
As cypress tree that rent is by the root,
As well-sown seed for drought that cannot sprout,
As branch or slip bitter from whence it grows,
As gaping ground that rainless cannot close;
As filth on land to whom no water flows,
As flowers do fade when Phoebus rarest shows,
As salamandra repulsed from the fire,
300   Wanting my wish, I die for my desire."
Speaking those words, Death seized him for his own,
Wherewith she thought her woes were overthrown;
Hero so thought, but yet she thought amiss:
Before she was beloved, now finds no bliss.
Duke Archilaüs being sudden dead,
Young Euristippus rulèd in his stead,
The next succeeding heir to what was his:
Then Hero's woes increased, and fled all bliss.

Look how the silly harmless bleating lamb,
310   Bereft from his kind make the gentle dam,
Left as a prey to butcher's cruelty,
In whom she finds not any drop of mercy;
Or like a warrior whom his soldiers flies
At his shrill echo of his foes' dread cries,
He all unable to withstand so many,
Not having wherewith to combat, nor any
Assurèd friend that dares to comfort him,
Nor any way for fear dares succor him;
But as a prey he yields to him he would not
320   If he had help, but, helpless, strive he could not.
So fared it with the meek distressèd Hero,
That sweet Leander banishèd her fro,
She had no Hercules to defend her cause,

She had no Brandamour disdaining laws
To combat for her safety; this sweet Io
Had no kind Jove to keep her from her foe;
This Psyches had no Cupid, love was banished,
And love from love exiled, love needs must famish.
Wood Euristippus for his brother's death,
Like as a toilèd huntsman wanting breath   330
Stormeth that bad chance in the game's pursuit
Should cause him panting rest as dead and mute;
Or like sad Orphey for Euridice,
Whom Cerberus bereft so hastily;
Like to the thundering threats of Hercules,
The world's admired prince, the great Alcides,
When Nessus got the height of his desire
By ravishing his fairest Deianire;
Such was his ire, and more if more may be,
Which he 'gainst Hero breathèd spitefully.   340
"Thou damnèd hag—" thus gan he to exclaim,
"Thou base-born strumpet, one of Circe's train,
Durst thou presume, poor silly simple fly,
With venom's force to force an eagle die?
What though my brother Leander banishèd,
Must he by thee therefore be poisonèd?
Die, cursèd wretch!" With that he cast her from him,
And would not suffer her to look upon him.
The still amazèd lady musing stood,
Admiring why the duke should be so wood.   350
Humbly she prostrates her at Anger's feet,
And with down-dropping tears like liquid sleet
She watereth the summer-thirsty ground,
Weeping so long she fell into a sound.
Again revivèd by the standers by,
She doth entreat them to resolve her why
Duke Euristippus wrongeth her so much
As to dishonor her with such a touch.
"Well know the gods my guiltless soul," quoth she;
"Was Archilaüs poisonèd by me?   360
If so, just heavens and immortal powers,

Rain vengeance down in all-consuming showers;
And cause that Hero that was counted fair
Like a mad hellish fury to despair."
The more she weeps, the more the heavens smile,
Scorning that beauty should take any soil,
Juno commanded Argus to defend her,
But Jupiter would not so much befriend her.
Argus stark dead, sweet Hero might not live,
370 For of her life the duke will her deprive.
Her doom was thus: ere three months' date took end,
If she found none that would her cause defend,
Untimely death should seize her as a prey,
And unresisting life should death obey.
Meantime within a rock-framed castle strong
She was imprisoned traitors vile among,
Where discontented when she should have rested,
Her food bad fare, with sighs and tears she feasted;
And when the breathless horses of the sun
380 Had made their stay, and Luna had begun
With cheerful smiling brows to grace dark night,
Clad in black sable weeds for want of light,
This all alone sad lady gan to play,
Framing sweet music to her welladay,
Th'effect whereof this sonnet plainly shows,
The fountain whence springs Hero's heavy woes.

Hero's Lamentation in Prison
Night's mourning black and misty veiling hue
Shadows the blessèd comfort of the sun,
At whose bright gaze I wonted to renew
390 My lifeless life when life was almost done.
Done is my life, and all my pleasure done,
For he is gone in whom my life begun:
Unhappy I, poor I, and none as I;
But pilgrim he, poor he, that should be by.

My love exiled, and I in prison fast,
Out-streaming tears break into weeping rain;

He too soon banished, I in dungeon cast,
He for me mourneth, I for him complain.
He's banishèd, yet lives at liberty,
And I exiled, yet live in misery: 400
He weeps for me far off, I for him here;
I would I were with him, and he more near.

But this imprisoning cave, this woeful cell,
This house of sorrow and increasing woe,
Grief's teary chamber where sad care doth dwell,
Where liquid tears like top-filled seas do flow,
Beating their waves 'gainst still relentless stone,
Still still they smile on me, and I still moan:
I weep to stone, and stone of stone I find;
Cold stone cold comfort yields, O most unkind.   410

Oft have I read that stone relents at rain,
And I implete their barren womb with store;
Tears streaming down, they wet and wet again,
Yet pitiless they harden all the more;
And when my longing soul looks they should sunder,
I touch the flinty stone and they seem stronger.
They strong, I weak; alas, what hope have I?
Hero wants comfort, Hero needs must die.

When the melodious shrill-tongued nightingale
With heavy cheer had warbled this sad tale,   420
Night's drowsy god an ivory canopy
Curtains before the windows of fair beauty.
Drowned thus in sleep, she spent the weary night;
There leave I Hero in a heavy plight.
Now to the woeful pilgrim I return,
Whose passions force the gentle birds to mourn;
They see Leander weep, with heavy note
They faintly sing, as when they sing by rote:
While he gan descant on his misery,
The pretty fowls do make him melody.   430

Leander's Complaint of his Restless Estate
Bright heaven's immortal moving spheres,
        and Phoebus all divine,
Rue on low Earth's unfainèd tears
        that issue from Earth's eyne.
Eyes were these no-eyes, whilst eye's eyesight
        lasted,
But these dark eyes' clear sight sad sorrow wasted.

What creature living lives in grief
        that breathes on Tellus' soil,
But heavens pity with relief,
440   save me, a slave to spoil?
Spoil do his worst, spoil cannot spoil me more;
Spoil never spoiled so true a love before.

The stricken deer stands not in awe
        of black grim ireful Death,
For he finds herbs that can withdraw
        the shaft, to save his breath.
The chasèd deer hath soil to cool his heat,
The toilèd steed is up in stable set.

The silly owls lurk in the leaves,
450   shine sun or night's queen weather;
The sparrow shrowds her in the eaves
        from storms of huffing weather.
Fowls comfort find, Leander finds no friend;
Then comfortless, Leander's life must end.

By this it pleased the smiling brows of heaven,
Whose deadly frowns him erst of joy beriven,
To set a period to Leander's toil.
Having enjoyed that long desired soil,
When he had viewed the stately territories,
460   And Delphos' sacred high erected towers,
Unto Apollo's oracle he goes,
In hope to find relief for many woes;

He craves long looked-for rest, or else to die,
To whom the oracle gan thus reply:

The Oracle
He loveth thine that loves not thee,
His love to thine shall fatal be.
Upon suspect she shall be slain
Unless thou do return again.

These harsh according rhymes to mickle pain
Did but renew Leander's woes again;   470
Yet as he might, with Fortune's sweet consent,
He gins return all dangers to prevent.
Within short time at Sestos he arriveth;
On love's light wings desire Leander driveth,
Desire that longs to view a blessèd end
Of Love and Fortune that so long contend.
This back-retired pilgrim lived secure,
And in unknown disguise he did endure
Full two months space, until the time drew nigh
To free fair Hero, or enforce her die.   480
The date outworn of the prefixèd day
When combatants their valor should display,
All things prepared, as blazing fame reported,
'Twere wonder to behold how men resorted;
Knights neighboring by, and ladies all divine,
Darting day's splendor from their sunlike eyne:
Spectatum veniunt, veniunt spectentur ut ipsae,
But wanting fair, they come to gaze on beauty,
Beauty, fair heaven's beauty, world's wonder,
Hero, whose beauty keeps all beauty under.   490
This fair-faced beauty from a foul-faced cell,
A loathsome dungeon like to night's dark hell,
At the fell duke's command in open view,
Was sent for, on whose never-spotted hue
Earth's mortal souls do feed and gaze upon her;
So long they gaze that they do surfeit on her.
For when this earth's admired immortal sun

To peep from under sable hold begun,
Like as the piercing eye of cloudy heaven,
500 Whose sight the black thick clouds have quite beriven,
But by the huffing winds being overblown,
And all their black expelled and overthrown,
The day doth gin be jocund, secure, playing,
The fair of heaven his beauty so displaying:
So when the fairest Hero did begin
(Whilom yclad in darkness' black-tanned skin)
To pass the noisome portal of the prison,
Like to the gorgeous Phoebus newly risen,
She doth illuminate the morning day,
510 Clad in a sable mantle of black say,
Which Hero's eyes transformèd to fair white,
Making the low'ring morn dark pure light.
As many mortal eyes beheld her eyes
As there are fiery tapers in the skies;
As many eyes gazed on fair Hero's beauty
As there be eyes that offer heaven duty;
As many servitors attended on her
As Venus' servants had to wait upon her.
Though by the stern duke she was dishonorèd,
520 Yet of the people she was honorèd;
Mongst whom exiled Leander all unseen
And all unknown attended on his queen.
When to the near-adjoining palace gate,
The place appointed for the princely combat,
They did approach, there might all eyes behold
The duke in armor of pure beaten gold,
Mounted upon a steed as white as snow,
The proud Duke Euristippus, Hero's foe;
Hero being seated in rich majesty,
530 A servile handmaid to captivity,
From whence she might behold that gentle knight
That for her sake durst hazard life in fight;
For this was all the comfort Hero had,
So many eyes shed tears to see her sad.
Her handmaid Hope persuaded her some one

Undaunted knight would be her champion.
Yet since her lord Leander was not nigh,
She was resolved either to live or die;
But her Leander, careful of his love,
Intending love's firm constancy to prove   540
(If to his lot the honor did befall)
Withdrew himself into the palace hall,
Where he was armèd to his soul's content,
And privily conducted to a tent,
From whence he issued forth at trumpet's sound,
Who, at the first encounter, on the ground
Forcèd the mazèd duke sore panting lie,
Drowned in the river of sad ecstasy.
At length reviving he doth mount again,
Whom young Leander in short time had slain.   550
The duke quite dead, this all unknown young knight
Was forthwith made the heir of Sestos right,
The Princess Hero set at liberty,
Kept by the late dead duke in misery,
Whose constancy Leander gan to prove,
And now anew begins to court his love.

"To walk on ground where danger is unseen
Doth make men doubt, where they have never been.
As blind men fear what footing they shall find,
So doth the wise mistrust the stranger's mind.   560
I strange to you, and you unknown to me,
Yet may not love twixt us two grafted be?
What I have done for Hero's love was done;
Say then you love, and end as I begun.
I hazard life to free thy beauty's fair
From tyrant's force and hellish soul despair:
Then, sacred fair, balance my good desert;
Enrich my soul with thy affecting heart."

Hero replied: "To rue on all false tears
And forgèd tales, wherein craft oft appears,   570
To trust each feignèd face and forcing charm

Betrays the simple soul that thinks no harm.
Not every tear doth argue inward pain,
Not every sigh warrants men do not feign,
Not every smoke doth prove a present fire,
Not all that glisters golden souls desire,
Not every word is drawn out of the deep,
For oft men smile when they do seem to weep:
Oft malice makes the mind to pour forth brine,
580 And envy leaks the conduits of the eyne.
Craft oft doth cause men make a seeming show
Of heavy woes where grief did never grow.
Then blame not those that wisely can beware
To shun dissimulation's dreadful snare.
Blame not the stoppèd ears 'gainst sirens' song,
Blame not the mind not moved with falsehood tongue;
But rest content and satisfied with this:
Whilst true Leander lives, true Hero's his."

"And thy Leander lives, sweet soul," said he,
590 "Praising thy all-admired chastity.
Though thus disguised, I am that banished knight
That for affecting thee was put to flight.
Hero, I am Leander, thy true fere,
As true to thee as life to me is dear."

When Hero all amazèd gan revive,
And she that then seemed dead was now alive,
With kind embracements kissing at each strain,
She welcomes him, and kisses him again.
"By thee my joys have shaken off despair;
600 All storms be past, and weather waxeth fair;
By thy return Hero receives more joy
Than Paris did when Helen was in Troy.
By thee my heavy doubts and thoughts are fled,
And now my wits with pleasant thoughts are fed."

"Feed, sacred saint, on nectar all divine,
While these my eyes," quoth he, "gaze on thy eyne.
And ever after may these eyes beware

That they on strangers' beauty never stare:
My wits I charm henceforth they take such heed,
They frame no toys my fancies new to feed.   610
Deaf be my ears to hear another voice,
To force me smile, or make my soul rejoice;
Lame be my feet when they presume to move
To force Leander seek another love.
And when thy fair, sweet fair, I gin disgrace,
Heaven to my soul afford no resting place."
What he to her, she vowed the like to him,
All sorrows fled, their joys anew begin.

Full many years those lovers lived in fame,
That all the world did much admire the same.   620
Their lives' spent date, and unresisted death
At hand to set a period to their breath,
They were transformed by all divine decrees
Into the form and shape of two pine trees,
Whose nature's such, the female pine will die
Unless the male be ever planted by:
A map for all succeeding times to come
To view true love, which in their loves begun.

Finis
Qualis vita, finis ita

ALL OVID'S ELEGIES

P. Ovidii Nasonis Amorum, Liber Primus

ELEGIA I

Quemadmodum a Cupidine pro bellis amoris scribere coactus sit

We which were Ovid's five books now are three,
For these before the rest preferreth he;
If reading five thou plain'st of tediousness,
Two ta'en away, thy labor will be less.

With Muse prepared I meant to sing of arms,
Choosing a subject fit for fierce alarms.
Both verses were alike till Love (men say)
Began to smile and took one foot away.
Rash boy, who gave thee power to change a line?
We are the Muses' prophets, none of thine.   10
What if thy mother take Diana's bow?
Shall Dian fan when love begins to glow?
In woody groves is 't meet that Ceres reign,
And quiver-bearing Dian till the plain?
Who'll set the fair-tressed Sun in battle ray,
While Mars doth take the Aonian harp to play?
Great are thy kingdoms, over-strong and large,
Ambitious imp, why seek'st thou further charge?
Are all things thine? the Muses' Tempe thine?
Then scarce can Phoebus say, "This harp is mine."   20
When in this work's first verse I trod aloft,

Love slacked my muse, and made my numbers soft.
I have no mistress nor no favorite,
Being fittest matter for a wanton wit.
Thus I complained, but Love unlocked his quiver,
Took out the shaft, ordained my heart to shiver,
And bent his sinewy bow upon his knee,
Saying, "Poet, here's a work beseeming thee."
O woe is me! he never shoots but hits;
30 I burn, Love in my idle bosom sits.
Let my first verse be six, my last five feet;
Farewell stern war, for blunter poets meet.
Elegian muse, that warblest amorous lays,
Girt my shine brow with sea-bank myrtle sprays.

ELEGIA II

*Quod primo amore correptus, in triumphum
duci se a Cupidine patiatur*

What makes my bed seem hard seeing it is soft?
Or why slips down the coverlet so oft?
Although the nights be long, I sleep not tho,
My sides are sore with tumbling to and fro.
Were Love the cause, it's like I should descry him,
Or lies he close, and shoots where none can spy him?
'Twas so, he struck me with a slender dart,
'Tis cruel Love turmoils my captive heart.
Yielding or struggling do we give him might;
10 Let's yield, a burden easily borne is light.
I saw a brandished fire increase in strength,
Which being not shaked, I saw it die at length.
Young oxen newly yoked are beaten more
Than oxen which have drawn the plough before;
And rough jades' mouths with stubborn bits are torn.
But managed horses' heads are lightly borne.
Unwilling lovers love doth more torment

Than such as in their bondage feel content.
Lo, I confess, I am thy captive, I,
And hold my conquered hands for thee to tie.   20
What need'st thou war? I sue to thee for grace;
With arms to conquer armless men is base.
Yoke Venus' doves, put myrtle on thy hair,
Vulcan will give thee chariots rich and fair;
The people thee applauding, thou shalt stand,
Guiding the harmless pigeons with thy hand;
Young men and women shalt thou lead as thrall,
So will thy triumph seem magnifical.
I, lately caught, will have a new-made wound,
And captive-like be manacled and bound;   30
Good Meaning, Shame, and such as seek love's wrack
Shall follow thee, their hands tied at their back.
Thee all shall fear, and worship as a king,
Io triumphing shall thy people sing.
Smooth Speeches, Fear and Rage shall by thee ride,
Which troops have always been on Cupid's side;
Thou with these soldiers conquerest gods and men,
Take these away, where is thine honor then?
Thy mother shall from heaven applaud this show,
And on their faces heaps of roses strow.   40
With beauty of thy wings, thy fair hair gilded,
Ride, golden Love, in chariots richly builded.
Unless I err, full many shalt thou burn,
And give wounds infinite at every turn.
In spite of thee, forth will thine arrows fly,
A scorching flame burns all the standers by.
So, having conquered Ind, was Bacchus' hue;
Thee pompous birds, and him two tigers drew.
Then seeing I grace thy show in following thee,
Forbear to hurt thyself in spoiling me.   50
Behold thy kinsman's Caesar's prosperous bands,
Who guards the conquered with his conquering
       hands.

ELEGIA III

Ad amicam

I ask but right: let her that caught me late
Either love, or cause that I may never hate.
I ask too much: would she but let me love her;
Love knows with such like prayers I daily
    move her.
Accept him that will serve thee all his youth,
Accept him that will love with spotless truth.
If lofty titles cannot make me thine,
That am descended but of knightly line—
Soon may you plough the little land I have;
I gladly grant my parents given to save—
Apollo, Bacchus and the Muses may,
And Cupid, who hath marked me for thy prey,
My spotless life, which but to gods gives place,
Naked simplicity, and modest grace.
I love but one, and her I love change never,
If men have faith, I'll live with thee for ever.
The years that fatal destiny shall give
I'll live with thee, and die, ere thou shalt grieve.
Be thou the happy subject of my books,
That I may write things worthy thy fair looks.
By verses hornèd Io got her name,
And she to whom in shape of swan Jove came,
And she that on a feigned bull swam to land,
Gripping his false horns with her virgin hand.
So likewise we will through the world be rung,
And with my name shall thine be always sung.

ELEGIA IV

Amicam, qua arte, quibusve nutibus in caena, presente viro uti debeat, admonet

Thy husband to a banquet goes with me,
Pray God it may his latest supper be.
Shall I sit gazing as a bashful guest,
While others touch the damsel I love best?
Wilt lying under him, his bosom clip?
About thy neck shall he at pleasure skip?
Marvel not, though the fair bride did incite
The drunken Centaurs to a sudden fight;
I am no half-horse, nor in woods I dwell,
Yet scarce my hands from thee contain I well.   10
But how thou shouldst behave thyself now know,
Nor let the winds away my warnings blow.
Before thy husband come, though I not see
What may be done, yet there before him be.
Lie with him gently, when his limbs he spread
Upon the bed, but on my foot first tread.
View me, my becks and speaking countenance;
Take and receive each secret amorous glance.
Words without voice shall on my eyebrows sit,
Lines thou shalt read in wine by my hand writ.   20
When our lascivious toys come in thy mind,
Thy rosy cheeks be to thy thumb inclined.
If aught of me thou speak'st in inward thought,
Let thy soft finger to thy ear be brought.
When I (my light) do or say aught that please thee,
Turn round thy gold ring, as it were to ease thee.
Strike on the board like them that pray for evil,
When thou dost wish thy husband at the devil.
What wine he fills thee, wisely will him drink;
Ask thou the boy what thou enough dost think.   30
When thou hast tasted, I will take the cup,

And where thou drink'st, on that part I will sup.
If he gives thee what first himself did taste,
Even in his face his offered gobbets cast.
Let not thy neck by his vile arms be pressed,
Nor lean thy soft head on his boist'rous breast.
Thy bosom's roseate buds let him not finger,
Chiefly on thy lips let not his lips linger.
If thou givest kisses, I shall all disclose,
Say they are mine and hands on thee impose.
40 Yet this I'll see, but if thy gown aught cover,
Suspicious fear in all my veins will hover.
Mingle not thighs nor to his leg join thine,
Nor thy soft foot with his hard foot combine.
I have been wanton, therefore am perplexed,
And with mistrust of the like measure vexed.
I and my wench oft under clothes did lurk,
When pleasure moved us to our sweetest work.
Do not thou so, but throw thy mantle hence,
50 Lest I should think thee guilty of offense.
Entreat thy husband drink, but do not kiss,
And while he drinks, to add more do not miss;
If he lies down with wine and sleep oppressed,
The thing and place shall counsel us the rest.
When to go homewards we rise all along,
Have care to walk in middle of the throng;
There will I find thee or be found by thee,
There touch whatever thou canst touch of me.
Aye me, I warn what profits some few hours,
60 But we must part when heav'n with black night lours.
At night thy husband clips thee: I will weep
And to the doors sight of thyself keep.
Then will he kiss thee, and not only kiss,
But force thee give him my stol'n honey bliss.
Constrained against thy will, give it the peasant;
Forbear sweet words, and be your sport unpleasant.
To him I pray it no delight may bring,
Or if it do, to thee no joy thence spring;

But though this night thy fortune be to try it,
To me tomorrow constantly deny it.   70

ELEGIA V

Corinnae concubitus

In summer's heat, and mid-time of the day,
To rest my limbs upon a bed I lay;
One window shut, the other open stood,
Which gave such light as twinkles in a wood,
Like twilight glimpse at setting of the sun,
Or night being past, and yet not day begun.
Such light to shamefast maidens must be shown,
Where they may sport and seem to be unknown.
Then came Corinna in a long loose gown,
Her white neck hid with tresses hanging down,   10
Resembling fair Semiramis going to bed,
Or Lais of a thousand wooers sped.
I snatched her gown; being thin, the harm was small,
Yet strived she to be covered therewithal,
And striving thus as one that would be cast,
Betrayed herself, and yielded at the last.
Stark naked as she stood before mine eye,
Not one wen in her body could I spy.
What arms and shoulders did I touch and see,
How apt her breasts were to be pressed by me!   20
How smooth a belly under her waist saw I,
How large a leg, and what a lusty thigh!
To leave the rest, all liked me passing well;
I clinged her naked body, down she fell.
Judge you the rest: being tired she bade me kiss;
Jove send me more such afternoons as this.

ELEGIA VI

Ad Janitorem, ut fores sibi aperiat

Unworthy porter, bound in chains full sore,
On movèd hooks set ope the churlish door.
Little I ask, a little entrance make;
The gate half-ope my bent side in will take.
Long love my body to such use makes slender,
And to get out doth like apt members render.
He shows me how unheard to pass the watch,
And guides my feet lest stumbling falls they catch.
But in times past I feared vain shades, and night,
Wond'ring if any walkèd without light.
Love hearing it laughed with his tender mother,
And smiling said, "Be thou as bold as other."
Forthwith Love came: no dark night-flying sprite,
Nor hands prepared to slaughter, me affright.
Thee fear I too much, only thee I flatter,
Thy lightning can my life in pieces batter.
Why enviest me? this hostile den unbar,
See how the gates with my tears watered are.
When thou stood'st naked, ready to be beat,
For thee I did thy mistress fair entreat;
But what entreats for thee sometimes took place
(O mischief) now for me obtain small grace.
Gratis thou mayst be free, give like for like,
Night goes away: the door's bar backward strike.
Strike, so again hard chains shall bind thee never,
Nor servile water shalt thou drink forever.
Hard-hearted porter, dost and wilt not hear?
With stiff oak propped the gate doth still appear.
Such rampired gates besiegèd cities aid,
In midst of peace why art of arms afraid?
Exclud'st a lover, how would'st use a foe?
Strike back the bar, night fast away doth go.
With arms or armèd men I come not guarded,

10

20

30

I am alone, were furious Love discarded.
Although I would, I cannot him cashier
Before I be divided from my gear.
See Love with me, wine moderate in my brain,
And on my hairs a crown of flowers remain.
Who fears these arms? who will not go to meet them?
Night runs away; with open entrance greet them.   40
Art careless? or is't sleep forbids thee hear,
Giving the winds my words running in thine ear?
Well I remember when I first did hire thee,
Watching till after midnight did not tire thee;
But now perchance thy wench with thee doth rest—
Ah, how thy lot is above my lot blest!
Though it be so, shut me not out therefore;
Night goes away, I pray thee ope the door.
Err we? or do the turnèd hinges sound,
And opening doors with creaking noise abound?   50
We err: a strong blast seemed the gates to ope;
Aye me, how high that gale did lift my hope!
If, Boreas, bears Oreithyia's rape in mind,
Come break these deaf doors with thy boisterous wind.
Silent the city is: night's dewy host
March fast away; the bar strike from the post,
Or I more stern than fire or sword will turn
And with my brand these gorgeous houses burn.
Night, love, and wine to all extremes persuade;
Night shameless, wine and love are fearless made.   60
All have I spent: no threats or prayers move thee;
O harder than the doors thou guard'st I prove thee.
No pretty wench's keeper mayst thou be:
The careful prison is more meet for thee.
Now frosty night her flight begins to take,
And crowing cocks poor souls to work awake;
But thou my crown, from sad hairs ta'en away,
On this hard threshold till the morning lay,
That when my mistress there beholds thee cast,
She may perceive how we the time did waste.   70
Whate'er thou art, farewell; be like me pained,

Careless, farewell, with my fault not distained!
And farewell cruel posts, rough threshold's block,
And doors conjoined with an hard iron lock!

ELEGIA VII

Ad pacandam amicam, quam verberaverat

Bind fast my hands, they have deservèd chains,
While rage is absent, take some friend the pains;
For rage against my wench moved my rash arm,
My mistress weeps whom my mad hand did harm.
I might have then my parents dear misused,
Or holy gods with cruel strokes abused.
Why, Ajax, master of the seven-fold shield,
Butchered the flocks he found in spacious field,
And he who on his mother venged his sire
10   Against the Destinies durst sharp darts require.
Could I therefore her comely tresses tear?
Yet was she gracèd with her ruffled hair.
So fair she was, Atalanta she resembled,
Before whose bow th' Arcadian wild beasts trembled;
Such Ariadne was, when she bewails
Her perjured Theseus' flying vows and sails;
So, chaste Minerva, did Cassandra fall,
Deflowered except, within thy temple wall.
That I was mad and barbarous all men cried,
20   She nothing said, pale fear her tongue had tied;
But secretly her looks with checks did trounce me,
Her tears, she silent, guilty did pronounce me.
Would of mine arms my shoulders had been scanted,
Better I could part of myself have wanted.
To mine own self have I had strength so furious,
And to myself could I be so injurious?
Slaughter and mischief's instruments, no better,
Deservèd chains these cursèd hands shall fetter.

Punished I am if I a Roman beat;
Over my mistress is my right more great?   30
Tydides left worst signs of villainy,
He first a goddess struck; another I.
Yet he harmed less; whom I professed to love
I harmed; a foe did Diomedes' anger move.
Go now, thou conqueror, glorious triumphs raise,
Pay vows to Jove, engirt thy hairs with bays,
And let the troops which shall thy chariot follow
"*Io*, a strong man conquered this wench," hollow.
Let the sad captive foremost with locks spread,
On her white neck but for hurt cheeks be led;   40
Meeter it were her lips were blue with kissing,
And on her neck a wanton's mark not missing.
But though I like a swelling flood was driven,
And as a prey unto blind anger given,
Was't not enough the fearful wench to chide,
Nor thunder in rough threatings' haughty pride,
Nor shamefully her coat pull o'er her crown,
Which to her waist her girdle still kept down?
But cruelly her tresses having rent,
My nails to scratch her lovely cheeks I bent.   50
Sighing she stood, her bloodless white looks showèd
Like marble from the Parian mountains hewèd;
Her half-dead joints and trembling limbs I saw,
Like poplar leaves blown with a stormy flaw,
Or slender ears with gentle Zephyr shaken,
Or waters' tops with the warm south wind taken.
And down her cheeks the trickling tears did flow
Like water gushing from consuming snow.
Then first I did perceive I had offended,
My blood the tears were that from her descended.   60
Before her feet thrice prostrate down I fell,
My fearèd hands thrice back she did repel.
But doubt thou not (revenge doth grief appease)
With thy sharp nails upon my face to seize;
Bescratch mine eyes, spare not my locks to break

(Anger will help thy hands though ne'er so weak),
And lest the sad signs of my crime remain,
Put in their place thy kembèd hairs again.

ELEGIA VIII

*Execratur lenam, quae puellam suam meretricia
arte instituebat*

There is—whoe'er will know a bawd aright,
Give ear—there is an old trot, Dipsas hight.
Her name comes from the thing: she being wise
Sees not the morn on rosy horses rise,
She magic arts and Thessale charms doth know,
And makes large streams back to their fountains flow;
She knows with grass, with threads on wrong
    wheels spun,
And what with mares' rank humor may be done.
When she will, clouds the darkened heav'n obscure;
10 When she will, day shines everywhere most pure.
If I have faith, I saw the stars drop blood,
The purple moon with sanguine visage stood.
Her I suspect among night's spirits to fly,
And her old body in birds' plumes to lie.
Fame saith as I suspect, and in her eyes
Two eyeballs shine and double light thence flies.
Great-grandsires from their ancient graves she chides,
And with long charms the solid earth divides.
She draws chaste women to incontinence,
20 Nor doth her tongue want harmful eloquence.
By chance I heard her talk; these words she said,
While closely hid betwixt two doors I laid:
"Mistress, thou know'st thou hast a blest youth
    pleased,
He stayed and on thy looks his gazes seized.
And why shouldst not please? none thy face exceeds;
Aye me, thy body hath no worthy weeds.

As thou art fair, would thou wert fortunate!
Wert thou rich, poor should not be my state.
Th' opposèd star of Mars hath done thee harm;
Now Mars is gone, Venus thy side doth warm,   30
And brings good fortune: a rich lover plants
His love on thee, and can supply thy wants.
Such is his form as may with thine compare,
Would he not buy thee, thou for him shouldst care."
She blushed. "Red shame becomes white cheeks,
    but this,
If feigned, doth well; if true, it doth amiss.
When on thy lap thine eyes thou dost deject,
Each one according to his gifts respect.
Perhaps the Sabines rude, when Tatius reigned,
To yield their love to more than one disdained;   40
Now Mars doth rage abroad without all pity,
And Venus rules in her Aeneas' city.
Fair women play, she's chaste whom none will have,
Or, but for bashfulness, herself would crave.
Shake off these wrinkles that thy front assault,
Wrinkles in beauty is a grievous fault.
Penelope in bows her youths' strength tried,
Of horn the bow was that approved their side.
Time flying slides hence closely, and deceives us,
And with swift horses the swift year soon leaves us.   50
Brass shines with use; good garments would be worn;
Houses not dwelt in are with filth forlorn.
Beauty not exercised with age is spent,
Nor one or two men are sufficient.
Many to rob is more sure, and less hateful,
From dog-kept flocks come preys to wolves most
    grateful.
Behold, what gives the poet but new verses?
And thereof many thousand he rehearses.
The poet's god, arrayed in robes of gold,
Of his gilt harp the well-tuned strings doth hold.   60
Let Homer yield to such as presents bring;
(Trust me) to give, it is a witty thing.

Nor, so thou mayst obtain a wealthy prize,
The vain name of inferior slaves despise.
Nor let the arms of ancient lives beguile thee;
Poor lover, with thy grandsires I exile thee.
Who seeks, for being fair, a night to have,
What he will give, with greater instance crave.
Make a small price, while thou thy nets dost lay,
70   Lest they should fly; being ta'en, the tyrant play.
Dissemble so, as loved he may be thought,
And take heed lest he gets that love for nought.
Deny him oft; feign now thy head doth ache:
And Isis now will show what scuse to make.
Receive him soon, lest patient use he gain,
Or lest his love oft beaten back should wane.
To beggars shut, to bringers ope thy gate;
Let him within hear barred-out lovers prate.
And as first wronged the wrongèd sometimes banish,
80   Thy fault with his fault so repulsed will vanish.
But never give a spacious time to ire,
Anger delayed doth oft to hate retire.
And let thine eyes constrainèd learn to weep,
That this or that man may thy cheeks moist keep.
Nor, if thou cozen'st one, dread to forswear:
Venus to mocked men lends a senseless ear.
Servants fit for thy purpose thou must hire,
To teach thy lover what thy thoughts desire.
Let them ask somewhat; many asking little,
90   Within a while great heaps grow of a tittle.
And sister, nurse, and mother spare him not,
By many hands great wealth is quickly got.
When causes fail thee to require a gift,
By keeping of thy birth make but a shift.
Beware lest he unrivaled loves secure;
Take strife away, love doth not well endure.
On all the bed men's tumbling let him view,
And thy neck with lascivious marks made blue;
Chiefly show him the gifts which others send;
100   If he gives nothing, let him from thee wend.

When thou hast so much as he gives no more,
Pray him to lend what thou mayst ne'er restore.
Let thy tongue flatter, while thy mind harm works:
Under sweet honey deadly poison lurks.
If this thou dost, to me by long use known,
Nor let my words be with the winds hence blown,
Oft thou wilt say, 'live well'; thou wilt pray oft
That my dead bones may in their grave lie soft."
As thus she spake, my shadow me betrayed,
With much ado my hands I scarcely stayed;   110
But her blear eyes, bald scalp's thin hoary fleeces,
And rivelled cheeks I would have pulled a-pieces.
The gods send thee no house, a poor old age,
Perpetual thirst, and winter's lasting rage.

ELEGIA IX

Ad Atticum, amantem non oportere desidiosum esse, sicuti nec militem

All lovers war, and Cupid hath his tent,
Attic, all lovers are to war far sent.
What age fits Mars, with Venus doth agree,
'Tis shame for eld in war or love to be.
What years in soldiers captains do require,
Those in their lovers pretty maids desire.
Both of them watch: each on the hard earth sleeps;
His mistress' doors this, that his captain's keeps.
Soldiers must travel far; the wench forth send,
Her valiant lover follows without end.   10
Mounts, and rain-doubled floods he passeth over,
And treads the deserts snowy heaps do cover.
Going to sea, east winds he doth not chide,
Nor to hoist sail attends fit time and tide.
Who but a soldier or a lover is bold
To suffer storm-mixed snows with night's sharp cold?
One as a spy doth to his enemies go,

The other eyes his rival as his foe.
He cities great, this thresholds lies before;
20   This breaks town gates, but he his mistress' door.
Oft to invade the sleeping foe 'tis good,
And armed to shed unarmèd people's blood.
So the fierce troops of Thracian Rhesus fell,
And captive horses bade their lord farewell.
Sooth, lovers watch till sleep the husband charms,
Who slumb'ring, they rise up in swelling arms.
The keeper's hands and corps-du-gard to pass,
The soldier's, and poor lover's work e'er was.
Doubtful is war and love: the vanquished rise,
30   And who thou never think'st should fall, down lies.
Therefore whoe'er love slothfulness doth call,
Let him surcease: love tries wit best of all.
Achilles burned, Briseis being ta'en away;
Trojans, destroy the Greek wealth while you may;
Hector to arms went from his wife's embraces,
And on Andromache his helmet laces.
Great Agamemnon was, men say, amazèd,
On Priam's loose-tressed daughter when he gazèd.
Mars in the deed the blacksmith's net did stable,
40   In heaven was never more notorious fable.
Myself was dull and faint, to sloth inclined,
Pleasure and ease had mollified my mind;
A fair maid's care expelled this sluggishness,
And to her tents willed me myself address.
Since mayst thou see me watch and night-wars move:
He that will not grow slothful, let him love.

ELEGIA X

Ad puellam, ne pro amore praemia poscat

Such as the cause was of two husbands' war,
Whom Trojan ships fetched from Europa far;
Such as was Leda, whom the god deluded

In snow-white plumes of a false swan included;
Such as Amymone through the dry fields strayed,
When on her head a water pitcher laid:
Such wert thou, and I feared the bull and eagle,
And whate'er love made Jove should thee inveigle.
Now all fear with my mind's hot love abates,
No more this beauty mine eyes captivates.   10
Ask'st why I change? because thou crav'st reward:
This cause hath thee from pleasing me debarred.
While thou wert plain, I loved thy mind and face,
Now inward faults thy outward form disgrace.
Love is a naked boy, his years sans stain,
And hath no clothes, but open doth remain.
Will you for gain have Cupid sell himself?
He hath no bosom, where to hide base pelf.
Love and Love's son are with fierce arms to odds;
To serve for pay beseems not wanton gods.   20
The whore stands to be bought for each man's money,
And seeks vile wealth by selling of her coney,
Yet greedy bawd's command she curseth still,
And doth, constrained, what you do of good will.
Take from irrational beasts a precedent;
'Tis shame their wits should be more excellent.
The mare asks not the horse, the cow the bull,
Nor the mild ewe gifts from the ram doth pull;
Only a woman gets spoils from a man,
Farms out herself on nights for what she can,   30
And lets what both delight, what both desire,
Making her joy according to her hire.
The sport being such as both alike sweet try it,
Why should one sell it and the other buy it?
Why should I lose, and thou gain by the pleasure
Which man and woman reap in equal measure?
Knights of the post of perjuries make sale,
The unjust judge for bribes becomes a stale.
'Tis shame sold tongues the guilty should defend,
Or great wealth from a judgment seat ascend;   40
'Tis shame to grow rich by bed merchandise,

Or prostitute thy beauty for bad prize.
Thanks worthily are due for things unbought,
For beds ill-hired we are indebted nought.
The hirer payeth all, his rent discharged,
From further duty he rests then enlarged.
Fair dames forbear rewards for nights to crave,
Ill-gotten goods good end will never have.
The Sabine gauntlets were too dearly won,
50   That unto death did press the holy nun.
The son slew her that forth to meet him went,
And a rich necklace caused that punishment.
Yet think no scorn to ask a wealthy churl;
He wants no gifts into thy lap to hurl.
Take clustered grapes from an o'er-laden vine,
May bounteous loam Alcinous' fruit resign.
Let poor men show their service, faith, and care;
All for their mistress, what they have, prepare.
In verse to praise kind wenches 'tis my part,
60   And whom I like eternize by mine art.
Garments do wear, jewels and gold do waste,
The fame that verse gives doth for ever last.
To give I love, but to be asked disdain;
Leave asking, and I'll give what I refrain.

ELEGIA XI

Napen alloquitur, ut paratas tabellas
ad Corinnam perferat

In skilful gathering ruffled hairs in order,
Nape, free-born, whose cunning hath no border,
Thy service for night's scapes is known commodious,
And to give signs dull wit to thee is odious.
Corinna clips me oft by thy persuasion,
Never to harm me made thy faith evasion.
Receive these lines, them to thy mistress carry,
Be sedulous, let no stay cause thee tarry.

Nor flint nor iron are in thy soft breast,
But pure simplicity in thee doth rest.   10
And 'tis supposed Love's bow hath wounded thee,
Defend the ensigns of thy war in me.
If what I do, she asks, say "hope for night";
The rest my hand doth in my letters write.
Time passeth while I speak, give her my writ,
But see that forthwith she peruseth it.
I charge thee mark her eyes and front in reading,
By speechless looks we guess at things succeeding.
Straight being read, will her to write much back,
I hate fair paper should writ matter lack.   20
Let her make verses, and some blotted letter
On the last edge, to stay mine eyes the better.
What need she tire her hand to hold the quill?
Let this word, "Come," alone the tables fill.
Then with triumphant laurel will I grace them,
And in the midst of Venus' temple place them,
Subscribing that to her I consecrate
My faithful tables, being vile maple late.

ELEGIA XII

Tabellas quas miserat execratur, quod amica noctem negabat

Bewail my chance: the sad book is returnèd,
This day denial hath my sport adjournèd.
Presages are not vain; when she departed,
Nape by stumbling on the threshold started.
Going out again, pass forth the door more wisely,
And somewhat higher bear thy foot precisely.
Hence, luckless tables, funeral wood, be flying,
And thou the wax stuffed full with notes denying,
Which I think gathered from cold hemlock's flower,
Wherein bad honey Corsic bees did pour.   10
Yet as if mixed with red lead thou wert ruddy,

That color rightly did appear so bloody.
As evil wood thrown in the highways lie,
Be broke with wheels of chariots passing by,
And him that hewed you out for needful uses
I'll prove had hands impure with all abuses.
Poor wretches on the tree themselves did strangle;
There sat the hangman for men's necks to angle.
To hoarse screech-owls foul shadows it allows,
20   Vultures and Furies nestled in the boughs.
To these my love I foolishly committed,
And then with sweet words to my mistress fitted;
More fitly had they wrangling bonds containèd,
From barbarous lips of some attorney strainèd.
Among day-books and bills they had lain better,
In which the merchant wails his bankrupt debtor.
Your name approves you made for such like things,
The number two no good divining brings.
Angry, I pray that rotten age you wracks,
30   And sluttish white-mold overgrow the wax.

ELEGIA XIII

Ad Auroram, ne properet.

Now o'er the sea from her old love comes she
That draws the day from heaven's cold axle-tree.
Aurora, whither slidest thou? down again,
And birds for Memnon yearly shall be slain.
Now in her tender arms I sweetly bide,
If ever, now well lies she by my side.
The air is cold, and sleep is sweetest now,
And birds send forth shrill notes from every bough:
Whither runn'st thou, that men and women love not?
10   Hold in thy rosy horses that they move not.
Ere thou rise, stars teach seamen where to sail,
But when thou comest, they of their courses fail.

Poor travelers, though tired, rise at thy sight,
And soldiers make them ready to the fight.
The painful hind by thee to field is sent,
Slow oxen early in the yoke are pent.
Thou cozen'st boys of sleep, and dost betray them
To pedants that with cruel lashes pay them.
Thou mak'st the surety to the lawyer run,
That with one word hath nigh himself undone.   20
The lawyer and the client hate thy view,
Both whom thou raisest up to toil anew.
By thy means women of their rest are barred,
Thou set'st their laboring hands to spin and card.
All could I bear; but that the wench should rise
Who can endure, save him with whom none lies?
How oft wished I night would not give thee place,
Nor morning stars shun thy uprising face.
How oft that either wind would break thy coach,
Or steeds might fall, forced with thick clouds'   30
    approach.
Whither goest thou, hateful nymph? Memnon the elf
Received his coal-black color from thyself.
Say that thy love with Cephalus were not known,
Then thinkest thou thy loose life is not shown?
Would Tithon might but talk of thee awhile,
Not one in heaven should be more base and vile.
Thou leav'st his bed because he's faint through age,
And early mount'st thy hateful carriage;
But held'st thou in thine arms some Cephalus,
Then wouldst thou cry, "Stay night, and run not thus."   40
Dost punish me because years make him wane?
I did not bid thee wed an aged swain.
The moon sleeps with Endymion every day;
Thou art as fair as she, then kiss and play.
Jove, that thou shouldst not haste but wait his leisure,
Made two nights one to finish up his pleasure.
I chid no more; she blushed, and therefore heard me,
Yet lingered not the day, but morning scared me.

ELEGIA XIV

Puellam consolatur cui prae nimia cura
comae deciderant

"Leave coloring thy tresses," I did cry;
Now hast thou left no hairs at all to dye.
But what had been more fair had they been kept?
Beyond thy robes thy dangling locks had swept.
Fear'dst thou to dress them being fine and thin,
Like to the silk the curious Seres spin,
Or threads which spider's slender foot draws out,
Fast'ning her light web some old beam about?
Not black, nor golden were they to our view,
Yet although neither, mixed of either's hue,
Such as in hilly Ida's wat'ry plains,
The cedar tall spoiled of his bark retains.
And they were apt to curl an hundred ways,
And did to thee no cause of dolor raise.
Nor hath the needle, or the comb's teeth reft them,
The maid that kembed them ever safely left them.
Oft was she dressed before mine eyes, yet never,
Snatching the comb to beat the wench, out drive her.
Oft in the morn, her hairs not yet digested,
Half-sleeping on a purple bed she rested;
Yet seemly, like a Thracian bacchanal,
That tired doth rashly on the green grass fall.
When they were slender, and like downy moss,
Thy troubled hairs, alas, endured great loss.
How patiently hot irons they did take,
In crooked trammels crispy curls to make.
I cried, " 'Tis sin, 'tis sin, these hairs to burn,
They well become thee, then to spare them turn.
Far off be force, no fire to them may reach,
Thy very hairs will the hot bodkin teach."
Lost are the goodly locks, which from their crown

10

20

30

Phoebus and Bacchus wished were hanging down.
Such were they as Diana painted stands
All naked holding in her wave-moist hands.
Why dost thy ill-kembed tresses' loss lament?
Why in thy glass dost look being discontent?
Be not to see with wonted eyes inclined;
To please thyself, thyself put out of mind.
No charmèd herbs of any harlot scathed thee,
No faithless witch in Thessale waters bathed thee.   40
No sickness harmed thee (far be that away!),
No envious tongue wrought thy thick locks decay.
By thine own hand and fault thy hurt doth grow,
Thou mad'st thy head with compound poison flow.
Now Germany shall captive hair-tires send thee,
And vanquished people curious dressings lend thee,
Which some admiring, O thou oft wilt blush,
And say, "He likes me for my borrowed bush,
Praising for me some unknown Guelder dame,
But I remember when it was my fame."   50
Alas she almost weeps, and her white cheeks,
Dyed red with shame, to hide from shame she seeks.
She holds, and views her old locks in her lap;
Aye me, rare gifts unworthy such a hap.
Cheer up thyself, thy loss thou mayst repair,
And be hereafter seen with native hair.

ELEGIA XV

Ad invidos, quod fama poetarum sit perennis

Envy, why carp'st thou my time is spent so ill,
And term'st my works fruits of an idle quill?
Or that unlike the line from whence I sprung,
War's dusty honors are refused, being young?
Nor that I study not the brawling laws,
Nor set my voice to sale in every cause?

Thy scope is mortal, mine eternal fame,
That all the world may ever chant my name.
Homer shall live while Tenedos stands and Ide,
10   Or into sea swift Simois doth slide.
Ascraeus lives while grapes with new wine swell,
Or men with crooked sickles corn down fell.
The world shall of Callimachus ever speak;
His art excelled, although his wit was weak.
For ever lasts high Sophocles' proud vein,
With sun and moon Aratus shall remain.
While bondmen cheat, fathers be hard, bawds whorish,
And strumpets flatter, shall Menander flourish.
Rude Ennius, and Plautus full of wit,
20   Are both in fame's eternal legend writ.
What age of Varro's name shall not be told,
And Jason's Argos and the fleece of gold?
Lofty Lucretius shall live that hour
That nature shall dissolve this earthly bower.
Aeneas' war, and Tityrus shall be read,
While Rome of all the conquered world is head.
Till Cupid's bow and fiery shafts be broken,
Thy verses, sweet Tibullus, shall be spoken.
And Gallus shall be known from east to west;
30   So shall Lycoris whom he lovèd best.
Therefore when flint and iron wear away,
Verse is immortal, and shall ne'er decay.
To verse let kings give place, and kingly shows,
And banks o'er which gold-bearing Tagus flows.
Let base-conceited wits admire vile things,
Fair Phoebus lead me to the Muses' springs.
About my head be quivering myrtle wound,
And in sad lovers' heads let me be found.
The living, not the dead, can envy bite,
40   For after death all men receive their right.
Then though death rakes my bones in funeral fire,
I'll live, and as he pulls me down mount higher.

The same by B.J.

Envy, why twitt'st thou me, my time's spent ill?
And call'st my verse fruits of an idle quill?
Or that (unlike the line from whence I sprung)
War's dusty honors I pursue not young?
Or that I study not the tedious laws,
And prostitute my voice in every cause?
Thy scope is mortal; mine eternal fame,
Which through the world shall ever chant my name.
Homer will live, whilst Tenedos stands, and Ide,
Or to the sea fleet Simois doth slide: 10
And so shall Hesiod too, while vines do bear,
Or crooked sickles crop the ripened ear;
Callimachus, though in invention low,
Shall still be sung, since he in art doth flow.
No loss shall come to Sophocles' proud vein;
With sun and moon Aratus shall remain.
Whilst slaves be false, fathers hard, and bawds be
        whorish,
Whilst harlots flatter, shall Menander flourish.
Ennius, though rude, and Accius' high-reared strain,
A fresh applause in every age shall gain.   20
Of Varro's name, what ear shall not be told?
Of Jason's Argo, and the fleece of gold?
Then shall Lucretius' lofty numbers die,
When earth and seas in fire and flames shall fry.
Tityrus, Tillage, Aeney shall be read,
Whilst Rome of all the conquered world is head.
Till Cupid's fires be out, and his bow broken,
Thy verses (neat Tibullus) shall be spoken.
Our Gallus shall be known from east to west;
So shall Lycoris, whom he now loves best.   30
The suffering ploughshare or the flint may wear,
But heavenly poesy no death can fear.
Kings shall give place to it, and kingly shows,
The banks o'er which gold-bearing Tagus flows.
Kneel hinds to trash: me let bright Phoebus swell,

With cups full flowing from the Muses' well.
The frost-drad myrtle shall impale my head,
And of sad lovers I'll be often read.
Envy the living, not the dead, doth bite,
For after death all men receive their right.
Then when this body falls in funeral fire,
My name shall live, and my best part aspire.

P. Ovidii Nasonis Amorum, Liber Secundus

ELEGIA I

Quod pro gigantomachia amores scribere sit coactus

I, Ovid, poet of my wantonness,
Born at Peligny, to write more address.
So Cupid wills; far hence be the severe:
You are unapt my looser lines to hear.
Let maids whom hot desire to husbands lead,
And rude boys touched with unknown love, me read,
That some youth hurt as I am with Love's bow
His own flame's best acquainted signs may know,
And long admiring say, "By what means learned
Hath this same poet my sad chance discerned?"   10
I durst the great celestial battles tell,
Hundred-hand Gyges, and had done it well,
With Earth's revenge, and how Olympus' top
High Ossa bore, Mount Pelion up to prop.
Jove and Jove's thunderbolts I had in hand,
Which for his heaven fell on the giants' band.
My wench her door shut, Jove's affairs I left,
Even Jove himself out of my wit was reft.
Pardon me, Jove, thy weapons aid me nought,
Her shut gates greater lightning than thine brought.   20
Toys and light elegies, my darts, I took,
Quickly soft words hard doors wide open strook.
Verses deduce the hornèd bloody moon,
And call the sun's white horses back at noon.

Snakes leap by verse from caves of broken mountains,
And turnèd streams run backward to their fountains.
Verses ope doors; and locks put in the post,
Although of oak, to yield to verses boast.
What helps it me of fierce Achill to sing?
30   What good to me will either Ajax bring?
Or he who warred and wandered twenty year?
Or woeful Hector, whom wild jades did tear?
But when I praise a pretty wench's face,
She in requital doth me oft embrace.
A great reward: heroes, O famous names,
Farewell; your favor nought my mind inflames.
Wenches, apply your fair looks to my verse,
Which golden Love doth unto me rehearse.

ELEGIA II

*Ad Bagoum, ut custodiam puellae sibi commissae
laxiorem habeat*

Bagous, whose care doth thy mistress bridle,
While I speak some few but fit words, be idle.
I saw the damsel walking yesterday
There where the porch doth Danaus' fact display.
She pleased me soon, I sent, and her did woo,
Her trembling hand writ back she might not do.
And asking why, this answer she redoubled,
Because thy care too much thy mistress troubled.
Keeper, if thou be wise, cease hate to cherish;
10   Believe me, whom we fear, we wish to perish.
Nor is her husband wise; what needs defense,
When unprotected there is no expense?
But furiously he follow his love's fire,
And thinks her chaste whom many do desire.
Stol'n liberty she may by thee obtain,
Which giving her, she may give thee again.

Wilt thou her fault learn, she may make thee tremble;
Fear to be guilty, then thou mayst dissemble.
Think when she reads, her mother letters sent her;
Let him go forth known, that unknown did enter;   20
Let him go see her though she do not languish,
And then report her sick and full of anguish.
If long she stays, to think the time more short,
Lay down thy forehead in thy lap to snort.
Enquire not what with Isis may be done,
Nor fear lest she to the theaters run.
Knowing her scapes, thine honor shall increase,
And what less labor than to hold thy peace?
Let him please, haunt the house, be kindly used,
Enjoy the wench, let all else be refused.   30
Vain causes feign of him, the true to hide,
And what she likes let both hold ratified.
When most her husband bends the brows and frowns,
His fawning wench with her desire he crowns.
But yet sometimes to chide thee let her fall
Counterfeit tears, and thee lewd hangman call.
Object thou then what she may well excuse,
To stain all faith in truth, by false crimes' use.
Of wealth and honor so shall grow thy heap;
Do this and soon thou shalt thy freedom reap.   40
On tell-tales' necks thou seest the link-knit chains,
The filthy prison faithless breasts restrains.
Water in waters, and fruit flying touch
Tantalus seeks, his long tongue's gain is such;
While Juno's watchman Io too much eyed,
Him timeless death took, she was deified.
I saw one's legs with fetters black and blue,
By whom the husband his wife's incest knew.
More he deserved; to both great harm he framed;
The man did grieve, the woman was defamed.   50
Trust me, all husbands for such faults are sad,
Nor make they any man that hear them glad.
If he loves not, deaf ears thou dost importune;

Or if he loves, thy tale breeds his misfortune.
Nor is it easily proved, though manifest,
She safe by favor of her judge doth rest.
Though himself see, he'll credit her denial,
Condemn his eyes, and say there is no trial.
Spying his mistress' tears, he will lament
60   And say, "This blab shall suffer punishment."
Why fight'st 'gainst odds? to thee, being cast, do hap
Sharp stripes; she sitteth in the judge's lap.
To meet for poison or vile facts we crave not,
My hands an unsheathed shining weapon have not.
We seek that, through thee, safely love we may;
What can be easier than the thing we pray?

ELEGIA III

Ad Eunuchum servantem dominam

Aye me, an eunuch keeps my mistress chaste,
That cannot Venus' mutual pleasure taste.
Who first deprived young boys of their best part,
With selfsame wounds he gave he ought to smart.
To kind requests thou wouldst more gentle prove,
If ever wench had made lukewarm thy love:
Thou wert not born to ride, or arms to bear,
Thy hands agree not with the warlike spear.
Men handle those; all manly hopes resign,
10   Thy mistress' ensigns must be likewise thine.
Please her, her hate makes others thee abhor;
If she discards thee, what use serv'st thou for?
Good form there is, years apt to play together,
Unmeet is beauty without use to wither.
She may deceive thee, though thou her protect,
What two determine never wants effect.
Our prayers move thee to assist our drift,
While thou hast time yet to bestow that gift.

ELEGIA IV

Quod amet mulieres, cuiuscunque formae sint

I mean not to defend the scapes of any,
Or justify my vices being many.
For I confess, if that might merit favor,
Here I display my lewd and loose behavior.
I loathe, yet after that I loathe I run;
O how the burden irks, that we should shun.
I cannot rule myself, but where love please
Am driven like a ship upon rough seas.
No one face likes me best, all faces move,
A hundred reasons make me ever love.   10
If any eye me with a modest look,
I blush, and by that blushful glance am took.
And she that's coy I like, for being no clown,
Methinks she would be nimble when she's down.
Though her sour looks a Sabine's brow resemble,
I think she'll do, but deeply can dissemble.
If she be learned, then for her skill I crave her;
If not, because she's simple I would have her.
Before Callimachus one prefers me far;
Seeing she likes my books, why should we jar?   20
Another rails at me, and that I write;
Yet would I lie with her if that I might.
Trips she, it likes me well; plods she, what then?
She would be nimbler, lying with a man.
And when one sweetly sings, then straight I long
To quaver on her lips even in her song.
Or if one touch the lute with art and cunning,
Who would not love those hands for their swift
        running?
And her I like that with a majesty
Folds up her arms and makes low courtesy.   30
To leave myself, that am in love with all,
Some one of these might make the chastest fall.

If she be tall, she's like an Amazon,
And therefore fills the bed she lies upon;
If short, she lies the rounder; to say troth,
Both short and long please me, for I love both.
I think what one undecked would be, being dressed;
Is she attired? then show her graces best.
A white wench thralls me, so doth golden yellow;
40 And nut-brown girls in doing have no fellow.
If her white neck be shadowed with black hair,
Why, so was Leda's, yet was Leda fair.
Amber-tressed is she? then on the morn think I;
My love alludes to every history.
A young wench pleaseth, and an old is good:
This for her looks, that for her womanhood.
Nay what is she that any Roman loves
But my ambitious ranging mind approves?

ELEGIA V

Ad amicam corruptam

No love is so dear (quivered Cupid, fly!)
That my chief wish should be so oft to die.
Minding thy fault, with death I wish to revel;
Alas, a wench is a perpetual evil.
No intercepted lines thy deeds display,
No gifts given secretly thy crime bewray:
O would my proofs as vain might be withstood,
Aye me, poor soul, why is my cause so good?
He's happy, that his love dares boldly credit,
10 To whom his wench can say, "I never did it."
He's cruel, and too much his grief doth favor,
That seeks the conquest by her loose behavior.
Poor wench, I saw when thou didst think I slumbered;
Not drunk, your faults on the spilt wine I numbered.
I saw your nodding eyebrows much to speak,
Even from your cheeks part of a voice did break.

Not silent were thine eyes, the board with wine
Was scribbled, and thy fingers writ a line.
I knew your speech (what do not lovers see?)
And words that seemed for certain marks to be.   20
Now many guests were gone, the feast being done,
The youthful sort to divers pastimes run.
I saw you then unlawful kisses join
(Such with my tongue it likes me to purloin).
None such the sister gives her brother grave,
But such kind wenches let their lovers have.
Phoebus gave not Diana such, 'tis thought,
But Venus often to her Mars such brought.
"What dost?" I cried, "transport'st thou my delight?
My lordly hands I'll throw upon my right.   30
Such bliss is only common to us two,
In this sweet good why hath a third to do?"
This, and what grief enforced me say, I said;
A scarlet blush her guilty face arrayed,
Even such as by Aurora hath the sky,
Or maids that their betrothèd husbands spy;
Such as a rose mixed with a lily breeds,
Or when the moon travails with charmèd steeds,
Or such as, lest long years should turn the dye,
Arachne stains Assyrian ivory.   40
To these, or some of these, like was her color,
By chance her beauty never shinèd fuller.
She viewed the earth: the earth to view beseemed her.
She lookèd sad: sad, comely I esteemed her.
Even kembèd as they were, her locks to rend,
And scratch her fair soft cheeks I did intend.
Seeing her face, mine upreared arms descended,
With her own armor was my wench defended.
I that erewhile was fierce, now humbly sue,
Lest with worse kisses she should me endue.   50
She laughed, and kissed so sweetly as might make
Wrath-kindled Jove away his thunder shake.
I grieve lest others should such good perceive,
And wish hereby them all unknown to leave.

Also much better were they than I tell,
And ever seemed as some new sweet befell.
'Tis ill they pleased so much, for in my lips
Lay her whole tongue hid, mine in hers she dips.
This grieves me not; no joinèd kisses spent
60 Bewail I only, though I them lament.
Nowhere can they be taught but in the bed;
I know no master of so great hire sped.

ELEGIA VI

In mortem psittaci

The parrot, from east India to me sent,
Is dead; all fowls her exequies frequent!
Go, godly birds, striking your breasts bewail,
And with rough claws your tender cheeks assail.
For woeful hairs let piece-torn plumes abound,
For long shrilled trumpets let your notes resound.
Why, Philomel, dost Tereus' lewdness mourn?
All-wasting years have that complaint outworn.
Thy tunes let this rare bird's sad funeral borrow,
10 Itys is great, but ancient cause of sorrow.
All you whose pinions in the clear air soar,
But most, thou friendly turtle dove, deplore;
Full concord all your lives was you betwixt,
And to the end your constant faith stood fixed.
What Pylades did to Orestes prove,
Such to the parrot was the turtle dove.
But what availed this faith? her rarest hue?
Or voice that how to change the wild notes knew?
What helps it thou wert given to please my wench?
20 Birds' hapless glory, death thy life doth quench.
Thou with thy quills mightst make green emeralds
        dark,
And pass our scarlet of red saffron's mark;
No such voice-feigning bird was on the ground,

Thou spokest thy words so well with stammering
    sound.
Envy hath rapt thee, no fierce wars thou movedst,
Vain babbling speech and pleasant peace thou lovedst.
Behold how quails among their battles live,
Which do perchance old age unto them give.
A little filled thee, and for love of talk,
Thy mouth to taste of many meats did balk.   30
Nuts were thy food, and poppy caused thee sleep,
Pure water's moisture thirst away did keep.
The ravenous vulture lives, the puttock hovers
Around the air, the cadess rain discovers,
And crows survive arms-bearing Pallas' hate,
Whose life nine ages scarce bring out of date.
Dead is that speaking image of man's voice,
The parrot given me, the far world's best choice.
The greedy spirits take the best things first,
Supplying their void places with the worst.   40
Thersites did Protesilaus survive,
And Hector died, his brothers yet alive.
My wench's vows for thee what should I show,
Which stormy south winds into sea did blow?
The seventh day came, none following mightst thou see,
And the Fate's distaff empty stood to thee;
Yet words in thy benumbèd palate rung:
"Farewell, Corinna," cried thy dying tongue.
Elysium hath a wood of holm-trees black,
Whose earth doth not perpetual green grass lack;   50
There good birds rest (if we believe things hidden)
Whence unclean fowls are said to be forbidden;
There harmless swans feed all abroad the river,
There lives the Phoenix one alone bird ever,
There Juno's bird displays his gorgeous feather,
And loving doves kiss eagerly together.
The parrot into wood received with these,
Turns all the goodly birds to what she please.
A grave her bones hides; on her corpse's great grave
The little stones these little verses have: 60

"This tomb approves I pleased my mistress well,
My mouth in speaking did all birds excel."

ELEGIA VII

Amicae se purgat quod ancillam non amet

Dost me of new crimes always guilty frame?
To overcome, so oft to fight I shame.
If on the marble theater I look,
One among many is to grieve thee took.
If some fair wench me secretly behold,
Thou arguest she doth secret marks unfold.
If I praise any, thy poor hairs thou tearest;
If blame, dissembling of my fault thou fearest.
If I look well, thou think'st thou dost not move;
If ill, thou say'st I die for others' love.
Would I were culpable of some offense,
They that deserve pain, bear't with patience.
Now rash accusing, and thy vain belief,
Forbid thine anger to procure my grief.
Lo, how the miserable great-eared ass,
Dulled with much beating, slowly forth doth pass.
Behold Cypassis, wont to dress thy head,
Is charged to violate her mistress' bed.
The gods from this sin rid me of suspicion,
To like a base wench of despised condition.
With Venus' game who will a servant grace?
Or any back made rough with stripes embrace?
Add she was diligent thy locks to braid,
And for her skill to thee a grateful maid,
Should I solicit her that is so just,
To take repulse, and cause her show my lust?
I swear by Venus, and the winged boy's bow,
Myself unguilty of this crime I know.

10

20

ELEGIA VIII

Ad Cypassim ancillam Corinnae

Cypassis, that a thousand ways trim'st hair,
Worthy to kemb none but a goddess fair,
Our pleasant scapes show thee no clown to be,
Apt to thy mistress, but more apt to me.
Who that our bodies were compressed bewrayed?
Whence knows Corinna that with thee I played?
Yet blushed I not, nor used I any saying
That might be urged to witness our false playing.
What if a man with bondwomen offend,
To prove him foolish did I e'er contend?   10
Achilles burned with face of captive Briseis,
Great Agamemnon loved his servant Chryseis.
Greater than these myself I not esteem;
What gracèd kings, in me no shame I deem.
But when on thee her angry eyes did rush,
In both thy cheeks she did perceive thee blush.
But being present, might that work the best,
By Venus' deity how did I protest!
Thou, goddess, dost command a warm south blast
My false oaths in Carpathian seas to cast.   20
For which good turn my sweet reward repay,
Let me lie with thee, brown Cypass, today.
Ungrate, why feignest new fears, and dost refuse?
Well mayst thou one thing for thy mistress use.
If thou deniest, fool, I'll our deeds express,
And as a traitor mine own fault confess,
Telling thy mistress where I was with thee,
How oft, and by what means we did agree.

ELEGIA IX

Ad Cupidinem

O Cupid, that dost never cease my smart,
O boy, that liest so slothful in my heart,
Why me that always was thy soldier found,
Dost harm, and in thy tents why dost me wound?
Why burns thy brand, why strikes thy bow
    thy friends?
More glory by thy vanquished foes ascends.
Did not Pelides whom his spear did grieve,
Being required, with speedy help relieve?
Hunters leave taken beasts, pursue the chase,
And than things found do ever further pace.
We people wholly given thee feel thine arms,
Thy dull hand stays thy striving enemies' harms.
Dost joy to have thy hookèd arrows shakèd
In naked bones? love hath my bones left naked.
So many men and maidens without love!
Hence with great laud thou mayst a triumph move.
Rome, if her strength the huge world had not filled,
With strawy cabins now her courts should build.
The weary soldier hath the conquered fields,
His sword laid by, safe, though rude places yields.
The dock inharbors ships drawn from the floods,
Horse freed from service range abroad the woods.
And time it was for me to live in quiet,
That have so oft served pretty wenches' diet.
Yet should I curse a god, if he but said,
"Live without love," so sweet ill is a maid.
For when my loathing it of heat deprives me,
I know not whither my mind's whirlwind drives me.
Even as a headstrong courser bears away
His rider vainly striving him to stay,
Or as a sudden gale thrusts into sea
The haven-touching bark now near the lea,

10

20

30

So wavering Cupid brings me back amain,
And purple Love resumes his darts again.
Strike, boy, I offer thee my naked breast,
Here thou hast strength, here thy right hand doth rest.
Here of themselves thy shafts come, as if shot;
Better than I their quiver knows them not.
Hapless is he that all the night lies quiet,
And slumb'ring, thinks himself much blessèd by it.   40
Fool, what is sleep but image of cold death?
Long shalt thou rest when Fates expire thy breath.
But me let crafty damsel's words deceive,
Great joys by hope I inly shall conceive.
Now let her flatter me, now chide me hard,
Let her enjoy me oft, oft be debarred.
Cupid, by thee Mars in great doubt doth trample,
And thy stepfather fights by thy example.
Light art thou, and more windy than thy wings;
Joys with uncertain faith thou takest and brings.   50
Yet, Love, if thou with thy fair mother hear,
Within my breast no desert empire bear;
Subdue the wand'ring wenches to thy reign,
So of both people shalt thou homage gain.

ELEGIA X

Ad Graecinum quod eodem tempore duas amet

Graecinus (well I wot) thou told'st me once
I could not be in love with two at once.
By thee deceived, by thee surprised am I,
For now I love two women equally.
Both are well favored, both rich in array,
Which is the loveliest it is hard to say.
This seems the fairest, so doth that to me,
And this doth please me most, and so doth she.
Even as a boat tossed by contrary wind,
So with this love and that, wavers my mind.   10

Venus, why doublest thou my endless smart?
Was not one wench enough to grieve my heart?
Why add'st thou stars to heaven, leaves to green
      woods,
And to the vast deep sea fresh water floods?
Yet this is better far than lie alone;
Let such as be mine enemies have none.
Yea, let my foes sleep in an empty bed,
And in the midst their bodies largely spread.
But may soft love rouse up my drowsy eyes,
20   And from my mistress' bosom let me rise.
Let one wench cloy me with sweet love's delight,
If one can do't, if not, two every night.
Though I am slender, I have store of pith,
Nor want I strength, but weight, to press her with.
Pleasure adds fuel to my lustful fire,
I pay them home with that they most desire.
Oft have I spent the night in wantonness,
And in the morn been lively ne'er the less.
He's happy who love's mutual skirmish slays,
30   And to the gods for that death Ovid prays.
Let soldiers chase their enemies amain,
And with their blood eternal honor gain;
Let merchants seek wealth with perjurèd lips,
Being wracked, carouse the sea tired by their ships;
But when I die, would I might droop with doing,
And in the midst thereof, set my soul going,
That at my funerals some may weeping cry,
"Even as he led his life, so did he die."

ELEGIA XI

Ad amicam navigantem

The lofty pine, from high Mount Pelion raught,
Ill ways by rough seas wond'ring waves first taught,
Which rashly 'twixt the sharp rocks in the deep

Carried the famous golden-fleecèd sheep.
O would that no oars might in seas have sunk,
The Argos wracked had deadly waters drunk.
Lo, country gods and known bed to forsake
Corinna means, and dangerous ways to take.
For thee the east and west winds make me pale,
With icy Boreas, and the southern gale.   10
Thou shalt admire no woods or cities there,
The unjust seas all bluish do appear.
The ocean hath no painted stones or shells,
The sucking shore with their abundance swells.
Maids, on the shore with marble-white feet tread,
So far 'tis safe; but to go farther dread.
Let others tell how winds fierce battles wage,
How Scylla's and Charybdis' waters rage,
And with what rocks the feared Cerannia threat,
In what gulf either Syrtes have their seat.   20
Let others tell this, and what each one speaks
Believe; no tempest the believer wreaks.
Too late you look back, when with anchors weighed,
The crooked bark hath her swift sails displayed.
The careful shipman now fears angry gusts,
And with the waters sees death near him thrusts.
But if that Triton toss the troubled flood,
In all thy face will be no crimson blood.
Then wilt thou Leda's noble twin-stars pray,
And he is happy whom the earth holds, say.   30
It is more safe to sleep, to read a book,
The Thracian harp with cunning to have strook;
But if my words with wingèd storms hence slip,
Yet, Galatea, favor thou her ship.
The loss of such a wench much blame will gather,
Both to the sea-nymphs and the sea-nymphs' father.
Go, minding to return with prosperous wind,
Whose blast may hither strongly be inclined,
Let Nereus bend the waves unto this shore,
Hither the winds blow, here the spring-tide roar.   40
Request mild Zephyr's help for thy avail,

And with thy hand assist thy swelling sail.
I from the shore thy known ship first will see,
And say it brings her that preserveth me.
I'll clip and kiss thee with all contentation,
For thy return shall fall the vowed oblation,
And in the form of beds we'll strew soft sand,
Each little hill shall for a table stand:
There wine being filled, thou many things shalt tell,
50   How almost wracked thy ship in main seas fell,
And hasting to me, neither darksome night,
Nor violent south winds did thee aught affright.
I'll think all true, though it be feignèd matter;
Mine own desires why should myself not flatter?
Let the bright day-star cause in heaven this day be,
To bring that happy time so soon as may be.

ELEGIA XII

Exultat, quod amica potitus sit

About my temples go, triumphant bays!
Conquered Corinna in my bosom lays,
She whom her husband, guard, and gate, as foes,
Lest art should win her, firmly did enclose.
That victory doth chiefly triumph merit,
Which without bloodshed doth the prey inherit.
No little ditchèd towns, no lowly walls,
But to my share a captive damsel falls.
When Troy by ten years' battle tumbled down,
10   With the Atrides many gained renown:
But I no partner of my glory brook,
Nor can another say his help I took.
I, guide and soldier, won the field and wear her,
I was both horseman, footman, standard-bearer.
Nor in my act hath fortune mingled chance;
O care-got triumph, hitherwards advance!
Nor is my war's cause new; but for a queen

Europe and Asia in firm peace had been.
The Lapiths and the Centaurs, for a woman,
To cruel arms their drunken selves did summon.   20
A woman forced the Trojans new to enter
Wars, just Latinus, in thy kingdom's center;
A woman against late-built Rome did send
The Sabine fathers, who sharp wars intend.
I saw how bulls for a white heifer strive,
She looking on them did more courage give.
And me with many, but yet me without murder,
Cupid commands to move his ensigns further.

ELEGIA XIII

Ad Isidem, ut parientem Corinnam iuvet

While rashly her womb's burden she casts out,
Weary Corinna hath her life in doubt.
She secretly with me such harm attempted,
Angry I was, but fear my wrath exempted.
But she conceived of me; or I am sure
I oft have done what might as much procure.
Thou that frequents Canopus' pleasant fields,
Memphis, and Pharos that sweet date trees yields,
And where swift Nile in his large channel skipping,
By seven huge mouths into the sea is slipping,   10
By feared Anubis' visage I thee pray,
So in thy temples shall Osiris stay,
And the dull snake about thy off'rings creep,
And in thy pomp horned Apis with thee keep:
Turn thy looks hither, and in one spare twain:
Thou givest my mistress life, she mine again.
She oft hath served thee upon certain days,
Where the French rout engirt themselves with bays.
On laboring women thou dost pity take,
Whose bodies with their heavy burdens ache.   20
My wench, Lucina, I entreat thee favor;

Worthy she is, thou shouldst in mercy save her.
In white, with incense I'll thine altars greet,
Myself will bring vowed gifts before thy feet,
Subscribing, "Naso with Corinna saved."
Do but deserve gifts with this title graved.
But if in so great fear I may advise thee,
To have this skirmish fought, let it suffice thee.

ELEGIA XIV

In amicam, quod abortivum ipsa fecerit

What helps it woman to be free from war,
Nor, being armed, fierce troops to follow far,
If without battle self-wrought wounds annoy them,
And their own privy-weaponed hands destroy them?
Who unborn infants first to slay invented,
Deserved thereby with death to be tormented.
Because thy belly should rough wrinkles lack,
Wilt thou thy womb-inclosèd offspring wrack?
Had ancient mothers this vile custom cherished,
All human kind by their default had perished;
Or stones, our stock's original, should be hurled
Again by some in this unpeopled world.
Who should have Priam's wealthy substance won,
If wat'ry Thetis had her child fordone?
In swelling womb her twins had Ilia killed,
He had not been that conquering Rome did build.
Had Venus spoiled her belly's Trojan fruit,
The earth of Caesars had been destitute.
Thou also, that wert born fair, hadst decayed,
If such a work thy mother had assayed.
Myself, that better die with loving may,
Had seen, my mother killing me, no day.
Why tak'st increasing grapes from vine-trees full?
With cruel hand why dost green apples pull?
Fruits ripe will fall, let springing things increase,

Life is no light price of a small surcease.
Why with hid irons are your bowels torn?
And why dire poison give you babes unborn?
At Colchis stained with children's blood men rail,
And mother-murdered Itys they bewail;   30
Both unkind parents, but for causes sad,
Their wedlock's pledges venged their husbands bad.
What Tereus, what Jason you provokes
To plague your bodies with such harmful strokes?
Armenian tigers never did so ill,
Nor dares the lioness her young whelps kill.
But tender damsels do it, though with pain;
Oft dies she that her paunch-wrapt child hath slain;
She dies, and with loose hairs to grave is sent,
And whoe'er see her, worthily lament.   40
But in the air let these words come to nought,
And my presages of no weight be thought.
Forgive her, gracious gods, this one delict,
And on the next fault punishment inflict.

ELEGIA XV

Ad annulum, quem dono amicae dedit

Thou ring that shalt my fair girl's finger bind,
Wherein is seen the giver's loving mind,
Be welcome to her, gladly let her take thee,
And her small joint's encircling round hoop make thee.
Fit her so well, as she is fit for me,
And of just compass for her knuckles be.
Blest ring, thou in my mistress' hand shalt lie;
Myself, poor wretch, mine own gifts now envy.
O would that suddenly into my gift
I could myself by secret magic shift!   10
Then would I wish thee touch my mistress' pap,
And hide thy left hand underneath her lap;
I would get off though strait, and sticking fast,

And in her bosom strangely fall at last.
Then I, that I may seal her privy leaves,
Lest to the wax the hold-fast dry gem cleaves,
Would first my beauteous wench's moist lips touch,
Only I'll sign nought that may grieve me much.
I would not out, might I in one place hit,
20 But in less compass her small fingers knit.
My life, that I will shame thee, never fear,
Or be a load thou shouldst refuse to bear.
Wear me, when warmest showers thy members wash,
And through the gem let thy lost waters pash.
But seeing thee, I think my thing will swell,
And even the ring perform a man's part well.
Vain things why wish I? go, small gift from hand,
Let her my faith with thee given understand.

ELEGIA XVI

Ad amicam, ut ad rura sua veniat

Sulmo, Peligny's third part, me contains,
A small, but wholesome soil with wat'ry veins.
Although the sun to rive the earth incline,
And the Icarian froward dog-star shine,
Pelignian fields with liquid rivers flow,
And on the soft ground fertile green grass grow.
With corn the earth abounds, with vines much more,
And some few pastures Pallas' olives bore.
And by the rising herbs, where clear springs slide,
10 A grassy turf the moistened earth doth hide.
But absent is my fire: lies I'll tell none,
My heat is here, what moves my heat is gone.
Pollux and Castor might I stand betwixt,
In heaven without thee would I not be fixed.
Upon the cold earth pensive let them lay
That mean to travel some long irksome way,
Or else will maidens, young men's mates, to go

If they determine to persever so.
Then on the rough Alps should I tread aloft,
My hard way with my mistress would seem soft.   20
With her I durst the Lybian Syrtes break through,
And raging seas in boist'rous south winds plough.
No barking dogs that Scylla's entrails bear,
Nor thy gulfs, crook'd Malea, would I fear;
No flowing waves with drownèd ships forth-pourèd
By cloyed Charybdis, and again devourèd.
But if stern Neptune's windy power prevail,
And waters' force force helping gods to fail,
With thy white arms upon my shoulders seize,
So sweet a burden I will bear with ease.   30
The youth oft swimming to his Hero kind,
Had then swum over, but the way was blind.
But without thee, although vine-planted ground
Contains me, though the streams in fields surround,
Though hinds in brooks the running waters bring,
And cool gales shake the tall trees' leafy spring,
Healthful Peligny I esteem nought worth,
Nor do I like the country of my birth.
Scythia, Cilicia, Britain are as good,
And rocks dyed crimson with Prometheus' blood.   40
Elms love the vines, the vines with elms abide,
Why doth my mistress from me oft divide?
Thou swarest division should not 'twixt us rise,
By me, and by my stars, thy radiant eyes.
Maids' words more vain and light than falling leaves,
Which, as it seems, hence wind and sea bereaves.
If any godly care of me thou hast,
Add deeds unto thy promises at last,
And with swift nags drawing thy little coach
(Their reins let loose), right soon my house approach.   50
But when she comes, you swelling mounts sink down,
And falling valleys be the smooth ways' crown.

ELEGIA XVII

Quod Corinnae soli sit serviturus

To serve a wench if any think it shame,
He being judge, I am convinced of blame.
Let me be slandered, while my fire she hides,
That Paphos, and the flood-beat Cythera guides.
Would I had been my mistress' gentle prey,
Since some fair one I should of force obey.
Beauty gives heart; Corinna's looks excel;
Aye me, why is it known to her so well?
But by her glass disdainful pride she learns,
10   Nor she herself, but first trimmed up, discerns.
Not though thy face in all things make thee reign
(O face, most cunning mine eyes to detain!),
Thou oughtst therefore to scorn me for thy mate:
Small things with greater may be copulate.
Love-snared Calypso is supposed to pray
A mortal nymph's refusing lord to stay.
Who doubts with Peleus Thetis did consort,
Egeria with just Numa had good sport,
Venus with Vulcan, though, smith's tools laid by,
20   With his stump foot he halts ill-favoredly.
This kind of verse is not alike, yet fit,
With shorter numbers the heroic sit.
And thou, my light, accept me howsoever,
Lay in the mid-bed, there be my lawgiver.
My stay no crime, my flight no joy shall breed,
Nor of our love to be ashamed we need.
For great revenues, I good verses have,
And many by me to get glory crave.
I know a wench reports herself Corinne:
30   What would not she give that fair name to win?
But sundry floods in one bank never go,
Eurotas cold, and poplar-bearing Po.

Nor in my books shall one but thou be writ,
Thou dost alone give matter to my wit.

ELEGIA XVIII

Ad Macrum, quod de amoribus scribat

To tragic verse while thou Achilles train'st,
And new-sworn soldiers' maiden arms retain'st,
We, Macer, sit in Venus' slothful shade,
And tender love hath great things hateful made.
Often at length my wench depart I bid,
She in my lap sits still as erst she did.
I said, "It irks me," half to weeping framed,
"Aye me," she cries, "to love why art ashamed?"
Then wreathes about my neck her winding arms,
And thousand kisses gives, that work my harms.   10
I yield, and back my wit from battles bring,
Domestic acts, and mine own wars to sing.
Yet tragedies and sceptres filled my lines,
But though I apt were for such high designs,
Love laughèd at my cloak, and buskins painted,
And rule so soon with private hands acquainted.
My mistress' deity also drew me fro it,
And Love triumpheth o'er his buskined poet.
What lawful is, or we profess love's art,
(Alas, my precepts turn myself to smart!)   20
We write, or what Penelope sends Ulysses,
Or Phyllis' tears that her Demophoön misses,
What thankless Jason, Macareus, and Paris,
Phaedra, and Hippolyte may read, my care is,
And what poor Dido with her drawn sword sharp
Doth say, with her that loved the Aonian harp.
As soon as from strange lands Sabinus came,
And writings did from divers places frame,
White-cheeked Penelope knew Ulysses' sign,
The stepdame read Hippolytus' lustless line,   30

Aeneas to Elisa answer gives,
And Phyllis hath to read, if now she lives.
Jason's sad letter doth Hypsipyle greet,
Sappho her vowed harp lays at Phoebus' feet.
Nor of thee, Macer, that resound'st forth arms,
Is golden love hid in Mars' mid-alarms:
There Paris is, and Helen's crime's record,
With Laodamia, mate to her dead lord.
Unless I err, to these thou more incline
40   Than wars, and from thy tents wilt come to mine.

ELEGIA XIX

Ad rivalem, cui uxor curae non erat

Fool, if to keep thy wife thou hast no need,
Keep her for me, my more desire to breed.
We scorn things lawful, stol'n sweets we affect,
Cruel is he that loves whom none protect.
Let us both lovers hope and fear alike,
And may repulse place for our wishes strike.
What should I do with fortune that ne'er fails me?
Nothing I love that at all times avails me.
Wily Corinna saw this blemish in me,
10   And craftily knows by what means to win me.
Ah often, that her hale head ached, she lying,
Willed me, whose slow feet sought delay, be flying;
Ah oft, how much she might, she feigned offense,
And, doing wrong, made show of innocence.
So having vexed she nourished my warm fire,
And was again most apt to my desire.
To please me, what fair terms and sweet words has she!
Great gods, what kisses, and how many gave she!
Thou also, that late took'st mine eyes away,
20   Oft cozen me, oft being wooed, say nay;
And on thy threshold let me lie dispread,
Suff'ring much cold by hoary night's frost bred.

So shall my love continue many years;
This doth delight me, this my courage cheers.
Fat love, and too much fulsome, me annoys,
Even as sweet meat a glutted stomach cloys.
In brazen tower had not Danae dwelt,
A mother's joy by Jove she had not felt;
While Juno Io keeps, when horns she wore,
Jove liked her better than he did before.   30
Who covets lawful things takes leaves from woods,
And drinks stol'n waters in surrounding floods.
Her lover let her mock that long will reign;
Aye me, let not my warnings cause my pain!
Whatever haps, by suff'rance harm is done;
What flies I follow, what follows me I shun.
But thou, of thy fair damsel too secure,
Begin to shut thy house at evening sure.
Search at the door who knocks oft in the dark,
In night's deep silence why the ban-dogs bark.   40
Whether the subtle maid lines brings and carries,
Why she alone in empty bed oft tarries.
Let this care sometimes bite thee to the quick,
That to deceits it may me forward prick.
To steal sands from the shore he loves alife,
That can affect a foolish wittol's wife.
Now I forewarn, unless to keep her stronger
Thou dost begin, she shall be mine no longer.
Long have I borne much, hoping time would beat thee
To guard her well, that well I might entreat thee.   50
Thou suffer'st what no husband can endure,
But of my love it will an end procure.
Shall I, poor soul, be never interdicted,
Nor never with night's sharp revenge afflicted?
In sleeping shall I fearless draw my breath?
Wilt nothing do, why I should wish thy death?
Can I but loathe a husband grown a bawd?
By thy default thou dost our joys defraud.
Some other seek that may in patience strive with thee;
To pleasure me, forbid me to corrive with thee.   60

P. Ovidii Nasonis Amorum, Liber Tertius

ELEGIA I

Deliberatio poetae, utrum elegos pergat scribere an potius tragedias

An old wood stands uncut, of long years' space,
'Tis credible some godhead haunts the place.
In midst thereof a stone-paved sacred spring,
Where round about small birds most sweetly sing.
Here while I walk, hid close in shady grove,
To find what work my muse might move, I strove.
Elegia came with hairs perfumèd sweet,
And one, I think, was longer of her feet;
A decent form, thin robe, a lover's look,
By her foot's blemish greater grace she took.   10
Then with huge steps came violent Tragedy:
Stern was her front, her cloak on ground did lie;
Her left hand held abroad a regal scepter,
The Lydian buskin in fit paces kept her.
And first she said, "When will thy love be spent,
O poet careless of thy argument?
Wine-bibbing banquets tell thy naughtiness,
Each cross-way's corner doth as much express.
Oft some points at the prophet passing by,
And, 'This is he whom fierce love burns,' they cry.   20
A laughing-stock thou art to all the city,
While without shame thou sing'st thy lewdness' ditty.
'Tis time to move grave things in lofty style,

Long hast thou loitered; greater works compile.
The subject hides thy wit; men's acts resound;
This thou wilt say to be a worthy ground.
Thy muse hath played what may mild girls content,
And by those numbers is thy first youth spent.
Now give the Roman Tragedy a name,
30   To fill my laws thy wanton spirit frame."
This said, she moved her buskins gaily varnished,
And seven times shook her head with thick locks
      garnished.
The other smiled (I wot) with wanton eyes;
Err I? or myrtle in her right hand lies.
"With lofty words, stout Tragedy," she said,
"Why tread'st me down? art thou aye gravely played?
Thou deign'st unequal lines should thee rehearse;
Thou fight'st against me using mine own verse;
Thy lofty style with mine I not compare,
40   Small doors unfitting for large houses are.
Light am I, and with me, my care, light Love,
Not stronger am I than the thing I move.
Venus without me should be rustical;
This goddess' company doth to me befall.
What gate thy stately words cannot unlock,
My flatt'ring speeches soon wide open knock.
And I deserve more than thou canst in verity,
By suff'ring much not borne by thy severity.
By me Corinna learns, cozening her guard,
50   To get the door with little noise unbarred;
And slipped from bed, clothed in a loose nightgown,
To move her feet unheard in setting down.
Ah, how oft on hard doors hung I engraved,
From no man's reading fearing to be saved!
But till the keeper went forth, I forget not,
The maid to hide me in her bosom let not.
What gift with me was on her birthday sent,
But cruelly by her was drowned and rent.
First of thy mind the happy seeds I knew,
60   Thou hast my gift, which she would from thee sue."

She left; I said, "You both I must beseech,
To empty air may go my fearful speech.
With scepters and high buskins th' one would
        dress me,
So through the world should bright renown
        express me.
The other gives my love a conquering name;
Come therefore, and to long verse shorter frame.
Grant, Tragedy, thy poet time's least tittle,
Thy labor ever lasts, she asks but little."
She gave me leave, soft loves in time make haste,
Some greater work will urge me on at last.   70

ELEGIA II

Ad amicam cursum equorum spectantem

I sit not here the noble horse to see,
Yet whom thou favor'st, pray may conqueror be.
To sit and talk with thee I hither came,
That thou mayst know with love thou mak'st me
        flame.
Thou view'st the course, I thee: let either heed
What please them, and their eyes let either feed.
What horse-driver thou favor'st most is best,
Because on him thy care doth hap to rest.
Such chance let me have: I would bravely run,
On swift steeds mounted till the race were done.   10
Now would I slack the reins, now lash their hide,
With wheels bent inward now the ring-turn ride;
In running if I see thee, I shall stay,
And from my hands the reins will slip away.
Ah, Pelops from his coach was almost felled,
Hippodamia's looks while he beheld,
Yet he attained by her support to have her:
Let us all conquer by our mistress' favor.
In vain, why fly'st back? force conjoins us now:

20 The place's laws this benefit allow.
    But spare my wench, thou at her right hand seated,
    By thy side's touching ill she is entreated.
    And sit thou rounder, that behind us see;
    For shame press not her back with thy hard knee.
    But on the ground thy clothes too loosely lie;
    Gather them up, or lift them, lo, will I.
    Envious garments so good legs to hide!
    The more thou look'st, the more the gown envied.
    Swift Atalanta's flying legs, like these,
30 Wish in his hands grasped did Hippomenes.
    Coat-tucked Diana's legs are painted like them,
    When strong wild beasts she stronger hunts to
        strike them.
    Ere these were seen, I burned; what will these do?
    Flames into flame, floods thou pour'st seas into.
    By these I judge delight me may the rest,
    Which lie hid under her thin veil suppressed.
    Yet in the meantime wilt small winds bestow,
    That from thy fan, moved by my hand, may blow?
    Or is my heat of mind, not of the sky?
40 Is't women's love my captive breast doth fry?
    While thus I speak, black dust her white robes ray;
    Foul dust, from her fair body go away.
    Now comes the pomp; themselves let all men cheer:
    The shout is nigh, the golden pomp comes here.
    First, Victory is brought with large spread wing:
    Goddess, come here, make my love conquering.
    Applaud you Neptune, that dare trust his wave,
    The sea I use not: me my earth must have.
    Soldier, applaud thy Mars: no wars we move,
50 Peace pleaseth me, and in mid-peace is love.
    With augurs Phoebus, Phoebe with hunters stands,
    To thee, Minerva, turn the craftsmen's hands;
    Ceres and Bacchus countrymen adore,
    Champions please Pollux, Castor loves horsemen more;
    Thee, gentle Venus, and the boy that flies
    We praise; great goddess, aid my enterprise.

Let my new mistress grant to be belovèd;
She becked, and prosperous signs gave as she movèd.
What Venus promised, promise thou we pray;
Greater than her, by her leave, th' art, I'll say.   60
The gods and their rich pomp witness with me,
For evermore thou shalt my mistress be.
Thy legs hang down, thou mayst, if that be best,
Awhile thy tiptoe on the footstool rest.
Now greatest spectacles the praetor sends,
Four-chariot horses from the lists' even ends.
I see whom thou affectest: he shall subdue;
The horses seem as thy desire they knew.
Alas, he runs too far about the ring;
What dost? thy wagon in less compass bring.   70
What dost, unhappy? her good wishes fade,
Let with strong hand the rein to bend be made.
One slow we favor; Romans, him revoke,
And each give signs by casting up his cloak.
They call him back; lest their gowns toss thy hair,
To hide thee in my bosom straight repair.
But now again the barriers open lie,
And forth the gay troops on swift horses fly.
At least now conquer, and outrun the rest;
My mistress' wish confirm with my request.   80
My mistress hath her wish; my wish remain:
He holds the palm, my palm is yet to gain.
She smiled, and with quick eyes behight some grace:
Pay it not here, but in another place.

ELEGIA III

De amica, quae periuraverat

What, are there gods? herself she hath forswore,
And yet remains the face she had before.
How long her locks were, ere her oath she took,
So long they be since she her faith forsook.

Fair white with rose red was before commixed;
Now shine her looks pure white and red betwixt.
Her foot was small: her foot's form is most fit;
Comely tall was she: comely tall she's yet.
Sharp eyes she had: radiant like stars they be,
10 By which she perjured oft hath lied to me.
In sooth th' eternal powers grant maids' society
Falsely to swear, their beauty hath some deity.
By her eyes, I remember, late she swore,
And by mine eyes, and mine were painèd sore.
Say, gods: if she unpunished you deceive,
For other's faults why do I loss receive?
But did you not so envy Cepheus' daughter,
For her ill-beauteous mother judged to slaughter?
'Tis not enough she shakes your record off,
20 And, unrevenged, mocked gods with me doth scoff.
But by my pain to purge her perjuries,
Cozened, I am the cozener's sacrifice.
God is a name, no substance, feared in vain,
And doth the world in fond belief detain,
Or if there be a God, he loves fine wenches,
And all things too much in their sole power drenches.
Mars girts his deadly sword on for my harm;
Pallas' lance strikes me with unconquered arm;
At me Apollo bends his pliant bow;
30 At me Jove's right hand lightning hath to throw.
The wrongèd gods dread fair ones to offend,
And fear those that to fear them least intend.
Who now will care the altars to perfume?
Tut, men should not their courage so consume.
Jove throws down woods and castles with his fire,
But bids his darts from perjured girls retire.
Poor Semele, among so many burned,
Her own request to her own torment turned;
But when her lover came, had she drawn back,
40 The father's thigh should unborn Bacchus lack.
Why grieve I? and of heaven reproaches pen?
The gods have eyes and breasts as well as men.

Were I a god, I should give women leave
With lying lips my godhead to deceive.
Myself would swear the wenches true did swear,
And I would be none of the gods severe.
But yet their gift more moderately use,
Or in mine eyes, good wench, no pain transfuse.

ELEGIA IV

Ad virum servantem coniugem

Rude man, 'tis vain thy damsel to commend
To keeper's trust: their wits should them defend.
Who, without fear, is chaste, is chaste in sooth:
Who, because means want, doeth not, she doth.
Though thou her body guard, her mind is stained:
Nor, lest she will, can any be restrained.
Nor canst by watching keep her mind from sin;
All being shut out, th' adulterer is within.
Who may offend, sins least; power to do ill
The fainting seeds of naughtiness doth kill.   10
Forbear to kindle vice by prohibition,
Sooner shall kindness gain thy will's fruition.
I saw a horse against the bit stiff-necked
Like lightning go, his struggling mouth being checked;
When he perceived the reins let slack, he stayed,
And on his loose mane the loose bridle laid.
How to attain what is denied we think,
Even as the sick desire forbidden drink.
Argus had either way an hundred eyes,
Yet by deceit love did them all surprise;   20
In stone and iron walls Danae shut,
Came forth a mother, though a maid there put.
Penelope, though no watch looked unto her,
Was not defiled by any gallant wooer.
What's kept, we covet more: the care makes theft;
Few love what others have unguarded left.

Nor doth her face please, but her husband's love;
I know not what men think should thee so move.
She is not chaste that's kept, but a dear whore;
30 Thy fear is than her body valued more.
Although thou chafe, stol'n pleasure is sweet play;
She pleaseth best, "I fear" if any say.
A free-born wench no right 'tis up to lock,
So use we women of strange nations' stock.
Because the keeper may come say, "I did it,"
She must be honest to thy servant's credit.
He is too clownish whom a lewd wife grieves,
And this town's well-known custom not believes,
Where Mars his sons not without fault did breed,
40 Remus and Romulus, Ilia's twin-born seed.
Cannot a fair one, if not chaste, please thee?
Never can these by any means agree.
Kindly thy mistress use, if thou be wise;
Look gently, and rough husbands' laws despise.
Honor what friends thy wife gives, she'll give many;
Least labor so shall win great grace of any;
So shalt thou go with youths to feast together,
And see at home much that thou ne'er brought'st thither.

ELEGIA V

Ad amnem, dum iter faceret ad amicam

Flood with reed-grown slime banks, till I be past
Thy waters stay; I to my mistress haste.
Thou hast no bridge, nor boat with ropes to throw,
That may transport me without oars to row.
Thee I have passed, and knew thy stream none such,
When thy wave's brim did scarce my ankles touch.
With snow thawed from the next hill now thou rushest,
And in thy foul deep waters thick thou gushest.
What helps my haste? what to have ta'en small rest?
10 What day and night to travel in her quest,

If standing here I can by no means get
My foot upon the further bank to set?
Now wish I those wings noble Perseus had,
Bearing the head with dreadful adders clad;
Now wish the chariot, whence corn seeds were found,
First to be thrown upon the untilled ground.
I speak old poets' wonderful inventions,
Ne'er was, nor shall be, what my verse mentions.
Rather, thou large bank-overflowing river,
Slide in thy bounds, so shalt thou run forever.   20
Trust me, land-stream, thou shalt no envy lack,
If I a lover be by thee held back.
Great floods ought to assist young men in love,
Great floods the force of it do often prove.
In mid-Bithynia, 'tis said, Inachus
Grew pale, and in cold fords hot lecherous.
Troy had not yet been ten years' siege outstander,
When nymph Neaera rapt thy looks, Scamander.
What, not Alpheus in strange lands to run
Th' Arcadian virgin's constant love hath won?   30
And Creusa unto Xanthus first affied,
They say Peneus near Phthia's town did hide.
What should I name Aesope, that Thebe loved,
Thebe who mother of five daughters proved.
If, Achelous, I ask where thy horns stand,
Thou say'st, broke with Alcides' angry hand.
Not Calydon, nor Aetolia did please;
One Deianira was more worth than these.
Rich Nile by seven mouths to the vast sea flowing,
Who so well keeps his water's head from knowing,   40
Is by Evadne thought to take such flame
As his deep whirlpools could not quench the same.
Dry Enipeus, Tyro to embrace,
Fly back his stream charged; the stream charged,
        gave place.
Nor pass I thee, who hollow rocks down tumbling,
In Tiber's field with wat'ry foam art rumbling,
Whom Ilia pleased, though in her looks grief reveled;

Her cheeks were scratched, her goodly hairs
    disheveled.
She, wailing Mars' sin and her uncle's crime,
50 Strayed barefoot through sole places on a time.
Her from his swift waves the bold flood perceived,
And from the mid-ford his hoarse voice upheaved,
Saying, "Why sadly tread'st my banks upon,
Ilia, sprung from Idaean Laomedon?
Where's thy attire? why wand'rest here alone?
To stay thy tresses white veil hast thou none?
Why weep'st, and spoil'st with tears thy wat'ry eyes,
And fiercely knock'st thy breast that open lies?
His heart consists of flint and hardest steel,
60 That seeing thy tears can any joy then feel.
Fear not: to thee our court stands open wide,
There shalt be loved: Ilia, lay fear aside.
Thou o'er a hundred nymphs or more shalt reign,
For five score nymphs or more our floods contain.
Nor, Roman stock, scorn me so much (I crave)
Gifts than my promise greater thou shalt have."
This said he: she her modest eyes held down,
Her woeful bosom a warm shower did drown.
Thrice she prepared to fly, thrice she did stay,
70 By fear deprived of strength to run away.
Yet rending with enragèd thumb her tresses,
Her trembling mouth these unmeet sounds expresses:
"O would in my forefathers' tomb deep laid
My bones had been, while yet I was a maid.
Why being a vestal am I wooed to wed,
Deflowered and stainèd in unlawful bed?
Why stay I? men point at me for a whore,
Shame, that should make me blush, I have no more."
This said, her coat hoodwinked her fearful eyes,
80 And into water desperately she flies.
'Tis said the slippery stream held up her breast,
And kindly gave her what she likèd best.
And I believe some wench thou hast affected,
But woods and groves keep your faults undetected.

While thus I speak the waters more abounded,
And from the channel all abroad surrounded.
Mad stream, why dost our mutual joys defer?
Clown, from my journey why dost me deter?
How wouldst thou flow wert thou a noble flood,
If thy great fame in every region stood?   90
Thou hast no name, but com'st from snowy
    mountains;
No certain house thou hast, nor any fountains.
Thy springs are nought but rain and melted snow,
Which wealth cold winter doth on thee bestow.
Either th' art muddy in mid-winter tide,
Or full of dust dost on the dry earth slide.
What thirsty traveler ever drunk of thee?
Who said with grateful voice, "Perpetual be"?
Harmful to beasts and to the fields thou proves;
Perchance these others, me mine own loss moves.   100
To this I fondly loves of floods told plainly,
I shame so great names to have used so vainly.
I know not what expecting, I erewhile
Named Achelous, Inachus, and Nile.
But for thy merits I wish thee, white stream,
Dry winters aye, and suns in heat extreme.

ELEGIA VI

Quod ab amica receptus cum ea coire non potuit, conqueritur

Either she was foul, or her attire was bad,
Or she was not the wench I wished t' have had.
Idly I lay with her, as if I loved not,
And like a burden grieved the bed that moved not.
Though both of us performed our true intent,
Yet could I not cast anchor where I meant.
She on my neck her ivory arms did throw,
Her arms far whiter than the Scythian snow,

And eagerly she kissed me with her tongue,
10 And under mine her wanton thigh she flung.
Yea, and she soothed me up, and called me "Sir,"
And used all speech that might provoke and stir.
Yet like as if cold hemlock I had drunk,
It mockèd me, hung down the head, and sunk.
Like a dull cipher or rude block I lay,
Or shade or body was I, who can say?
What will my age do, age I cannot shun,
When in my prime my force is spent and done?
I blush, that being youthful, hot and lusty,
20 I prove neither youth nor man, but old and rusty.
Pure rose she, like a nun to sacrifice,
Or one that with her tender brother lies.
Yet boarded I the golden Chie twice,
And Libas, and the white-cheeked Pitho thrice.
Corinna craved it in a summer's night,
And nine sweet bouts we had before daylight.
What, waste my limbs through some Thessalian charms?
May spells and drugs do silly souls such harms?
With virgin wax hath some imbased my joints,
30 And pierced my liver with sharp needles' points?
Charms change corn to grass and make it die;
By charms are running springs and fountains dry.
By charms mast drops from oaks, from vines grapes fall,
And fruit from trees when there's no wind at all.
Why might not then my sinews be enchanted,
And I grow faint as with some spirit haunted?
To this add shame: shame to perform it quailed me,
And was the second cause why vigor failed me.
My idle thoughts delighted her no more
40 Than did the robe or garment which she wore.
Yet might her touch make youthful Pylius fire,
And Tithon livelier than his years require.
Even her I had and she had me in vain,
What might I crave more, if I ask again?
I think the great gods grieved they had bestowed
The benefit which lewdly I forslowed.

I wished to be received in, in I get me;
To kiss, I kiss; to lie with her she let me.
Why was I blest? why made king to refuse it?
Chuff-like had I not gold and could not use it?   50
So in a spring thrives he that told so much,
And looks upon the fruits he cannot touch.
Hath any rose so from a fresh young maid,
As she might straight have gone to church and prayed?
Well, I believe she kissed not as she should,
Nor used the sleight and cunning which she could.
Huge oaks, hard adamants might she have moved,
And with sweet words cause deaf rocks to have loved.
Worthy she was to move both gods and men,
But neither was I man nor livèd then.   60
Can deaf ear take delight when Phaemius sings,
Or Thamyris in curious painted things?
What sweet thought is there but I had the same?
And one gave place still as another came.
Yet notwithstanding, like one dead it lay,
Drooping more than a rose pulled yesterday.
Now, when he should not jet, he bolts upright,
And craves his task, and seeks to be at fight.
Lie down with shame, and see thou stir no more,
Seeing thou wouldst deceive me as before.   70
Thou cozenest me: by thee surprised am I,
And bide sore loss with endless infamy.
Nay more, the wench did not disdain a whit
To take it in her hand and play with it,
But when she saw it would by no means stand,
But still drooped down, regarding not her hand,
"Why mock'st thou me," she cried, "or being ill,
Who bade thee lie down here against thy will?
Either th' art witched with blood of frogs new dead,
Or jaded cam'st thou from some other's bed."   80
With that, her loose gown on, from me she cast her;
In skipping out her naked feet much graced her.
And lest her maid should know of this disgrace,
To cover it, spilt water on the place.

ELEGIA VII

Quod ab amica non recipiatur, dolet

What man will now take liberal arts in hand,
Or think soft verse in any stead to stand?
Wit was sometimes more precious than gold,
Now poverty great barbarism we hold.
When our books did my mistress fair content,
I might not go whither my papers went.
She praised me, yet the gate shut fast upon her,
I here and there go, witty with dishonor.
See a rich chuff, whose wounds great wealth inferred,
10   For bloodshed knighted, before me preferred!
Fool, canst thou him in thy white arms embrace?
Fool, canst thou lie in his enfolding space?
Knowest not this head a helm was wont to bear?
This side that serves thee, a sharp sword did wear.
His left hand, whereon gold doth ill alight,
A target bore; blood-sprinkled was his right.
Canst touch that hand wherewith someone lie dead?
Ah whither is thy breast's soft nature fled?
Behold the signs of ancient fight, his scars,
20   Whate'er he hath his body gained in wars.
Perhaps he'll tell how oft he slew a man,
Confessing this, why dost thou touch him then?
I, the pure priest of Phoebus and the Muses,
At thy deaf doors in verse sing my abuses.
Not what we slothful knew, let wise men learn,
But follow trembling camps and battles stern,
And for a good verse draw the first dart forth:
Homer without this shall be nothing worth.
Jove, being admonished gold had sovereign power,
30   To win the maid came in a golden shower.
Till then, rough was her father, she severe,
The posts of brass, the walls of iron were;
But when in gifts the wise adulterer came,

She held her lap ope to receive the same.
Yet when old Saturn heaven's rule possessed,
All gain in darkness the deep earth suppressed.
Gold, silver, iron's heavy weight, and brass,
In hell were harbored; here was found no mass.
But better things it gave, corn without ploughs,
Apples, and honey in oaks' hollow boughs.   40
With strong ploughshares no man the earth did cleave,
The ditcher no marks on the ground did leave,
Nor hanging oars the troubled seas did sweep;
Men kept the shore, and sailed not into deep.
Against thyself, man's nature, thou wert cunning,
And to thine own loss was thy wit swift running.
Why gird'st thy cities with a towered wall?
Why let'st discordant hands to armor fall?
What dost with seas? with th' earth thou wert content;
Why seek'st not heaven, the third realm, to frequent?   50
Heaven thou affects; with Romulus, temples brave
Bacchus, Alcides, and now Caesar have.
Gold from the earth instead of fruits we pluck;
Soldiers by blood to be enriched have luck.
Courts shut the poor out; wealth gives estimation;
Thence grows the judge, and knight of reputation.
All they possess: they govern fields and laws,
They manage peace, and raw war's bloody jaws.
Only our loves let not such rich churls gain;
'Tis well if some wench for the poor remain.   60
Now, Sabine-like, though chaste she seems to live,
One her commands, who many things can give.
For me, she doth keeper and husband fear;
If I should give, both would the house forbear.
If of scorned lovers god be venger just,
O let him change goods so ill got to dust.

ELEGIA VIII

Tibulli mortem deflet

If Thetis and the Morn their sons did wail,
And envious Fates great goddesses assail,
Sad Elegia, thy woeful hairs unbind:
Ah now a name too true thou hast, I find.
Tibullus, thy work's poet, and thy fame,
Burns his dead body in the funeral flame.
Lo Cupid brings his quiver spoilèd quite,
His broken bow, his firebrand without light.
How piteously with drooping wings he stands,
And knocks his bare breast with self-angry hands.
The locks spread on his neck receive his tears,
And shaking sobs his mouth for speeches bears.
So at Aeneas' burial, men report,
Fair-fac'd Iulus, he went forth thy court.
And Venus grieves, Tibullus' life being spent,
As when the wild boar Adon's groin had rent.
The gods' care we are called, and men of piety,
And some there be that think we have a deity.
Outrageous death profanes all holy things,
And on all creatures obscure darkness brings.
To Thracian Orpheus what did parents good,
Or songs amazing wild beasts of the wood?
Where Linus by his father Phoebus laid
To sing with his unequaled harp is said.
See Homer from whose fountain ever filled
Pierian dew to poets is distilled:
Him the last day in black Averne hath drowned;
Verses alone are with continuance crowned.
The work of poets lasts Troy's labor's fame,
And that slow web night's falsehood did unframe.
So Nemesis, so Delia famous are:
The one his first love, th' other his new care.
What profit to us hath our pure life bred?

10

20

30

What to have lain alone in empty bed?
When bad fates take good men, I am forbod
By secret thoughts to think there is a god.
Live godly, thou shalt die; though honor heaven,
Yet shall thy life be forcibly bereaven.
Trust in good verse: Tibullus feels death's pains,
Scarce rests of all what a small urn contains.   40
Thee, sacred poet, could sad flames destroy?
Nor fearèd they thy body to annoy?
The holy gods' gilt temples they might fire,
That durst to so great wickedness aspire.
Eryx' bright empress turned her looks aside,
And some that she refrained tears have denied.
Yet better is 't, than if Corcyra's isle
Had thee unknown interred in ground most vile.
Thy dying eyes here did thy mother close,
Nor did thy ashes her last off'rings lose.   50
Part of her sorrow here thy sister bearing
Comes forth her unkembed locks asunder tearing.
Nemesis and thy first wench join their kisses
With thine, nor this last fire their presence misses.
Delia departing, "Happier loved," she saith,
"Was I: thou liv'dst, while thou esteem'dst my faith."
Nemesis answers, "What's my loss to thee?
His fainting hand in death engraspèd me."
If aught remains of us but name and spirit,
Tibullus doth Elysium's joy inherit.   60
Your youthful brows with ivy girt to meet him,
With Calvus, learn'd Catullus come, and greet him,
And thou, if falsely charged to wrong thy friend,
Gallus, that car'st not blood and life to spend.
With these thy soul walks: souls if death release,
The godly sweet Tibullus doth increase.
Thy bones I pray may in the urn safe rest,
And may th' earth's weight thy ashes nought molest.

ELEGIA IX

Ad Cererem, conquerens quod eius sacris cum amica concumbere non permittatur

Come were the times of Ceres' sacrifice:
In empty bed alone my mistress lies.
Golden-haired Ceres, crowned with ears of corn,
Why are our pleasures by thy means forborne?
Thee, goddess, bountiful all nations judge,
Nor less at man's prosperity any grudge.
Rude husbandmen baked not their corn before,
Nor on the earth was known the name of floor;
On mast of oaks, first oracles, men fed,
10 This was their meat, the soft grass was their bed.
First Ceres taught the seed in fields to swell,
And ripe-eared corn with sharp-edged scythes to fell;
She first constrained bulls' necks to bear the yoke,
And untilled ground with crooked ploughshares broke.
Who thinks her to be glad at lovers' smart,
And worshipped by their pain and lying apart?
Nor is she, though she loves the fertile fields,
A clown, nor no love from her warm breast yields.
Be witness Crete (nor Crete doth all things feign),
20 Crete proud that Jove her nursery maintain.
There he who rules the world's star-spangled towers,
A little boy, drunk teat-distilling showers.
Faith to the witness Jove's praise doth apply;
Ceres, I think, no known fault will deny.
The goddess saw Iasion on Candian Ide,
With strong hand striking wild beasts' bristled hide;
She saw, and as her marrow took the flame,
Was divers ways distract with love and shame.
Love conquered shame, the furrows dry were burned,
30 And corn with least part of itself returned.
When well-tossed mattocks did the ground prepare,
Being fit broken with the crooked share,

And seeds were equally in large fields cast,
The ploughman's hopes were frustrate at the last.
The grain-rich goddess in high woods did stray,
Her long hair's ear-wrought garland fell away.
Only was Crete fruitful that plentious year;
Where Ceres went, each place was harvest there.
Ida, the seat of groves, did sing with corn,
Which by the wild boar in the woods was shorn.   40
Law-giving Minos did such years desire,
And wished the goddess long might feel love's fire.
Ceres, what sports to thee so grievous were,
As in thy sacrifice we them forbear?
Why am I sad, when Proserpine is found,
And Juno-like with Dis reigns underground?
Festival days ask Venus, songs and wine,
These gifts are meet to please the powers divine.

ELEGIA X

Ad amicam, a cuius amore discedere non potest

Long have I borne much, mad thy faults me make:
Dishonest love, my wearied breast forsake!
Now have I freed myself, and fled the chain,
And what I have borne, shame to bear again.
We vanquish, and tread tamed Love under feet,
Victorious wreaths at length my temples greet.
Suffer, and harden: good grows by this grief,
Oft bitter juice brings to the sick relief.
I have sustained so oft thrust from the door,
To lay my body on the hard moist floor.   10
I know not whom thou lewdly didst embrace,
When I to watch supplied a servant's place;
I saw when forth a tired lover went,
His side past service, and his courage spent.
Yet this is less than if he had seen me;
May that shame fall mine enemies' chance to be.

When have not I, fixed to thy side, close laid?
I have thy husband, guard, and fellow played.
The people by my company she pleased;
20   My love was cause that more men's love she seized.
What should I tell her vain tongue's filthy lies,
And, to my loss, god-wronging perjuries?
What secret becks in banquets with her youths,
With privy signs, and talk dissembling truths?
Hearing her to be sick, I thither ran,
But with my rival sick she was not then.
These hardened me, with what I keep obscure;
Some other seek, who will these things endure.
Now my ship in the wishèd haven crowned,
30   With joy hears Neptune's swelling waters sound.
Leave thy once powerful words, and flatteries;
I am not as I was before, unwise.
Now love and hate my light breast each way move,
But victory, I think, will hap to love.
I'll hate, if I can; if not, love 'gainst my will:
Bulls hate the yoke, yet what they hate have still.
I fly her lust, but follow beauty's creature;
I loathe her manners, love her body's feature.
Nor with thee, nor without thee can I live,
40   And doubt to which desire the palm to give.
Or less fair, or less lewd would thou mightst be;
Beauty with lewdness doth right ill agree.
Her deeds gain hate, her face entreateth love;
Ah, she doth more worth than her vices prove.
Spare me, O by our fellow-bed, by all
The gods who by thee to be perjured fall,
And by thy face to me a power divine,
And by thine eyes whose radiance burns out mine.
Whate'er thou art, mine art thou: choose this course,
50   Wilt have me willing, or to love by force?
Rather I'll hoist up sail, and use the wind,
That I may love yet, though against my mind.

ELEGIA XI

Dolet amicam suam ita suis carminibus innotuisse
ut rivales multos sibi pararit

What day was that which, all sad haps to bring,
White birds to lovers did not always sing?
Or is I think my wish against the stars?
Or shall I plain some god against me wars?
Who mine was called, whom I loved more than any,
I fear with me is common now to many.
Err I? or by my books is she so known?
'Tis so: by my wit her abuse is grown.
And justly: for her praise why did I tell?
The wench by my fault is set forth to sell.   10
The bawd I play, lovers to her I guide:
Her gate by my hands is set open wide.
'Tis doubtful whether verse avail or harm,
Against my good they were an envious charm.
When Thebes, when Troy, when Caesar should
      be writ,
Alone Corinna moves my wanton wit.
With Muse opposed, would I my lines had done,
And Phoebus had forsook my work begun.
Nor, as use will not poets' record hear,
Would I my words would any credit bear.   20
Scylla by us her father's rich hair steals,
And Scylla's womb mad raging dogs conceals.
We cause feet fly, we mingle hairs with snakes,
Victorious Perseus a winged steed's back takes.
Our verse great Tityus a huge space outspreads,
And gives the viper-curlèd dog three heads.
We make Enceladus use a thousand arms,
And men enthralled by mermaids' singing charms.
The east winds in Ulysses' bags we shut,
And blabbing Tantalus in mid-waters put.   30
Niobe flint, Callist we make a bear,

Bird-changèd Progne doth her Itys tear;
Jove turns himself into a swan, or gold,
Or his bull's horns Europa's hand doth hold.
Proteus what should I name? teeth, Thebes' first seed?
Oxen in whose mouths burning flames did breed?
Heav'n star Electra, that bewailed her sisters?
The ships whose godhead in the sea now glisters?
The sun turned back from Atreus' cursed table?
40 And sweet touched harp that to move stones was able?
Poets' large power is boundless and immense,
Nor have their words true history's pretense.
And my wench ought to have seemed falsely praised.
Now your credulity harm to me hath raised.

ELEGIA XII

De Iunonis festo

When fruit-filled Tuscia should a wife give me,
We touched the walls, Camillus, won by thee.
The priests to Juno did prepare chaste feasts,
With famous pageants, and their home-bred beasts.
To know their rites well recompensed my stay,
Though thither leads a rough steep hilly way.
There stands an old wood with thick trees dark clouded:
Who sees it grants some deity there is shrouded.
An altar takes men's incense and oblation,
10 An altar made after the ancient fashion.
Here, when the pipe with solemn tunes doth sound,
The annual pomp goes on the covered ground.
White heifers by glad people forth are led,
Which with the grass of Tuscan fields are fed,
And calves from whose feared front no threat'ning flies,
And little pigs, base hogsties' sacrifice,
And rams with horns their hard heads wreathèd back;
Only the goddess-hated goat did lack,

By whom disclosed, she in the high woods took,
Is said to have attempted flight forsook.   20
Now is the goat brought through the boys with darts,
And given to him that the first wound imparts.
Where Juno comes, each youth and pretty maid
Show large ways, with their garments there displayed.
Jewels and gold their virgin tresses crown,
And stately robes to their gilt feet hang down.
As is the use, the nuns in white veils clad,
Upon their heads the holy mysteries had.
When the chief pomp comes, loud the people hollow,
And she her vestal virgin priests doth follow.   30
Such was the Greek pomp, Agamemnon dead,
Which fact, and country wealth Halesus fled,
And having wandered now through sea and land,
Built walls high towered with a prosperous hand.
He to th' Hetrurians Juno's feast commended;
Let me, and them by it be aye befriended.

ELEGIA XIII

Ad amicam, si peccatura est, ut occulte peccet

Seeing thou art fair, I bar not thy false playing,
But let not me, poor soul, know of thy straying.
Nor do I give thee counsel to live chaste,
But that thou wouldst dissemble, when 'tis past.
She hath not trod awry that doth deny it.
Such as confess have lost their good names by it.
What madness is 't to tell night's pranks by day,
And hidden secrets openly to bewray?
The strumpet with the stranger will not do
Before the room be clear, and door put to.   10
Will you make shipwrack of your honest name,
And let the world be witness of the same?
Be more advised, walk as a puritan,

And I shall think you chaste, do what you can.
Slip still, only deny it when 'tis done,
And before folk immodest speeches shun.
The bed is for lascivious toyings meet;
There use all tricks, and tread shame under feet.
When you are up and dressed, be sage and grave,
20   And in the bed hide all the faults you have.
Be not ashamed to strip you, being there,
And mingle thighs, yours ever mine to bear.
There in your rosy lips my tongue entomb,
Practice a thousand sports when there you come.
Forbear no wanton words you there would speak,
And with your pastime let the bedstead creak.
But with your robes put on an honest face,
And blush, and seem as you were full of grace.
Deceive all; let me err, and think I am right,
30   And like a wittol think thee void of sleight.
Why see I lines so oft received and given?
This bed and that by tumbling made uneven?
Like one start up, your hair tossed and displaced,
And with a wanton's tooth your neck new-raced?
Grant this, that what you do I may not see;
If you weigh not ill speeches, yet weigh me.
My soul fleets when I think what you have done,
And thorough every vein doth cold blood run.
Then thee whom I must love, I hate in vain,
40   And would be dead, but dead with thee remain.
I'll not sift much, but hold thee soon excused,
Say but thou wert injuriously accused.
Though while the deed be doing you be took,
And I see when you ope the two-leaved book,
Swear I was blind, deny, if you be wise,
And I will trust your words more than mine eyes.
From him that yields, the palm is quickly got,
Teach but your tongue to say, "I did it not,"
And being justified by two words, think
50   The cause acquits you not, but I that wink.

ELEGIA XIV

Ad Venerem, quod elegis finem imponat

Tender Love's mother, a new poet get;
This last end to my elegies is set,
Which I, Peligny's foster-child, have framed
(Nor am I by such wanton toys defamed),
Heir of an ancient house, if help that can,
Not only by war's rage made gentleman.
In Virgil Mantua joys, in Catull Verone,
Of me Peligny's nation boasts alone,
Whom liberty to honest arms compelled,
When careful Rome in doubt their prowess held.   10
And some guest, viewing wat'ry Sulmo's walls,
Where little ground to be enclosed befalls,
"How such a poet could you bring forth?" says;
"How small soe'er, I'll you for greatest praise."
Both loves to whom my heart long time did yield,
Your golden ensigns pluck out of my field.
Horned Bacchus greater fury doth distill,
A greater ground with great horse is to till.
Weak elegies, delightful Muse, farewell;
A work that after my death here shall dwell.   20

LUCAN'S FIRST BOOK
TRANSLATED
LINE FOR LINE

Blount: I purpose to be blunt with you, and out of my dull-
ness to encounter you with a dedication in the memory of
that pure elemental wit Chr. Marlowe, whose ghost or ge-
nius is to be seen walk the churchyard in (at the least) three
or four sheets. Methinks you should presently look wild
now, and grow humorously frantic upon the taste of it.
Well, lest you should, let me tell you. This spirit was some-
time a familiar of your own, *Lucan's first book translated,*
which (in regard of your old right in it) I have raised in the
circle of your patronage. But stay now, Edward: if I mistake   10
not, you are to accommodate yourself with some few in-
structions touching the property of a patron, that you are
not yet possessed of, and to study them for your better
grace as our gallants do fashions. First, you must be proud,
and think you have merit enough in you, though you are
ne'er so empty; then, when I bring you the book, take
physic, and keep state, assign me a time by your man to
come again, and afore the day be sure to have changed your
lodging; in the meantime sleep little, and sweat with the in-
vention of some pitiful dry jest or two which you may hap-   20
pen to utter, with some little (or not at all) marking of your
friends, when you have found a place for them to come in
at; or if by chance something has dropped from you worthy

the taking up, weary all that come to you with the often repetition of it; censure scornfully enough, and somewhat like a traveler; commend nothing lest you discredit your (that which you would seem to have) judgment. These things if you can mold yourself to them, Ned, I make no question but they will not become you. One special virtue 30 in our patrons of these days I have promised myself you shall fit excellently, which is to give nothing; yes, thy love I will challenge as my peculiar object, both in this, and (I hope) many more succeeding offices. Farewell: I affect not the world should measure my thoughts to thee by a scale of this nature: leave to think good of me when I fall from thee.

Thine in all rites of perfect friendship,

THOM. THORPE

Wars worse than civil on Thessalian plains,
And outrage strangling law, and people strong
We sing, whose conquering swords their own breasts
    launched,
Armies allied, the kingdom's league uprooted,
Th' affrighted world's force bent on public spoil,
Trumpets and drums like deadly threat'ning other,
Eagles alike displayed, darts answering darts.

Romans, what madness, what huge lust of war,
Hath made barbarians drunk with Latin blood?
Now Babylon (proud through our spoil) should stoop,   10
While slaughtered Crassus' ghost walks unrevenged,
Will ye wage war, for which you shall not triumph?
Aye me, O what a world of land and sea
Might they have won whom civil broils have slain!
As far as Titan springs, where night dims heaven,
Aye, to the torrid zone where mid-day burns,
And where stiff winter, whom no spring resolves,
Fetters the Euxine Sea with chains of ice;
Scythia and wild Armenia had been yoked,
And they of Nilus' mouth (if there live any).   20
Rome, if thou take delight in impious war,
First conquer all the earth, then turn thy force
Against thyself: as yet thou wants not foes.
That now the walls of houses half-reared totter,
That rampires fallen down, huge heaps of stone
Lie in our towns, that houses are abandoned,

And few live that behold their ancient seats,
Italy many years hath lien untilled
And choked with thorns, that greedy earth
        wants hinds,
30   Fierce Pyrrhus, neither thou nor Hannibal
Art cause; no foreign foe could so afflict us;
These plagues arise from wreak of civil power.
But if for Nero (then unborn) the Fates
Would find no other means (and gods not slightly
Purchase immortal thrones, nor Jove joyed heaven
Until the cruel Giants' war was done)
We plain not heavens, but gladly bear these evils
For Nero's sake: Pharsalia groan with slaughter,
And Carthage souls be glutted with our bloods;
40   At Munda let the dreadful battles join;
Add, Caesar, to these ills, Perusian famine,
The Mutin toils, the fleet at Leuca sunk,
And cruel field near burning Aetna fought.
Yet Rome is much bound to these civil arms,
Which made thee emperor, thee (seeing thou,
        being old,
Must shine a star) shall heaven (whom thou lovest)
Receive with shouts, where thou wilt reign as king,
Or mount the sun's flame-bearing chariot,
And with bright restless fire compass the earth,
50   Undaunted though her former guide be changed;
Nature and every power shall give thee place,
What god it please thee be, or where to sway.
But neither choose the north t' erect thy seat,
Nor yet the adverse reeking southern pole,
Whence thou shouldst view thy Rome with
        squinting beams.
If any one part of vast heaven thou swayest,
The burdened axis with thy force will bend;
The midst is best; that place is pure and bright.
There, Caesar, mayst thou shine and no cloud
        dim thee,

Then men from war shall bide in league and ease,   60
Peace through the world from Janus' fane shall fly,
And bolt the brazen gates with bars of iron.
Thou, Caesar, at this instant art my god:
Thee if I invocate, I shall not need
To crave Apollo's aid or Bacchus' help,
Thy power inspires the Muse that sings this war.

The causes first I purpose to unfold
Of these garboils, whence springs a long discourse,
And what made madding people shake off peace.
The Fates are envious, high seats quickly perish,   70
Under great burdens falls are ever grievous;
Rome was so great it could not bear itself.
So when this world's compounded union breaks,
Time ends, and to old Chaos all things turn,
Confusèd stars shall meet, celestial fire
Fleet on the floods, the earth shoulder the sea,
Affording it no shore, and Phoebe's wain
Chase Phoebus, and enraged affect his place,
And strive to shine by day, and full of strife
Dissolve the engines of the broken world.   80
All great things crush themselves; such end the gods
Allot the height of honor, men so strong
By land and sea no foreign force could ruin.
O Rome, thyself art cause of all these evils,
Thyself thus shivered out to three men's shares:
Dire league of partners in a kingdom last not.
O faintly-joined friends, with ambition blind,
Why join you force to share the world betwixt you?
While th' earth the sea, and air the earth sustains,
While Titan strives against the world's swift course,   90
Or Cynthia, night's queen, waits upon the day,
Shall never faith be found in fellow kings.
Dominion cannot suffer partnership;
This need no foreign proof nor far-fet story:
Rome's infant walls were steeped in brother's blood;

Nor then was land, or sea, to breed such hate,
A town with one poor church set them at odds.

Caesar's and Pompey's jarring love soon ended,
'Twas peace against their wills; betwixt them both
100 Stepped Crassus in, even as the slender Isthmus
Betwixt the Aegean and the Ionian sea
Keeps each from other, but being worn away,
They both burst out, and each encounter other:
So whenas Crassus' wretched death, who stayed
        them,
Had filled Assyrian Carra's walls with blood,
His loss made way for Roman outrages.
Parthians, y' afflict us more than ye suppose:
Being conquered, we are plagued with civil war.
Swords share our empire; Fortune, that made Rome
110 Govern the earth, the sea, the world itself,
Would not admit two lords; for Julia,
Snatched hence by cruel fates with ominous howls,
Bare down to hell her son, the pledge of peace,
And all bands of that death-presaging alliance.
Julia, had heaven given thee longer life,
Thou hadst restrained thy headstrong husband's rage,
Yea, and thy father too, and, swords thrown down,
Made all shake hands as once the Sabines did;
Thy death broke amity, and trained to war
120 These captains emulous of each other's glory.
Thou fear'dst, great Pompey, that late deeds
        would dim
Old triumphs, and that Caesar's conquering France
Would dash the wreath thou wear'st for pirates'
        wrack.
Thee war's use stirred, and thoughts that always
        scorned
A second place; Pompey could bide no equal,
Nor Caesar no superior: which of both
Had justest cause unlawful 'tis to judge.
Each side had great partakers: Caesar's cause

The gods abetted, Cato liked the other.
Both differed much: Pompey was struck in years,   130
And by long rest forgot to manage arms,
And being popular sought by liberal gifts
To gain the light unstable commons' love,
And joyed to hear his theater's applause;
He lived secure, boasting his former deeds,
And thought his name sufficient to uphold him,
Like to a tall oak in a fruitful field,
Bearing old spoils and conquerors' monuments,
Who though his root be weak, and his own weight
Keep him within the ground, his arms all bare,   140
His body (not his boughs) send forth a shade;
Though every blast it nod, and seem to fall,
When all the woods about stand bolt upright,
Yet he alone is held in reverence.
Caesar's renown for war was less, he restless,
Shaming to strive but where he did subdue;
When ire or hope provoked, heady and bold,
At all times charging home, and making havoc;
Urging his fortune, trusting in the gods,
Destroying what withstood his proud desires,   150
And glad when blood and ruin made him way:
So thunder which the wind tears from the clouds,
With crack of riven air and hideous sound
Filling the world, leaps out and throws forth fire,
Affrights poor fearful men, and blasts their eyes
With overthwarting flames, and raging shoots
Alongst the air, and, nought resisting it,
Falls, and returns, and shivers where it lights.
Such humors stirred them up; but this war's seed
Was even the same that wracks all great dominions.   160
When Fortune made us lords of all, wealth flowed,
And when we grew licentious and rude;
The soldiers' prey and rapine brought in riot;
Men took delight in jewels, houses, plate,
And scorned old sparing diet, and ware robes
Too light for women; Poverty (who hatched

Rome's greatest wits) was loathed, and all the world
Ransacked for gold, which breeds the world decay;
And then large limits had their butting lands,
170   The ground which Curius and Camillus tilled
Was stretched unto the fields of hinds unknown.
Again, this people could not brook calm peace,
Them freedom without war might not suffice;
Quarrels were rife, greedy desire, still poor,
Did vile deeds; then 'twas worth the price of blood,
And deemed renown to spoil their native town;
Force mastered right, the strongest governed all.
Hence came it that th' edicts were overruled,
That laws were broke, tribunes with consuls strove,
180   Sale made of offices, and people's voices
Bought by themselves and sold, and every year
Frauds and corruption in the field of Mars;
Hence interest and devouring usury sprang,
Faith's breach, and hence came war, to most men
        welcome.

Now Caesar overpassed the snowy Alps;
His mind was troubled, and he aimed at war,
And coming to the ford of Rubicon,
At night in dreadful vision fearful Rome
Mourning appeared, whose hoary hairs were torn,
190   And on her turret-bearing head dispersed,
And arms all naked, who with broken sighs,
And staring, thus bespoke: "What mean'st thou,
        Caesar?
Whither goes my standard? Romans if ye be,
And bear true hearts, stay here!" This spectacle
Struck Caesar's heart with fear, his hair stood up,
And faintness numbed his steps there on the brink.
He thus cried out: "Thou thunderer that guard'st
Rome's mighty walls built on Tarpeian rock,
Ye gods of Phrygia and Iulus' line,
200   Quirinus' rites and Latian Jove advanced
On Alba hill, O vestal flames, O Rome,

My thought's sole goddess, aid mine enterprise!
I hate thee not, to thee my conquests stoop;
Caesar is thine, so please it thee, thy soldier;
He, he afflicts Rome that made me Rome's foe."
This said, he laying aside all lets of war,
Approached the swelling stream with drum and
    ensign;
Like to a lion of scorched desert Afric,
Who, seeing hunters, pauseth till fell wrath
And kingly rage increase, then having whisked   210
His tail athwart his back, and crest heaved up,
With jaws wide open ghastly roaring out
(Albeit the Moor's light javelin or his spear
Sticks in his side), yet runs upon the hunter.

In summer time the purple Rubicon,
Which issues from a small spring, is but shallow,
And creeps along the vales dividing just
The bounds of Italy from Cisalpine France;
But now the winter's wrath, and wat'ry moon
Being three days old, enforced the flood to swell,   220
And frozen Alps thawed with resolving winds.
The thunder-hoofed horse, in a crooked line,
To scape the violence of the stream, first waded,
Which being broke the foot had easy passage.
As soon as Caesar got unto the bank.
And bounds of Italy, "Here, here," saith he,
"An end of peace; here end polluted laws;
Hence, leagues and covenants; Fortune, thee I follow,
War and the Destinies shall try my cause."
This said, the restless general through the dark   230
(Swifter than bullets thrown from Spanish slings,
Or darts which Parthians backward shoot)
    marched on,
And then (when Lucifer did shine alone,
And some dim stars) he Ariminum entered.
Day rose, and viewed these tumults of the war;
Whether the gods or blust'ring south were cause

I know not, but the cloudy air did frown.
The soldiers having won the market-place,
There spread the colors, with confusèd noise
240   Of trumpet's clange, shrill cornets, whistling fifes.
The people started; young men left their beds,
And snatched arms near their household gods
          hung up,
Such as peace yields: worm-eaten leathern targets
Through which the wood peered, headless darts,
          old swords
With ugly teeth of black rust foully scarred.
But seeing white eagles, and Rome's flags well
          known,
And lofty Caesar in the thickest throng,
They shook for fear, and cold benumbed their limbs,
And muttering much, thus to themselves complained:
250   "O walls unfortunate, too near to France,
Predestinate to ruin! all lands else
Have stable peace, here war's rage first begins,
We bide the first brunt. Safer might we dwell
Under the frosty Bear, or parching East,
Wagons or tents, than in this frontier town.
We first sustained the uproars of the Gauls
And furious Cimbrians, and of Carthage Moors;
As oft as Rome was sacked, here 'gan the spoil."
Thus sighing whispered they, and none durst speak
260   And show their fear or grief; but as the fields,
When birds are silent through winter's rage,
Or sea far from the land, so all were whist.
Now light had quite dissolved the misty night,
And Caesar's mind unsettled musing stood;
But gods and Fortune pricked him to this war,
Infringing all excuse of modest shame,
And laboring to approve his quarrel good.
The angry Senate, urging Gracchus' deeds,
From doubtful Rome wrongly expelled the tribunes
270   That crossed them; both which now approached
          the camp,

And with them Curio, sometime tribune too,
One that was fee'd for Caesar, and whose tongue
Could tune the people to the nobles' mind.
"Caesar," said he, "while eloquence prevailed,
And I might plead, and draw the commons' minds
To favor thee, against the Senate's will,
Five years I lengthened thy command in France;
But law being put to silence by the wars,
We, from our houses driven, most willingly
Suffered exile: let thy sword bring us home.   280
Now, while their part is weak and fears, march
        hence:
Where men are ready, lingering ever hurts.
In ten years won'st thou France; Rome may be won
With far less toil, and yet the honor's more;
Few battles fought with prosperous success
May bring her down, and with her all the world.
Nor shalt thou triumph when thou com'st to Rome,
Nor Capitol be adorned with sacred bays.
Envy denies all; with thy blood must thou
Aby thy conquest past: the son decrees   290
To expel the father; share the world thou canst not;
Enjoy it all thou mayst." Thus Curio spake,
And therewith Caesar, prone enough to war,
Was so incensed as are Eleius steeds
With clamors, who, though locked and chained
        in stalls,
Souse down the walls, and make a passage forth.
Straight summoned he his several companies
Unto the standard; his grave look appeased
The wrestling tumult, and right hand made silence,
And thus he spake: "You that with me have borne   300
A thousand brunts, and tried me full ten years,
See how they quit our blood shed in the north,
Our friends' death, and our wounds, our wintering
Under the Alps! Rome rageth now in arms
As if the Carthage Hannibal were near.
Cornets of horse are mustered for the field,

Woods turned to ships; both land and sea against us.
Had foreign wars ill-thrived, or wrathful France
Pursued us hither, how were we bested,
310 When, coming conqueror, Rome afflicts me thus?
Let come their leader whom long peace hath quailed,
Raw soldiers lately pressed, and troops of gowns;
Brabbling Marcellus; Cato whom fools reverence;
Must Pompey's followers, with strangers' aid
(Whom from his youth he bribed), needs make
        him king?
And shall he triumph long before his time,
And having once got head still shall he reign?
What should I talk of men's corn reaped by force,
And by him kept of purpose for a dearth?
320 Who sees not war sit by the quivering judge,
And sentence given in rings of naked swords,
And laws assailed, and armed men in the Senate?
'Twas his troop hemmed in Milo being accused;
And now, lest age might wane his state, he casts
For civil war, wherein through use he's known
To exceed his master, that arch-traitor Sulla.
A brood of barbarous tigers, having lapped
The blood of many a herd, whilst with their dams
They kenneled in Hircania, evermore
330 Will rage and prey: so Pompey, thou having licked
Warm gore from Sulla's sword, art yet athirst;
Jaws fleshed with blood continue murderous.
Speak, when shall this thy long-usurped power end?
What end of mischief? Sulla teaching thee,
At last learn, wretch, to leave thy monarchy.
What, now Sicilian pirates are suppressed,
And jaded king of Pontus poisoned slain,
Must Pompey as his last foe plume on me,
Because at his command I wound not up
340 My conquering eagles? say I merit nought,
Yet, for long service done, reward these men,
And so they triumph, be 't with whom ye will.
Whither now shall these old bloodless souls repair?

What seats for their deserts? what store of ground
For servitors to till? what colonies
To rest their bones? say, Pompey, are these worse
Than pirates of Sicilia? they had houses.
Spread, spread these flags that ten years' space have
    conquered!
Let's use our tried force; they that now thwart right,
In wars will yield to wrong: the gods are with us.   350
Neither spoil nor kingdom seek we by these arms,
But Rome at thraldom's feet to rid from tyrants."
This spoke, none answered; but a murmuring buzz
Th' unstable people made: their household gods
And love to Rome (though slaughter steeled their
    hearts,
And minds were prone) restrained them; but war's
    love
And Caesar's awe dashed all. Then Laelius,
The chief centurion, crowned with oaken leaves
For saving of a Roman citizen,
Stepped forth, and cried: "Chief leader of Rome's
    force,   360
So be I may be bold to speak a truth,
We grieve at this thy patience and delay.
What doubt'st thou us? even now when youthful
    blood
Pricks forth our lively bodies, and strong arms
Can mainly throw the dart, wilt thou endure
These purple grooms, that Senate's tyranny?
Is conquest got by civil war so heinous?
Well, lead us then to Syrtes' desert shore,
Or Scythia, or hot Libya's thirsty sands.
This hand, that all behind us might be quailed,   370
Hath with thee passed the swelling ocean,
And swept the foaming breast of Arctic's Rhene.
Love overrules my will, I must obey thee,
Caesar; he whom I hear thy trumpets charge
I hold no Roman; by these ten blest ensigns
And all thy several triumphs, shouldst thou bid me

Entomb my sword within my brother's bowels,
Or father's throat, or women's groaning womb,
This hand (albeit unwilling) should perform it;
380 Or rob the gods, or sacred temples fire.
These troops should soon pull down the church of
        Jove.
If to encamp on Tuscan Tiber's streams,
I'll boldly quarter out the fields of Rome;
What walls thou wilt be leveled with the ground,
These hands shall thrust the ram, and make them fly,
Albeit the city thou wouldst have so razed
Be Rome itself." Here every band applauded,
And with their hands held up all jointly cried
They'll follow where he please. The shouts rent
        heaven,
390 As when against pine-bearing Ossa's rocks
Beats Thracian Boreas, or when trees bowed down
And rustling swing up as the wind fets breath.

When Caesar saw his army prone to war,
And Fates so bent, lest sloth and long delay
Might cross him, he withdrew his troops from
        France,
And in all quarters musters men for Rome.
They by Lemannus' nook forsook their tents;
They whom the Lingones foiled with painted spears,
Under the rocks by crooked Vogesus;
400 And many came from shallow Isara,
Who, running long, falls in a greater flood,
And ere he sees the sea loseth his name;
The yellow Ruthens left their garrisons;
Mild Atax glad it bears not Roman boats,
And frontier Varus that the camp is far,
Sent aid; so did Alcides' port, whose seas
Eat hollow rocks, and where the north-west wind
Nor Zephyr rules not, but the north alone
Turmoils the coast, and enterance forbids;
410 And others came from that uncertain shore

Which is nor sea, nor land, but ofttimes both,
And changeth as the ocean ebbs and flows;
Whether the sea rolled always from that point
Whence the wind blows, still forcèd to and fro,
Or that the wandering main follow the moon,
Or flaming Titan (feeding on the deep)
Pulls them aloft, and makes the surge kiss heaven,
Philosophers, look you, for unto me,
Thou cause, whate'er thou be whom God assigns
This great effect, art hid. They came that dwell   420
By Nemes' fields, and banks of Satirus,
Where Tarbel's winding shores embrace the sea;
The Santons that rejoice in Caesar's love,
Those of Bituriges and light Axon pikes;
And they of Rhene and Leuca, cunning darters,
And Sequana that well could manage steeds;
The Belgians apt to govern British cars;
Th' Averni too, which boldly feign themselves
The Romans' brethren, sprung of Ilian race;
The stubborn Nervians stained with Cotta's blood,   430
And Vangions who, like those of Sarmata,
Wear open slops; and fierce Batavians,
Whom trumpets' clange incites, and those that dwell
By Cinga's stream, and where swift Rhodanus
Drives Araris to sea; they near the hills
Under whose hoary rocks Gebenna hangs;
And Trevier, thou being glad that wars are past thee;
And you, late-shorn Ligurians, who were wont
In large-spread hair to exceed the rest of France;
And where to Hesus and fell Mercury   440
They offer human flesh, and where Jove seems
Bloody like Dian, whom the Scythians serve.
And you, French Bardi, whose immortal pens
Renown the valiant souls slain in your wars,
Sit safe at home and chant sweet poesy.
And, Druides, you now in peace renew
Your barbarous customs and sinister rites;
In unfelled woods and sacred groves you dwell,

And only gods and heavenly powers you know,
450   Or only know you nothing. For you hold
That souls pass not to silent Erebus
Or Pluto's bloodless kingdom, but elsewhere
Resume a body: so (if truth you sing)
Death brings long life. Doubtless these northern men,
Whom death, the greatest of all fears, affright not,
Are blest by such sweet error; this makes them
Run on the sword's point and desire to die,
And shame to spare life which being lost is won.
You likewise that repulsed the Cayc foe,
460   March towards Rome; and you, fierce men of Rhene,
Leaving your country open to the spoil.
These being come, their huge power made him bold
To manage greater deeds; the bordering towns
He garrisoned, and Italy he filled with soldiers.
Vain fame increased true fear, and did invade
The people's minds, and laid before their eyes
Slaughter to come, and swiftly bringing news
Of present war, made many lies and tales.
One swears his troops of daring horsemen fought
470   Upon Mevania's plain, where bulls are grazed;
Other that Caesar's barbarous bands were spread
Along Nar flood that into Tiber falls,
And that his own ten ensigns and the rest
Marched not entirely, and yet hide the ground;
And that he's much changed, looking wild and big,
And far more barbarous than the French (his vassals)
And that he lags behind with them of purpose
Born 'twixt the Alps and Rhene, which he hath
    brought
From out their northern parts, and that Rome,
480   He looking on, by these men should be sacked.
Thus in his fright did each man strengthen Fame,
And, without ground, feared what themselves had
    feigned.
Nor were the commons only struck to heart
With this vain terror, but the Court, the Senate:

The fathers' selves leaped from their seats, and, flying,
Left hateful war decreed to both the consuls.
Then, with their fear and danger all distract,
Their sway of flight carries the heavy rout
That in chained troops break forth at every port;
You would have thought their houses had been fired,   490
Or, dropping-ripe, ready to fall with ruin;
So rushed the inconsiderate multitude
Thorough the city, hurried headlong on,
As if the only hope that did remain
To their afflictions were t' abandon Rome.
Look how when stormy Auster from the breach
Of Libyan Syrtes rolls a monstrous wave,
Which makes the mainsail fall with hideous sound,
The pilot from the helm leaps in the sea,
And mariners, albeit the keel be sound,   500
Shipwrack themselves: even so, the city left,
All rise in arms, nor could the bedrid parents
Keep back their sons, or women's tears their
    husbands;
They stayed not either to pray or sacrifice,
Their household gods restrain them not, none
    lingered
As loath to leave Rome whom they held so dear;
Th' irrevocable people fly in troops.
O gods, that easy grant men great estates,
But hardly grace to keep them: Rome, that flows
With citizens and captives, and would hold   510
The world (were it together) is by cowards
Left as a prey, now Caesar doth approach.
When Romans are besieged by foreign foes,
With slender trench they escape night stratagems,
And sudden rampire raised of turf snatched up
Would make them sleep securely in their tents.
Thou, Rome, at name of war runn'st from thyself,
And wilt not trust thy city walls one night:
Well might these fear, when Pompey feared and fled.
Now evermore, lest some one hope might ease   520

The commons' jangling minds, apparent signs arose,
Strange sights appeared, the angry threat'ning gods
Filled both the earth and seas with prodigies;
Great store of strange and unknown stars were seen
Wandering about the north, and rings of fire
Fly in the air, and dreadful bearded stars,
And comets that presage the fall of kingdoms;
The flattering sky glittered in often flames,
And sundry fiery meteors blazed in heaven,
530 Now spear-like, long, now like a spreading torch;
Lightning in silence stole forth without clouds,
And from the northern climate snatching fire
Blasted the Capitol; the lesser stars,
Which wont to run their course through empty night,
At noonday mustered; Phoebe, having filled
Her meeting horns to match her brother's light,
Struck with th' earth's sudden shadow, waxèd pale;
Titan himself throned in the midst of heaven
His burning chariot plunged in sable clouds,
540 And whelmed the world in darkness, making men
Despair of day, as did Thyestes' town,
Mycenae, Phoebus flying through the east.
Fierce Mulciber unbarrèd Aetna's gate,
Which flamèd not on high, but headlong pitched
Her burning head on bending Hespery.
Coal-black Charybdis whirled a sea of blood;
Fierce mastiffs howled; the vestal fires went out;
The flame in Alba, consecrate to Jove,
Parted in twain, and with a double point
550 Rose like the Theban brothers' funeral fire;
The earth went off her hinges, and the Alps
Shook the old snow from off their trembling laps.
The ocean swelled as high as Spanish Calpe,
Or Atlas' head. Their saints and household gods
Sweat tears to show the travails of their city.
Crowns fell from holy statues, ominous birds
Defiled the day, and wild beasts were seen,
Leaving the woods, lodge in the streets of Rome.

Cattle were seen that muttered human speech;
Prodigious births with more and ugly joints   560
Than nature gives, whose sight appals the mother;
And dismal prophecies were spread abroad;
And they whom fierce Bellona's fury moves
To wound their arms, sing vengeance; Sibyl's priests,
Curling their bloody locks, howl dreadful things;
Souls quiet and appeased sighed from their graves;
Clashing of arms was heard; in untrod woods
Shrill voices shright, and ghosts encounter men.
Those that inhabited the suburb fields
Fled; foul Erinnys stalked about the walls,   570
Shaking her snaky hair and crooked pine
With flaming top, much like that hellish fiend
Which made the stern Lycurgus wound his thigh,
Or fierce Agave mad; or like Megaera
That scared Alcides, when by Juno's task
He had before looked Pluto in the face.
Trumpets were heard to sound; and with what noise
An armèd battle joins, such and more strange
Black night brought forth in secret: Sulla's ghost
Was seen to walk, singing sad oracles;   580
And Marius' head above cold Tav'ron peering
(His grave broke open) did affright the boors.
To these ostents (as their old custom was)
They call th' Etrurian augurs, amongst whom
The gravest, Arruns, dwelt in forsaken Luca,   *or Luna*
Well skilled in pyromancy, one that knew
The hearts of beasts, and flight of wand'ring fowls.
First he commands such monsters Nature hatched
Against her kind (the barren mule's loathed issue)
To be cut forth and cast in dismal fires;   590
Then, that the trembling citizens should walk
About the city; then the sacred priests
That with divine lustration purged the walls,
And went the round, in and without the town.
Next, an inferior troop, in tucked-up vestures,
After the Gabine manner; then the nuns

And their veiled matron, who alone might view
Minerva's statue; then, they that keep and read
Sibylla's secret works, and washed their saint
600   In Almo's flood; next, learned augurs follow,
Apollo's soothsayers, and Jove's feasting priests,
The skipping Salii with shields like wedges,
And flamens last, with network woolen veils.
While these thus in and out had circled Rome,
Look, what the lightning blasted Arruns takes,
And it inters with murmurs dolorous,
And calls the place bidental; on the altar
He lays a ne'er-yoked bull, and pours down wine,
Then crams salt leaven on his crooked knife;
610   The beast long struggled, as being like to prove
An awkward sacrifice, but by the horns
The quick priest pulled him on his knees and
          slew him.
No vein sprung out, but from the yawning gash,
Instead of red blood, wallowed venomous gore.
These direful signs made Arruns stand amazed,
And searching farther for the gods' displeasure,
The very color scared him; a dead blackness
Ran through the blood, that turned it all to jelly,
And stained the bowels with dark loathsome spots;
620   The liver swelled with filth, and every vein
Did threaten horror from the host of Caesar:
A small thin skin contained the vital parts;
The heart stirred not, and from the gaping liver
Squeezed matter; through the caul the entrails peered,
And which (aye me) ever pretendeth ill,
At that bunch where the liver is, appeared
A knob of flesh, whereof one half did look
Dead and discolored, th' other lean and thin.
By these he seeing what mischiefs must ensue
630   Cried out, "O gods! I tremble to unfold
What you intend: great Jove is now displeased,
And in the breast of this slain bull are crept
Th' infernal powers. My fear transcends my words,

Yet more will happen than I can unfold.
Turn all to good, be augury vain, and Tages,
Th' art's master, false!" Thus, in ambiguous terms
Involving all, did Arruns darkly sing.
But Figulus, more seen in heavenly mysteries,
Whose like Egyptian Memphis never had
For skill in stars and tuneful planeting,   640
In this sort spake: "The world's swift course is
    lawless
And casual; all the stars at random rage;
Or if Fate rule them, Rome, thy citizens
Are near some plague. What mischief shall ensue?
Shall towns be swallowed? shall the thickened air
Become intemperate? shall the earth be barren?
Shall water be congealed and turned to ice?
O gods, what death prepare ye? with what plague
Mean ye to rage? the death of many men
Meets in one period. If cold noisome Saturn   650
Were now exalted, and with blue beams shined,
Then Ganymede would renew Deucalion's flood,
And in the fleeting sea the earth be drenched.
O Phoebus, shouldst thou with thy rays now singe
The fell Nemean beast, th' earth would be fired,
And heaven tormented with thy chafing heat;
But thy fires hurt not. Mars, 'tis thou inflam'st
The threatening Scorpion with the burning tail,
And fir'st his cleyes. Why art thou thus enraged?
Kind Jupiter hath low declined himself;   660
Venus is faint; swift Hermes retrograde;
Mars only rules the heaven. Why do the planets
Alter their course, and vainly dim their virtue?
Sword-girt Orion's side glisters too bright:
War's rage draws near, and to the sword's strong
    hand
Let all laws yield, sin bear the name of virtue.
Many a year these furious broils let last;
Why should we wish the gods should ever end them?
War only gives us peace. O Rome, continue

670   The course of mischief, and stretch out the date
      Of slaughter; only civil broils make peace."
      These sad presages were enough to scare
      The quivering Romans, but worse things affright
          them.
      As Maenas full of wine on Pindus raves,
      So runs a matron through th' amazèd streets,
      Disclosing Phoebus' fury in this sort:
      "Paean, whither am I haled? where shall I fall,
      Thus borne aloft? I see Pangaeus' hill
      With hoary top, and under Haemus' mount
680   Philippi plains. Phoebus, what rage is this?
      Why grapples Rome, and makes war, having no foes?
      Whither turn I now? thou lead'st me toward th' east,
      Where Nile augmenteth the Pelusian sea;
      This headless trunk that lies on Nilus' sand
      I know. Now throughout the air I fly
      To doubtful Syrtes and dry Afric, where
      A fury leads the Emathian bands; from thence
      To the pine-bearing hills, hence to the mounts
      Pyrene, and so back to Rome again.
690   See, impious war defiles the Senate-house,
      New factions rise; now through the world again
      I go; O Phoebus, show me Neptune's shore,
      And other regions, I have seen Philippi."
      This said, being tired with fury she sunk down.

      Finis

THE
PASSIONATE SHEPHERD
TO HIS LOVE

FROM

The Passionate Pilgrim
(1599)

Live with me and be my love,
And we will all the pleasures prove
That hills and valleys, dales and fields,
And all the craggy mountains yield.

There will we sit upon the rocks
And see the shepherds feed their flocks
By shallow rivers, by whose falls
Melodious birds sing madrigals.

There will I make thee a bed of roses
With a thousand fragrant posies,   10
A cap of flowers, and a kirtle
Embroidered all with leaves of myrtle.

A belt of straw and ivy buds
With coral clasps and amber studs,
And if these pleasures may thee move,
Then live with me and be my love.

The Passionate Shepherd to His Love

Come live with me, and be my love,
And we will all the pleasures prove
That valleys, groves, hills and fields,
Woods, or steepy mountain yields.

And we will sit upon the rocks,
Seeing the shepherds feed their flocks
By shallow rivers, to whose falls
Melodious birds sing madrigals.

And I will make thee beds of roses,
And a thousand fragrant posies,   10
A cap of flowers, and a kirtle,
Embroidered all with leaves of myrtle.

A gown made of the finest wool
Which from our pretty lambs we pull,
Fair linèd slippers for the cold,
With buckles of the purest gold.

A belt of straw and ivy-buds,
With coral clasps and amber studs,
And if these pleasures may thee move,
Come live with me, and be my love.   20

The shepherd swains shall dance and sing
For thy delight each May morning.
If these delights thy mind may move,
Then live with me, and be my love.

SIR WALTER RALEGH
The Nymph's Reply

If all the world and love were young,
And truth in every shepherd's tongue,
These pretty pleasures might me move
To live with thee and be thy love.

But Time drives flocks from field to fold,
When rivers rage and rocks grow cold,
And Philomel becometh dumb;
The rest complains of cares to come.

The flowers do fade, and wanton fields
To wayward winter reckoning yields;   10
A honey tongue, a heart of gall
Is fancy's spring, but sorrow's fall.

Thy gowns, thy shoes, thy beds of roses,
Thy cap, thy kirtle, and thy posies,
Soon break, soon wither, soon forgotten,
In folly ripe in reason rotten.

Thy belt of straw and ivy buds,
Thy coral clasps and amber studs,
All these in me no means can move
To come to thee and be thy love.   20

But could youth last and love still breed,
Had joys no date, nor age no need,
Then these delights my mind might move
To live with thee and be thy love.

ANONYMOUS

Another of the Same Nature, Made Since

Come live with me and be my dear,
And we will revel all the year,
In plains and groves, on hills and dales,
Where fragrant air breeds sweetest gales.

There shall you have the beauteous pine,
The cedar and the spreading vine,
And all the woods to be a screen,
Lest Phoebus kiss my summer's queen.

The seat for your disport shall be
Over some river, in a tree,   10
Where silver sands and pebbles sing
Eternal ditties with the spring.

There shall you see the nymphs at play,
And how the satyrs spend the day,
The fishes gliding on the sands,
Offering their bellies to your hands.

The birds with heavenly tuned throats
Possess woods-echoes with sweet notes,
Which to your senses will impart
A music to inflame the heart.   20

Upon the bare and leafless oak
The ring-doves' wooings will provoke

A colder blood than you possess
To play with me and do no less.

In bowers of laurel trimly dight
We will outwear the silent night,
While Flora busy is to spread
Her richest treasure on our bed.

Ten thousand glow-worms shall attend,
And all their sparkling lights shall spend,
All to adorn and beautify
Your lodging with most majesty.

Then in mine arms will I enclose
Lilies' fair mixture with the rose,
Whose nice perfections in love's play
Shall tune me to the highest key.

Thus as we pass the welcome night
In sportful pleasures and delight,
The nimble fairies on the grounds
Shall dance and sing melodious sounds.

If these may serve for to entice
Your presence to love's paradise,
Then come with me and be my dear,
And we will straight begin the year.

JOHN DONNE

The Bait

Come live with me and be my love,
And we will some new pleasures prove,
Of golden sands and crystal brooks,
With silken lines and silver hooks.

There will the river whispering run,
Warmed by thine eyes more than the sun;
And there th' enamored fish will stay,
Begging themselves they may betray.

When thou wilt swim in that live bath,
Each fish, which every channel hath,   10
Will amorously to thee swim,
Gladder to catch thee than thou him.

If thou to be so seen beest loath
By sun or moon, thou dark'nest both;
And if myself have leave to see,
I need not their light, having thee.

Let others freeze with angling reeds,
And cut their legs with shells and weeds,
Or treacherously poor fish beset
With strangling snare, or windowy net: 20

Let coarse bold hands from slimy nest
The bedded fish in banks out-wrest,

Or curious traitors, sleave-silk flies
Bewitch poor fishes' wand'ring eyes.

For thee, thou need'st no such deceit,
For thou thyself art thine own bait;
That fish that is not catched thereby,
Alas, is wiser far than I.

J. PAULIN

Love's Contentment

Come, my Clarinda, we'll consume
Our joys no more at this low rate;
More glorious titles let's assume
And love according to our state.

For if Contentment wears a crown
Which never tyrant could assail,
How many monarchs put we down
In our Utopian commonweal?

As princes rain down golden showers
On those in whom they take delight,   10
So in this happier court of ours,
Each is the other's favorite.

Our privacies no eye dwells near,
But unobservèd we embrace,
And no sleek courtier's pen is there
To set down either time or place.

No midnight fears disturb our bliss,
Unless a golden dream awake us,
For care we know not what it is,
Unless to please doth careful make us.   20

We fear no enemy's invasion,
Our counsel's wise and politic;

With timely force, if not persuasion,
We cool the homebred schismatic.

All discontent thus to remove
What monarch boasts but thou and I?
In this content we live and love,
And in this love resolve to die:

That when, our souls together fled,
30   One urn shall our mixed dust enshrine,
In golden letters may be read,
Here lie Content's late King and Queen.

On the Death of
Sir Roger Manwood

IN OBITUM HONORATISSIMI VIRI ROGERI

MANWOOD MILITIS QUAESTORII REGINALIS

CAPITALIS BARONIS

Noctivagi terror, ganeonis triste flagellum,
Et Jovis Alcides, rigido vulturque latroni,
Urna subtegitur. Scelerum gaudete nepotes!
Insons, luctifica sparsis cervice capillis
Plange! fori lumen, venerandae gloria legis,
Occidit: heu, secum effoetas Acherontis ad oras
Multa abiit virtus. Pro tot virtutibus uni,
Livor, parce viro; non audacissimus esto
Illius in cineres, cuius tot millia vultus
Mortalium attonuit: sic cum te nuntia Ditis   10
Vulneret exsanguis, feliciter ossa quiescant,
Famaque marmorei superet monumenta sepulchri.

ON THE DEATH OF THE MOST NOBLE

GENTLEMAN SIR ROGER MANWOOD, LORD CHIEF

BARON OF THE QUEEN'S EXCHEQUER

Within this urn lies the terror of vagabonds, the harsh
scourge of the profligate, a vulture to the hardened criminal,
Jove's Alcides. Rejoice, sons of the wicked! and you who are
guiltless, weep with head bowed in grief and disheveled

hair! The light of government, the glory of reverend law is
dead: alas, much virtue went with him to the dim shores of
Acheron. O Envy, for so many virtues spare one man; do
not insult over the ashes of one whose countenance terrified
so many thousands of mortals. So, though the pale messen-
ger of Dis assails you, may your bones rest peacefully, and
your fame outlast the monuments of your marble sepulchre.

Notes

HERO AND LEANDER

The text of Marlowe's poem and of Chapman's continuation has been prepared from the edition printed by Felix Kingston for Paul Linley, London, 1598.

DEDICATION

Walsingham   Marlowe's friend and patron.
8   *make*   contribute.

Sestiad I

ARGUMENT
The arguments and the division of the poem into Sestiads are by Chapman.

Sestiad   From Sestos, on the model of *Iliad*.
4   *hight*   named.
31   *Buskins*   boots.
40   *mother*   Venus.
50   *black*   either dark-haired or ugly.
52   *Musaeus*   The original of *Hero and Leander* is by Musaeus the Grammarian, a fifth-century Alexandrian Greek commonly confused until the seventeenth century with the mythical ur-poet Musaeus, contemporary of Orpheus, and hence "divine."
59   *Cynthia*   the moon; Leander is being compared with Endymion.
62   *Jove . . . hand*   Leander as Ganymede.
65   *Pelops' shoulder*   Pelops was killed by his father, Tantalus, cut up, cooked, and served at a dinner of the gods. Only Demeter partook, however, and ate his shoulder. When Hermes subsequently reconstituted Pelops, he supplied a shoulder of ivory. The story is told in Ovid, *Metamorphoses,* VI 403–11.

68   *curious*   elaborately beautiful.
72   *slack*   weak.
73   *orient*   glowing.
     his   Narcissus'.
77   *Hippolytus*   A chaste hunter who scorned love.
80   *uplandish*   wild.
101 *Phaëthon*   Son of Apollo, the sun god. He undertook to
     drive the chariot of the sun, but lost control of the horses, and
     was destroyed by Jove lest he set the world on fire. See Ovid,
     Metamorphoses, II 30ff.
107 *star*   the moon.
108 *thirling*   whirling.
111 *overrules*   rules over.
114 *Ixion's . . . race*   the Centaurs. Ixion was an ungrateful and
     treacherous king of Thessaly. When he was ostracized by his
     countrymen for the murder of his father-in-law, Jove took pity
     on him and brought him to Olympus; but Ixion repaid his
     kindness by trying to seduce Juno. Apprised of the attempt,
     Jove created a false Juno out of cloud and sent it to Ixion, and
     from this union the Centaurs were born. Ixion was punished by
     being bound on a wheel perpetually turning in hell.
136 *discolored*   multicolored.
137 *Proteus*   A sea god, the embodiment of continual change.
139 *Bacchus*   God of wine and ecstatic poetry.
146 *Danae*   A mortal wooed by Jupiter as a shower of gold.
148 *Idalian*   either from Mount Ida, or from Idalium, where
     there was a grove sacred to Venus.
     Ganymede   Youth carried off by Jupiter as an eagle.
149 *Europa*   Mortal carried off by Jupiter as a bull.
150 *tumbling . . . Rainbow*   Jupiter as rain-god, with Iris, the
     rainbow.
151–2 *Mars . . . Cyclops*   Vulcan devised a net to entrap his adul-
     terous wife Venus with Mars. The story is in the *Odyssey*,
     VIII 266ff., retold by Ovid, *Metamorphoses*, IV 171–89.
154 *Sylvanus . . . boy*   God of woods, in love with the youth
     Cyparissus (*Metamorphoses*, X 120–421).
158 *turtles'*   turtle doves'.
159 *vailed*   lowered.
161 *golden head*   According to Ovid, Cupid has arrows of two
     sorts, the gold-tipped to kindle love, the lead-tipped to extin-
     guish it (*Metamorphoses*, I 470–1).

171 *affect* prefer.

189 *Acheron* A river in Hades.

255 *One . . . number* According to Aristotle, *Metaphysics,* 1080a. The concept was greatly elaborated by neo-Platonic philosophy, and is discussed by Chapman in V 323–40.

258 *Hymen* God of marriage.

270 *essence* something real: Aristotelian terminology.

296 *tralucent* translucent.

298 *trace* walk.

301 *Doric* solemn and heroic; perhaps Marlowe's error for Lydian.

312 *put* put off.
     mo more.

321 *Pallas* Athena.

326 *nice* coy.

346 *whist* silent.

349 *Morpheus* God of sleep.

353 *beldam* old woman.

386ff. The story is apparently Marlowe's invention.

388 *Argus* A hundred-eyed monster sent by Juno to watch Io, with whom Jove was in love, and slain at Jove's command by Mercury.

392 *glose* deceive.

402 *fancy to assay* to try her love.

434 *Hebe* Jove's cupbearer before Ganymede.

440 *terms* state.

450 *upweighed* raised.

452 *father* Saturn.

456 *Ops* wife of Saturn.

458 *Stygian empery* the kingdom of hell.

465 *Learning* Hermes is also patron of learning.

473 *sisters* the Fates.

475 *Midas' brood* rich fools. Midas preferred the music of Pan to that of Apollo, and as a reward for his stupidity, Apollo gave him an ass's ears. Earlier, when Dionysus had offered to grant him any wish, Midas had asked that whatever he touched might turn to gold; but he had to beg for the gift to be rescinded when even his food was transformed.

480 *surprised* delighted.

481 *still* continually.
     clown boor.

Sestiad II

1   *by*   at.

9   *light*   immodest.

12   *train*   encourage.

20   *pointed*   appointed.

26   *affied*   engaged.

32   *fancy*   love.
     peised   poised.

46   *Salmacis*   A nymph who pursued the youth Hermaphrodi-
     tus. She wooed him when he came to bathe in her spring,
     and he ignored her. But she embraced him, and prayed that
     they might be forever joined. The gods granted her wish,
     and transformed them into the hermaphrodite (*Metamor-
     phoses*, IV 285 ff).

51   *Aesop's cock*   The fable is about a rooster that finds both a
     jewel and a barleycorn in the dirt, and while admiring the
     luster of the former, prefers the latter. The point is that
     Leander does not realize the value of Hero's "jewel."

56   *appetence*   affinity.

61   *rude*   inexperienced.

73   *put . . . it*   deflected him.

75   *Tantalus*   King of Lydia, and a son of Jupiter. He stole nec-
     tar from the gods to give to men (or, according to another
     story, revealed the gods' secrets to men), and was punished
     by being condemned in hell to suffer intense hunger and
     thirst with fruit and water just out of reach.

87   *Morn . . . steeds*   Aurora and Apollo in his chariot, though
     their liaison appears to be Marlowe's invention. Possibly he
     is conflating two stories about the parentage of Phaëthon, in
     one of which he is the child of Aurora and Cephalus, in the
     other of Apollo and Clymene.

105 *Cupid's myrtle*   Myrtle was sacred to Venus, and therefore
     the emblem of the lover.

107 *she*   Hero.

116 *reeking*   steaming.

118-20 *air . . . violence*   The image is of air rushing to fill a
     vacuum.

118 *his*   its.

120 *Alcides*   Hercules.

123-8 *sun . . . burns*   The sun is conceived as being closest when
     at the horizon (and hence "shining lat'rally") and farthest

away when directly overhead. But it is at noon that the sun's rays are hottest.

135   *apparently*   clearly.
143   *ringled*   ringed.
144   *checks*   stamps.
146   *What . . . dares*   i.e., now Leander dares do anything.
150   *toiling*   raging.
155   *sapphire-visaged god*   Neptune.
156   *Triton*   A sea god, Neptune's trumpeter.
179   *Helle*   Drowned in the Hellespont, which was named for her.
203   *Thetis' . . . bower*   the sea.
218   *hinds*   boors.
242   *lawn*   sheer fabric of her gown.
255   *fet*   fetched.
258   *dreary*   bloody.
261   *Actaeon*   As punishment for seeing Diana bathing, he was turned into a stag and killed by his own hounds.
270   *harpy played*   i.e., withdrew the dainties.
274   *empaled*   surrounded.
277   *Sisyphus*   Condemned in hell to roll a rock endlessly up a mountain.
298   *orchard . . . Hesperides*   Where the golden apples of immortality grew. Obtaining them was one of the labors of Hercules.
305   *Erycine*   Venus, who had a shrine on Mount Eryx in Sicily.
326   *Dis*   Plutus, god of wealth.
327   *this*   this time.
329   *Hesperus*   the evening star.
334   *danged*   hurled.
335   *Desunt nonnulla*   Some sections are missing.

Sestiad III

DEDICATION

Lady Walsingham   Wife of Sir Thomas Walsingham, to whom Marlowe's fragment is dedicated.
3   *strange instigation*   mystical inspiration.
8   *sign that for*   refer to that as.
10–11 *money-monger*   man interested only in worldly wealth.
11–12 *concluded*   included.
20   *silly*   untutored.

38–9   *This . . . him*   This dedication has married the two sections of the poem, as you are married to Sir Thomas.

42   *circular*   perfect.

ARGUMENT

4   *Thesme*   law.

6   *improving*   reproving.

SESTIAD

16   *that*   that which.

17   *this*   this time.

36   *virtue*   (marginal) power.

43   *limit*   hold.

57   *moist*   fruitful.

60   *Time's . . . thigh*   "Time's *order* is the harmony of creation, a harmony expressed in terms of the intervals of the musical scale by Pythagoras. Chapman combines this tradition with the legend that Pythagoras had a golden thigh . . ." (Millar MacLure, ed., *Marlowe's Poems*, p. 47).

69   *Hermione*   Leander's sister is Chapman's invention.

72   *seised for*   legally possessed by.

89   *virtual*   powerful.

96   *prefer*   offer.

99   *characters*   letters.

102   *carcanet*   necklace.

112   *the goddess Ceremony*   Chapman's creation.

123   *disparent*   variegated.

131   *mathematic*   geometric.

158   *close*   secretly.
       flatly   unceremoniously.

175   *het*   heated.

189   *his*   Marlowe's.

190   *Pierian flood*   the muses' spring.

204   *Iberian city*   Cadiz, in 1596.

223   *expugnèd*   conquered.

234   *intire*   within.

237–8   *shows . . . us*   reveals our ideas ("in-forms") to the external world.

241   *rorid*   dewy.

242   *T' event*   for giving forth.

252   *wrought*   revealed.

261   *lapwing*   deceitful.

263   *moorish*   marsh; i.e., any ordinary bird.
265   *apoplexy*   last illness.
266   *bedrid*   diseased.
273   *list*   wished.
284   *these . . . cinctures*   the worldly philosophy just expressed.
287   *impulsive*   penetrating.
293   *cypress*   crape.
297   *heart-bowing*   toward which her heart bowed.
299   *that . . . that*   her two hands.
301   *No . . . sight*   her outward form could not be descried, and
       her own sight was turned wholly inward.
307   *imitating*   reflecting.
312   *enginous*   ingenious.
315   *Jove's son*   Hercules.
320   *called again*   recalled.
326   *With . . . sail*   sails pregnant with wind.
335   *fresh heat*   freshly heated.
336-7 *Neptune's . . . wandered*   i.e., how Leander swam in the sea.
348   *dog-fees meat*   meat from the killed game given to hunting
       dogs.
388   *weight*   weighty.
391   *skillful glance*   knowledgeable gleam.
392   *imperance*   power.
402   *Turned to*   both returned to and turned into.
409   *orbicular*   spherical.

Sestiad IV

ARGUMENT

4   *Ostents*   omens.
7   *Cyprides*   Venus, born on the island of Cyprus.
13   *wreak*   both avenge and bring about.

SESTIAD

18   *queen-light . . . east*   Venus.
27   *subtle*   delicate.
29   *different concord*   harmony of variety.
79   *affects*   emotions.
80   *in . . . body*   personified as the moon.
90   *was . . . sped*   only caught a serpent.
99   *scrip*   satchel.

105   *overslip* ignore.
114   *lawn* fine linen.
117   *eyas* youthful.
121   *Arachnean* elaborately woven (from Arachne, a superlative weaver who was transformed into the spider).
130   *ostents* omens.
       success event.
153   *continent* contents.
154   *approved* agreed.
165   *doubt* fear.
182   *forego* precede.
185   *self* own.
186   *naught* wicked.
190   *brain-bald* brainless.
192   *singularity* eccentricity.
193   *singular* alone.
196   *less* lesser men.
197   *bear . . . out* support them.
199   *atones* reconciles.
213   *scuse* excuse.
       slubbered bungled.
227   *feres* companions.
235   *proin* preen.
250   *current* legal tender.
254   *for* instead of.
256   *antic* grotesque.
265   *turtles* doves.
267   *epicedians* funeral elegists.
275   *that . . . used* what Venus herself did.
294   *brakes* harnesses.
300   *Cares* Caria, in southwest Asia Minor.
302   *Arachne* A superlative weaver, who competed with Athena, and was turned into the spider.
304   *hold* to grasp.
316   *her* Hero.
317   *she choosed* whom she had chosen.
324   *upbraid* charge.
328   *Cynthia* Diana, the moon.
330   *Phoebe* the moon.
334   *day's . . . verse* Apollo, god of the sun and of poetry.
336   *anademe* wreath.

346   *Persean*   Perseus viewed the gorgon Medusa reflected in his shield because to look at her directly was death.

347   *worst success*   failure.

Sestiad V

ARGUMENT

1   *date*   length.

SESTIAD

2   *Olympiad*   four years, the period between the Olympic games.

3   *Sol*   the sun.

5   *Aurora*   the dawn.

6   *Phoebus*   the sun.

12   *full of note*   noteworthy.

14   *humors*   fluids.

44   *after . . . fingers*   as Music played.

50   *abide*   suffer.

62   *Teras*   the name means portent.
      ebon   here (incorrectly) ivory.

64   *consort*   accompany.

78   *estate*   importance.

79   *forewent*   preceded.

101   *responsible*   correspondingly beautiful.

122   *transmission*   transport.

124   *interminate*   limitless.

125   *For*   as to.

128   *prove*   test.

142   *To . . . prayers*   as he most wished.

166   *Do . . . rites*   perform the Eleusinian mysteries.

171   *yellow . . . sky*   stars.

178   *Morpheus*   God of sleep.

206   *Proteus*   God of disguise.

207   *Ingled*   cajoled, fondled.

215   *spring*   cause to spring. The lily was created (or, in another version, changed from purple to white) when Jupiter gave Juno the infant Hercules to suckle, and a drop of milk fell on the earth.

224   *Amongst . . . spirits*   in her mind.

246   *contents*   contentments.

248–9   *Which . . . strike*   which even Love's favor could scarcely entice to strike a blow.

274   *prove*   learn.
279   *so . . . derived*   from such a distance.
281   *carriage*   burden.
282   *occurrents*   (news of) events.
285   *incur . . . harm*   risk harming themselves.
287   *Adolesche*   The name means chatterer.
312   *proving*   experiencing.
314   *Cyprias*   Venus (from Cyprus, her birthplace).
315   *crushed out*   produced.
321   *efficient right*   proper function.
339   *one . . . is*   see I 255.
342   *rock*   distaff.
344   *piece*   girl.
355   *disparent*   variegated.
381   *Phemonoe*   Apollo's daughter.
390   *sphere*   belt.
391   *weed*   garment.
392   *Minerva's knot*   symbolic of chastity.
407   *saffron mirror*   moon.
408   *Tellus*   earth.
418   *take . . . toy*   feel so slighted.
420   *free love*   indiscriminate energy.
426   *sprung*   produced.
428   *line*   activities.
432   *tire*   attire.
440   *outfacing*   superlative.
454   *Thetis . . . thee*   The allusion is profoundly ambiguous: Thetis attempted unsuccessfully to make her son Achilles immortal by dipping him in the Styx, or in another story, by burning away his mortality.

Sestiad VI

ARGUMENT

2   *from . . . binds*   in the name of the Fates, commands the winds to remain calm.
7   *Ate*   Discord.
10   *surprise*   overthrow.
13   *just ruth*   proper compassion.
14   *Acanthides*   goldfinches.

SESTIAD

3   *humorous*   moist; also capricious.
18   *obsequious*   with a quibble on obsequies, funeral rites.
19   *fleering*   smirking.
20   *warping*   weaving.
21   *devotes*   devotion.
22   *pricks . . . descant*   writes his melody.
24   *owl*   Considered stupid and deceitful by the Elizabethans.
27   *quean*   whore.
29   *antic*   grotesque.
     repair   move on to.
30   *fawns*   fawning.
31   *whips*   runs about.
35   *Eurus*   the east wind.
40   *fenny Notus*   wet south wind.
45   *Zephyr*   the west wind.
46   *Boreas*   the north wind.
47   *ravished love*   Oreithyia.
53   *curious price*   especially high esteem.
64   *pined*   neglected.
77   *The . . . delight*   we do not apprehend the essential meaning of
     things, but only the pleasure they give us.
80   *rule*   standard.
90   *opposed*   opposite.
98   *addressed*   offered.
109   *form*   mere ceremonies.
116   *rampires*   ramparts.
120   *Rhene*   the Rhineland.
129   *bird-bolt*   small short-range arrow for shooting birds.
      keeping . . . coil   making more fuss.
132   *vacantry*   emptiness.
144   *cockhorse*   presumptuous.
174   *licorously*   lecherously.
      clept   embraced.
180   *either's right*   both their claims.
186   *braves*   boasts.
188   *statists*   politicians.
191   *Atthaea*   Oreithyia, Boreas' wife; Chapman coined the name
      because she was princess of Attica.
214   *his*   the wind's.
216   *bating*   abating.

230   *rased*   destroyed.
238   *sense-sport*   sports to please the senses (here, bear-baiting).
260   *mixèd*   confused.
276   *Acanthides*   goldfinch, from the Greek for thistle, hence Chapman's "thistle-warps."
283   *so little*   little as they are.
289   *yellow*   emblematic of inconstancy.

PETOWE: THE SECOND PART OF
HERO AND LEANDER

Petowe's continuation of *Hero and Leander* appeared as *The Second Part of Hero and Leander,* 1598. This was the only edition.

DEDICATION

15   *go*   walk.
28   *Desunt nonnulla*   Some sections are missing (see *Hero and Leander*, II 335).
29   *true Italian discourse*   There is no Italian source for Petowe's story.
63   *censures*   judgments.

 3   *fair*   beauty.
      Tellus   earth.
11   *Earth shamed*   shamed by Earth.
18   *mermaids*   sirens.
19   *Tisiphone*   One of the Furies.
32   *I'll . . . will*   I may not have my way.
36   *beriven*   taken away.
52   *period*   end.
65–6   *thy . . . dearth*   earth is both the object of *on* and the subject of *finds.* (The figure is called *apo koinu.*)
76   *For . . . trade*   because they were not skillful enough poets.
82   *according*   harmonizing.
92   *Mercury*   God of prose.
103   *Nil refert*   it doesn't matter.
149   *fere*   companion.
178   *proved*   experienced.
185   *make*   mate.
216   *rind*   bark.

218   *cleas*   claws.
220   *Hermaphroditus*   A youth loved by Salmacis, nymph of the
       fountain where he bathed. At her prayer, the gods united
       them in a single body.
248   *make*   mate.
256   *coy*   unresponsive.
285   *kind*   nature.
289   *cock-boat*   ship's rowboat.
290   *growned of*   grown from.
298   *Phoebus*   the sun.
299   *salamandra*   The salamander was said to live in fire.
310   *make*   mate.
322   *That . . . fro*   since Leander was banished from her.
324   *Brandamour*   Possibly Brandimarte, companion of Orlando
       and lover of Fiordelisa in Boiardo's *Orlando Innamorato*.
325   *Io*   Beloved of Jupiter, who transformed her into a cow to
       protect her from Juno.
327   *Psyches*   Psyche, beloved of Cupid.
329   *Wood*   mad.
330   *toilèd*   exhausted.
333   *Orphey*   Orpheus.
334   *Cerberus*   watchdog of Hades.
335–8 *Hercules . . . Deianire*   Deianira, wife of Hercules (or Al-
       cides), was carried off by the centaur Nessus.
350   *Admiring*   wondering.
354   *sound*   swoon.
358   *touch*   charge.
367   *Argus*   The hundred-eyed guard set by Juno to watch Io;
       slain by Mercury.
380   *Luna*   the moon.
384   *welladay*   lament.
412   *implete*   fill.
       store   great quantity.
438   *Tellus*   earth.
440   *spoil*   destruction.
448   *toilèd*   exhausted.
449   *silly*   innocent.
450   *night's queen*   the moon.
455   *this*   this time.
456   *him . . . beriven*   first bereaved him of joy.
457   *period*   end.
467   *suspect*   suspicion.

469 *mickle*   much.
481 *date outworn*   time elapsed.
486 *eyne*   eyes.
487 *Spectatum . . . ipsae*   They come as spectators, and to be watched themselves (Ovid, *Ars Amatoria*, I 99).
488 *wanting fair*   lacking beauty.
500 *beriven*   bereaved.
506 *whilom*   formerly.
510 *say*   light serge.
548 *ecstasy*   unconsciousness.
555 *prove*   test.
593 *fere*   mate.
621 *spent date*   time expired.
622 *period*   end.
630 *Qualis . . . ita*   As the life is, so is its end.

ALL OVID'S ELEGIES

The bibliographical situation, as the Table of Dates indicates, is very complex. My basic text is the Huntington Library's copy of *All Ovids Elegies: 3. Bookes . . .* , Middleborough, n.d. But, as Roma Gill has pointed out (*Review of English Studies*, vol. 21, no. 83, pp. 346–8) the relation between the early editions is unclear, and the primacy of the Huntington volume's text is by no means established.

Book I

ELEGIA I

How he was forced by Cupid to write of love instead of war.

2 *these . . . he*   i.e., Ovid prefers it this way. The first version of the *Amores* contained five books rather than three.
8 *took . . . away*   epics are written in hexameters, love elegies in alternating hexameter and pentameter lines.
11 *thy mother*   Venus.
13 *Ceres*   goddess of agriculture.
15 *ray*   array.
16 *Aonian*   belonging to the muses: their sacred spring Helicon was in Aonia.
19 *Tempe*   A valley in Thessaly famous for its beauty.
34 *shine*   shining.
       myrtle   sacred to Venus.

ELEGIA II
*First captured by love, he endures being led
in triumph by Cupid.*

3   *tho*   then.
26 *pigeons*   Venus' doves.
34 *Io*   the Roman cry of triumph.
35 *Fear*   "terrorque" in Marlowe's text; modern editions read
    "errorque."
47 *having . . . hue*   Bacchus was said to have ridden victoriously
    as far as the Ganges.
48 *tigers*   Bacchus' chariot was drawn by tigers.

ELEGIA III
To his mistress.

21 *hornèd Io*   to protect her from Juno, Jupiter transformed his
    beloved Io into a cow.
22 *she*   Leda.
23 *she*   Europa.
24 *false horns*   Marlowe translates "cornua falsa"; modern texts
    read "vara" (bent).

ELEGIA IV
*He advises his love what devices and signals they ought to
employ when they are at a dinner with her husband
present.*

7–8 *fair . . . fight*   at the wedding of Peirithous, king of the Lapiths,
    and Hippodamia, resulting in the battle of Lapiths and Cen-
    taurs.
16 *bed*   the couch on which Romans reclined at dinner.
30 *Ask . . . think*   ask for only as much wine as you think is
    enough.
34 *gobbets*   morsels.
61 *clips*   embraces.

ELEGIA V
Sex with Corinna.

11 *Semiramis*   Queen of Assyria, a famous beauty.
12 *Lais*   Celebrated Greek courtesan.
15 *cast*   taken.
18 *wen*   blemish.
24 *clinged*   clung to.

ELEGIA VI
To her porter, to open the door for him.

2   *hooks*   hinges.
17 *enviest*   Marlowe translates "ut invideas"; modern texts read "et ut videas" (and so that you may see).
21 *entreats*   entreaties.
29 *rampired*   fortified.
36 *my gear*   i.e., my body.
41 *Art careless?*   do you not care?
53 *bears*   thou bearest.
    Oreithyia   Carried off by Boreas, the north wind, to be his wife.
72 *Careless*   uncaring.
    with . . . distained   i.e., not guilty of letting me in.

ELEGIA VII
That his mistress, whom he has beaten, should make peace with him.

7–8 *Ajax . . . flocks*   Ajax, enraged at being denied the armor of Achilles, went mad and slew a flock of sheep thinking they were his enemies.
9   *he*   Orestes.
13   *Atalanta*   Mythical beauty, huntress of the Calydonian boar.
15   *Ariadne*   Princess of Crete, who rescued Theseus from the labyrinth of Minos, and was subsequently abandoned by him on the island of Naxos.
18   *Deflowered . . . wall*   i.e., the fact that the rape took place in Diana's temple was the only sort of chastity left to her. Marlowe omits the Latin's "nisi vittatis . . . capillis," "except that fillets [tokens of chastity] bound her hair."
31   *Tydides*   Diomedes, son of Tydeus.
32   *goddess*   Aphrodite (Venus), wounded by Diomedes in battle.
38   *hollow*   cry out.
40   *On . . . cheeks*   i.e., her flesh is white except for her cheeks.
54   *flaw*   squall.
63   *doubt*   hesitate.
68   *kembèd*   combed.

ELEGIA VIII
He reviles the bawd who has been introducing his mistress to the courtesan's art.

2   *trot*   old hag.
    hight   named.
3   *name . . . thing*   Dipsas means thirsty. The point is that she is always drunk.

5   *Thessale* Thessaly, reputedly the home of witchcraft.

7   *wrong* crooked.

8   *rank humor* foul-smelling discharge of a mare in heat.

11   *have faith* am trustworthy.

15   *Fame* gossip.

16   *eyeballs* pupils.

23   *blest* well endowed.

26   *weeds* clothes.

29–30   *Th' opposèd . . . warm* Mars has been unfavorable to you, but now Venus is in the ascendant.

34   *Would he* even if he would.

39   *Tatius* King of the Sabines.

42   *Aeneas' city* Rome, founded by Aeneas.

45   *front* forehead.

48   *approved . . . side* proved their valor.

49   *closely* secretly.

62   *witty* wise.

64   *vain name* "nomen inane" in Marlowe's text; modern editions read "crimen inane," empty reproach.

74   *Isis* The moon goddess, controlling the menstrual cycle.

75   *patient . . . gain* he grew used to suffering.

86   *to mocked men* Translating "illusis"; modern texts read "in lusis," to (love's) deceptions.

94   *By . . . shift* say it is your birthday.

112   *rivelled* wrinkled.

ELEGIA IX

To Atticus: that a lover may not be lazy, any more than a soldier.

2   *Attic* Atticus.

3   *What . . . Mars* the age that is suitable for being a soldier.

5   *years* Marlowe's text reads "annos"; modern editions have "animos" (spirits).

9   *the . . . send* send the wench forth.

23   *fell* Slain by Odysseus and Diomedes (*Iliad*, X. 435 ff.).

33   *Briseis* Achilles' captive, expropriated by Agamemnon (*Iliad*, I 391–2).

36   *on* on Hector.

38   *Priam's . . . daughter* Cassandra.

39   *Mars . . . stable* Vulcan (the blacksmith) trapped (did stable) Mars in bed with Venus.

43   *A . . . care* caring for a fair maid.

ELEGIA X

To his girl, that she should not demand money for her love.

1   *cause*   Helen of Troy.

4   *included*   enclosed.

5   *Amymone*   One of the Danaides, rescued from the attack of
    a satyr by Poseidon, and loved by him.

7   *bull and eagle*   Forms in which Jove carried off Europa and
    Ganymede.

18   *pelf*   riches.

19   *to*   at.

22   *coney*   The obscenity is Marlowe's; the Latin reads simply
     "body."

31   *lets*   rents.

37   *Knights . . . post*   perjurers.

38   *becomes a stale*   i.e., prostitutes himself.

46   *enlarged*   freed.

49–50   *Sabine . . . nun*   Tarpeia, daughter of the Roman governor,
        admitted the Sabine invaders to Rome, and as a reward she
        asked for what they wore on their arms. Instead of giving her
        their rich bracelets, the Sabines crushed her with their shields
        to punish her treachery.

51–2   *son . . . punishment*   Eriphyle was the wife of Amphiarus.
       When the Argives marched against Thebes, Amphiarus hid,
       sensing that he was doomed if he accompanied them. But Eri-
       phyle allowed Polynices, one of the Argive generals, to bribe
       her with a golden necklace, and revealed Amphiarus' hiding
       place. He was thus forced to join the expedition, but he or-
       dered his son Alcmaeon to murder Eriphyle when news of his
       death arrived. Alcmaeon carried out his father's orders, and
       subsequently went mad.

54   *wants*   lacks.

56   *Alcinous' fruit*   which grew all the year (*Odyssey*, VII
     114 ff.).

61   *wear*   wear out.

64   *refrain*   hold back.

ELEGIA XI

He pleads with Nape to carry a letter to Corinna.

3   *scapes*   escapades.

4   *to . . . odious*   i.e., she is clever at signaling.

5   *clips*   embraces.

6   *Never . . . evasion*   i.e., you never betrayed me.

10   *But*   Marlowe's text reads "sed"; modern texts have "nec": she is *not* naïve.

17   *front*   brow.

24   *tables*   pages.

25   *laurel*   the crown of poetry.

27   *Subscribing*   testifying (literally, writing underneath).

28   *being . . . late*   formerly humble wood.

ELEGIA XII

He curses his writing tablets, which he deplores because
his mistress has refused to spend the night with him.

8   *wax*   Roman writing tablets were made of wood coated with wax.

10   *bad honey*   Corsican honey was notoriously bitter.

27   *Your name*   "tabellar duplices," hence they are duplicitous, i.e., folded double.

ELEGIA XIII

To Dawn, not to hurry.

1   *old love*   Aurora's husband, Tithonus, had been granted immortality but not eternal youth.

4   *birds . . . slain*   Memnon was the son of Aurora and Tithonus. He was killed by Achilles at Troy, but Jupiter granted him immortality. A flock of birds rose from his funeral pyre and fought until half of them fell into the blaze to appease his spirit. The birds were said to return annually to the tomb of Memnon and repeat the battle.

9   *that*   so that.

14   *them*   themselves.

33   *Cephalus*   Loved by Aurora (*Metamorphoses*, VII 711 ff.).

45–6   *Jove . . . one*   when he slept with Alcmena and conceived Hercules.

ELEGIA XIV

He consoles his girl, whose hair has fallen out
from excessive hair-dressing.

6   *curious Seres*   skillful Chinese.

16   *kembed*   combed.

18   *drive*   drove.

21   *Thracian bacchanal*   celebrant of the Thracian rites of Dionysus.

22   *rashly*   heedlessly.

30   *hot bodkin*   curling iron.

33 *Diana* Marlowe misunderstands Ovid's reference to a painting by Apelles of *Dione*, or Venus, rising from the sea.

45 *captive hair-tires* wigs from the hair of captives.

46 *curious* elegant.

49 *Guelder* German.

50 *fame* glory.

ELEGIA XV
To those who begrudge the poet eternal fame.

9–10 *Tenedos, Ide* (Ida), *Simois* all places described in the *Iliad*.

11 *Ascraeus* Hesiod, born in Ascra, in Boeotia.

13 *Callimachus* Alexandrian elegiac poet (third century B.C.).

14 *wit* inspiration.

16 *Aratus* Greek poet (third century B.C.).

19 *Ennius* Founder of Roman epic poetry (second century B.C.).

21 *Varro* Roman poet, lexicographer and antiquarian (first century B.C.).

22 *Argos* Argo, Jason's ship.

25 *Tityrus* Traditionally Virgil's name for himself in the *Eclogues*.

29 *Gallus* Roman amatory poet (first century B.C.).

34 *Tagus* Spanish river traditionally said to have golden sands.

37 *myrtle* sacred to Venus.

B.J. *Ben Jonson.* The poem reappears in *Poetaster,* I i 43 ff.

16 *With sun and moon* Aratus's poem *Phaenomena* was about astronomy.

25 *Tityrus, Tillage* Virgil's *Eclogues* and *Georgics* respectively.

37 *drad* fearing.

Book II

ELEGIA I
Why he is impelled to write of love rather than of titanic struggles.

2 *Peligny* Paeligni: not a place-name, but a tribe inhabiting the Abruzzi.
   address undertake.

12 *Gyges* Properly Gyes, a giant, son of Uranus.

13–14 *Olympus, Ossa, Pelion* mountains; by piling them on top of each other the giants hoped to climb to heaven and overthrow the gods.

21 *Toys* trifles.

23   *deduce*   draw down.

25   *Snakes . . . mountains*   Ovid says, "carmine dissiliunt abrup-
     tis faucibus angues," "by song the serpents' jaws are burst
     open and their fangs drawn." Marlowe is confused by "fau-
     cibus" (jaws): *faux* can be used metaphorically for a chasm.

30   *either Ajax*   The son of Telamon, and the son of Oileus. But
     modern texts read "Atrides" instead of "Aiaces"; the refer-
     ence is to Agamemnon and Menelaus.

31   *he*   Odysseus.

32   *jades*   horses.

38   *rehearse*   dictate.

ELEGIA II

To Bagous, to keep a more lax watch over his mistress,
who has been entrusted to him.

4   *Danaus' fact*   The temple of Apollo in Rome was adorned
     with sculptures of the Danaides.
     fact   deed.

7   *redoubled*   returned.

8   *thy care*   Bagous' watchfulness.

13   *he follow*   he may follow.

17–18   *Wilt . . . dissemble*   The general sense is, turn a blind eye to
        her actions; but the translation is very confused.

25   *what . . . done*   what she is doing at the temple of Isis.

27   *scapes*   escapades.

29   *him*   the lover.

31   *of him*   for her husband.

35   *fall*   weep.

37   *Object . . . excuse*   charge her with small offenses for which
     she may easily be excused.

38   *To . . . use*   if she is charged with false crimes her true
     crimes will not be believed.

44   *Tantalus*   Condemned in hell to suffer thirst and hunger in a
     pond whose waters recede when he tries to drink, and with
     fruit trees nearby that withdraw as he reaches for them.
     long tongue   He was punished for revealing the secrets of
     the gods.

45   *Juno's watchman*   hundred-eyed Argus, set to watch Jove's
     love Io, who had been transformed into a cow.

46   *timeless*   untimely: he was killed by Mercury at the com-
     mand of Jove.
     deified   Io became the goddess Isis.

56   *her judge*   the husband.
61   *cast*   defeated.
63   *vile facts*   evil deeds.

ELEGIA III
To the eunuch serving his mistress.

13   Good . . . *together*   there is beauty, and an age appropriate to making love.

ELEGIA IV
That he loves women of all sorts.

5   *that*   what.
9   *likes*   attracts.
13   *clown*   coarse girl, peasant.
15   *Sabine*   Sabine women were known for their modesty.
16   *do*   i.e., sleep with him.
19   *Callimachus*   "his wit was weak" (I xv 14).
21   *that*   what.
31   *To . . . myself*   leaving myself aside.
38   *attired*   in elegant clothes.
43   *morn*   Aurora.

ELEGIA V
To his faithless mistress.

24   *it likes me*   I like.
35   *Aurora*   dawn.
38   *travails*   struggles.
40   *Arachne*   a superlative weaver and dyer.
45   *kembèd*   combed.
54, 55   *them, they*   the kisses.
61–2   *Nowhere . . . sped*   i.e., she could only have learned such techniques in bed, and her expert teacher is no one I know. *sped*   enjoyed.

ELEGIA VI
On the death of his parrot.

5   *For . . . hairs*   instead of hair disheveled (in mourning).
7–10   *Philomel, Tereus, Itys*   Tereus, king of Thrace, was the husband of Procne, sister of Philomel. While conducting Philomel from Athens to visit her sister, Tereus fell in love with her and raped her. He then cut out her tongue so that she could not reveal the crime, imprisoned her, and told Procne that her sister was dead. But Philomel wove the story into a tapestry and sent

it to Procne, who, in revenge, murdered her son Itys and served him up to Tereus at dinner. Tereus' own revenge on the two sisters was forestalled by the metamorphosis of all the figures in the tragedy into birds: Tereus into a hawk, Philomel a nightingale, Procne a swallow, and Itys a sandpiper.

15 *Pylades, Orestes*   Archetypes of friendship.

22 *pass*   surpass.
   mark   dye: in Ovid it is the bird's beak ("rostra") that is red. But Marlowe's text reads "nostra," hence "our scarlet."

23 *on . . . ground*   in the world.

29 *filled*   satisfied.

33 *puttock*   kite.

34 *cadess*   jackdaw.

35 *Pallas' hate*   because the crow revealed the birth and hiding place of Erichthonius, who was created when Vulcan attempted to rape Minerva (*Metamorphoses*, II 552 ff.).

36 *nine ages*   Crows were said to have immense life spans.

38 *far*   wide.

41 *Thersites*   the ignoble railer of the *Iliad*.
   Protesilaus   first Greek hero killed upon landing at Troy.

43 *what*   why.

49 *holm-trees*   ilex.

53 *harmless*   innocent.

55 *Juno's bird*   the peacock.

61 *approves*   proves.

ELEGIA VII

He swears to his mistress that he has not made love to her maid.

4 *One . . . took*   i.e., you think I am looking at a particular girl.

9 *thou . . . move*   you have no effect on me.

18 *to violate*   of violating.

24 *grateful*   satisfactory.

26 *show*   to reveal.

ELEGIA VIII

To Cypassis, Corinna's maid.

2 *kemb*   comb.

3 *clown*   fool, peasant.

11, 12 *Briseis, Chryseis*   Chryseis was Agamemnon's prisoner; when forced to return her to Troy to avert a plague, he took Achilles' prisoner Briseis instead, thus prompting Achilles' wrath and retirement from the war.

17 *might . . . best* i.e., my reaction was much better.
20 *Carpathian seas* the Aegean between Crete and Rhodes.
24 *for* in place of.

ELEGIA IX
To Cupid.

7 *Pelides* Achilles, son of Peleus, who wounded Telephus and then cured him.
   whom him whom, Telephus.
16 *laud* praise.
20 *though . . . yields* The sense is that he no longer seeks to tame the wilderness; but the translation of lines 19–22 is very confused.
34 *purple* ruddy, blushing.
47 *in . . . trample* vacillates.
48 *stepfather* Mars.

ELEGIA X
To Graecinus, that he can love two at once.

19 *soft* The Latin verse says "saevus," fierce.
34 *wracked . . . sea* when they are shipwrecked, let them drink the sea.
35 *doing* sexual activity.

ELEGIA XI
To his mistress sailing.

1 *raught* taken.
2 *Ill . . . taught* Ovid says, "first taught the evil ways of the sea, while the waves marveled."
4 *Carried . . . sheep* in the Argonauts' expedition.
6 *wracked* shipwrecked.
10 *Boreas* the north wind.
19 *Cerannia* Ceraunian mountains, on the coast of Epirus.
20 *Syrtes* Two gulfs in North Africa notoriously difficult to navigate.
22 *wreaks* harms.
24 *crooked* curved.
27 *Triton* A sea god.
29 *Leda's . . . stars* Castor and Pollux, sons of Leda and patrons of navigation.
32 *Thracian* Orpheus was Thracian.
33 *slip* slip away.

34   *Galatea*   the sea-nymph.
36   *father*   Nereus.
41   *avail*   benefit.
45   *clip*   embrace.

ELEGIA XII
He rejoices that he has conquered his mistress.

10   *Atrides*   Agamemnon and Menelaus, sons of Atreus.
17   *queen*   Helen.
19   *woman*   Hippodamia: the war between the Lapiths and the Centaurs was begun during her wedding to Pirithous, king of the Lapiths.
21–2   *woman . . . center*   Lavinia, daughter of King Latinus, and wife of Aeneas. She had been engaged to her kinsman Turnus, but an oracle said she must marry a foreign prince, and Latinus determined to give her to Aeneas. To prevent the marriage Turnus attempted to drive the Trojans from Italy, and was killed in the war.
     new   once again.
23   *A woman*   i.e., the Sabine women, because of their abduction by the Romans.
27–8   *without . . . further*   Cupid commands me to pursue the war, but without shedding blood.

ELEGIA XIII
To Isis, to aid Corinna in childbirth.

3   *secretly . . . me*   keeping it secret from me.
4   *exempted*   removed.
7–8   *Canopus, Memphis, Pharos*   in Egypt, home of Isis.
11   *Anubis*   dog-headed god of the dead, son of Isis's husband Osiris.
14   *Apis*   the holy bull.
18   *French rout*   "There was a temple to Isis in the Campus Martius. About it were laurels, and the Gallic squadron may refer to Roman riders on Gallic horses in the neighbouring exercise grounds" (Ovid, *Heroides and Amores*, trans. G. Showerman, Loeb Library, London, 1914, pp. 422–3).
21   *Lucina*   goddess of childbirth.
25   *Naso . . . Corinna*   coming from Ovid and Corinna.
27   *thee*   Corinna.
28   *To . . . thee*   i.e., don't do it again.

ELEGIA XIV
To his mistress, who has attempted an abortion.

3   *annoy*   harm.
8   *wrack*   torture.
11 *stones . . . original*   Deucalion and his wife Pyrrha repeopled the world after the universal flood by flinging behind them stones, which became men and women.
14 *Thetis*   a sea-nymph, mother of Achilles.
15 *Ilia*   Rhea Silvia, mother of Romulus and Remus.
17 *fruit*   Aeneas, founder of Rome, son of Venus and Anchises.
23 *increasing*   ripening.
26 *surcease*   delay.
27 *bowels*   innards.
29 *Colchis*   home of Medea, who murdered her two children.
30 *Itys*   son of Tereus and Procne, murdered by his mother.
35 *Armenian tigers*   proverbially fierce.
43 *delict*   dereliction.

ELEGIA XV
To a ring, which he has given his mistress.

11 *pap*   breast.
13 *strait*   tight.
15 *privy leaves*   private letters.
16 *hold-fast*   tenacious.
19 *I . . . hit*   confused; the sense is, I won't leave her finger if her intention is to put me away.
20 *in . . . knit*   i.e., I'll make myself tighter.
24 *pash*   splash.

ELEGIA XVI
To his mistress, to come to his country estate.

1   *Sulmo*   Ovid's birthplace in the Abruzzi.
    Peligny   Paeligni, the tribe inhabiting the area.
2   *veins*   streams.
3   *rive*   crack.
4   *Icarian . . . dog-star*   Canicula, the dog of Icarius. He discovered and revealed his master's murdered body, and was translated to the heavens as a reward for his fidelity.
8   *Pallas' olives*   The olive tree was created by Athena.
13 *Pollux and Castor*   These spend alternate days in heaven.
15 *pensive*   sleepless.

17   *will . . . go*   i.e., let their girls accompany them.

21   *Syrtes*   waters dangerous to navigation.

24   *Malea*   the southern tip of the Spartan peninsula.

28   *helping gods*   the tutelary figureheads on the stern.

31   *youth*   Leander.

32   *blind*   because Hero's torch had been extinguished.

35   *hinds*   peasants.

43   *swarest*   sworest.

46   *as it seems*   Marlowe's text reads "ut visum est"; modern editions have "qua visum est," "by the whim of (wind . . .)."
      bereaves   carries off.

51–2 *you . . . crown*   i.e., make her way easy.

ELEGIA XVII
That he will serve only Corinna.

2   *convinced*   convicted.

3   *while . . . hides*   if Venus moderate the fire I burn with.

4   *Paphos, Cythera*   homes of Venus.

5   *my . . . prey*   prey of a gentle mistress.

6   *of force*   perforce.

7   *heart*   high spirits.

10   *but . . . up*   until she has her makeup on.

14   *copulate*   suited.

15   *Calypso*   in love with Odysseus, who is presumably the "mortal nymph's refusing lord" of line 16.

17   *Peleus, Thetis*   parents of Achilles.

18   *Egeria*   a water-nymph.
      Numa   king of Rome.

19–20 *Venus . . . ill-favoredly*   Venus was "copulate" with Vulcan, even though he was ungainly when not working at his forge.

21   *not alike*   because Latin elegiacs alternate hexameters and pentameters.

22   *shorter numbers*   pentameters.
      heroic   hexameters.

27   *For*   in place of.

ELEGIA XVIII
To Macer, writing of his love poems.

1   *To . . . train'st*   i.e., while you write heroic poetry.

2   *maiden*   first.

15   *buskins*   the boots of the tragedian.

16   *rule . . . acquainted*   majesty . . . adopted.
17   *mistress' deity*   divine mistress.
19–21   *What . . . Ulysses*   The syntax is, we write what is lawful, or what Ulysses sends, etc., or we profess love's art.
19   *love's art*   Ovid's *Ars Amatoria*.
21–6   *what . . . harp*   all epistles from Ovid's *Heroides*.
26   *her*   Sappho.
     Aonian   of the muses; Mount Helicon was in Aonia.
27   *Sabinus*   Poet and friend of Ovid, who composed answers to several of the *Heroides*.
29   *sign*   handwriting.
30   *stepdame*   Phaedra.
31   *Elisa*   Dido.
32   *Phyllis*   Queen of Thrace, abandoned by Demophoön, king of Athens.
34   *Sappho . . . feet*   because her love has been reciprocated.
35   *of thee*   by thee.
38   *Laodamia*   wife of Protesilaus, killed in the landing at Troy.

ELEGIA XIX
To his rival, her husband, who does not guard his wife.

5   *us . . . lovers*   i.e., we are both lovers.
6   *may . . . strike*   may her refusals provide opportunities for our wishes to succeed.
8   *avails*   is available to.
13   *how . . . might*   as much as she could.
20   *cozen me*   Marlowe's text reads "fac insidias"; modern editions have "time insidias," "be afraid of plots."
21   *dispread*   stretched out.
27   *Danae*   Jupiter made love to her as a shower of gold.
29   *Juno . . . wore*   Juno set a guard over Io, transformed by Jupiter into a cow.
35   *suff'rance*   indulgence.
40   *ban-dogs*   watchdogs.
41   *lines*   messages.
45   *alife*   dearly.
46   *wittol*   cuckold.
50   *entreat*   handle, i.e., cheat.
60   *corrive*   share.

Book III

ELEGIA I

The poet's deliberation whether to continue writing elegies
or to turn to tragedy.

8   *longer . . . feet*   because the elegiac meter alternates hexame-
ter and pentameter lines.

12   *front*   forehead.
on . . . lie   reached to the ground.

14   *buskin*   the high boot of tragedy.
fit   translating "apta"; modern editions read "alta," high.

18   *cross-way's corner*   street corner.

19   *some*   somebody.

34   *myrtle*   sacred to Venus and hence emblematic of love.

36   *art . . . played*   do you always play such heavy parts?

37   *Thou . . . rehearse*   you permit tragedies to be written in
lines of mixed lengths.

42   *thing I move*   i.e., love.

43   *should*   would.

56   *let*   failed.

60   *she*   Tragedy.
thee   the poet. In Ovid, Elegy says, "You owe it to me that
Tragedy now claims you."

61   *left*   ceased.

ELEGIA II
To his mistress, watching the races.

12   *ring-turn*   post where the track turns.

15–17   *Pelops . . . her*   Hippodamia's suitors had to compete with
her father in a chariot race; Hippodamia rode as a distracting
passenger with the suitor. But one wooer, Pelops, won her
heart, and she helped him to win and to contrive the death of
her father.

19   *force . . . now*   i.e., the place is crowded.

22   *entreated*   treated.

28   *thou look'st*   one looks.

29–30   *Swift . . . Hippomenes*   Atalanta's suitors were required to
race with her. Hippomenes won by throwing three golden ap-
ples in her way.

31   *Coat-tucked*   with coat tucked up.

34   *seas into*   into the sea.

41   *ray*   soil.
55   *boy . . . flies*   Cupid.
58   *She becked*   Venus nodded.
63   *if . . . best*   if you like that best.
66   *lists' . . . ends*   the starting points.
69   *too far about*   i.e., on the outside.
71   *unhappy*   unfortunate man.
73   *One . . . favor*   we have picked a slow horse.
73–4   *Romans . . . cloak*   The spectators could call for the race to be started again by throwing their cloaks in the air.
80   *my . . . request*   i.e., grant both our wishes.
83   *behight*   promised.

ELEGIA III
On his mistress, who has lied to him.

17   *Cepheus' daughter*   Andromeda, exposed on a rock to assuage the gods' anger against her mother Cassiopeia, who had claimed to be more beautiful than the Nereids.
19   *shakes . . . off*   spoils your record.
20   *mocked . . . scoff*   scoffs both at the gods she has mocked and at me.
24   *fond*   foolish.
26   *in . . . drenches*   overwhelms with their power alone.
37–40   *Semele . . . lack*   Semele wished Jupiter to make love to her in his real form, and was consumed by his fire. Their child Bacchus was born from Jupiter's thigh.
48   *transfuse*   transmit.

ELEGIA IV
To a man who guards his wife.

6   *lest . . . will*   against her will.
19   *Argus*   set by Juno to guard Io, Jupiter's love.
     either way   in all directions.
21   *Danae*   loved by Jupiter as a golden shower.
29   *dear*   valuable.
36   *honest*   chaste.
39–40   *Mars . . . seed*   Rhea Silvia (*Ilia*) was the mother of Romulus and Remus by Mars. The affair was "not without fault" because Rhea Silvia was a vestal virgin.
42   *these*   beauty and chasteness.
45   *gives*   brings you.

46   *Least . . . any*   i.e., anyone will be your good friend with no
     effort on your part.
48   *much*   i.e., presents.

ELEGIA V
To a torrent, while he is on the way to his mistress.

14   *head . . . adders*   of the gorgon Medusa. Perseus killed her
     and carried her head on his shield.
15   *chariot*   Ceres' chariot.
24   *prove*   test.
25–44   A summary of the loves of the various river gods.
36   *Alcides*   Hercules: Achelous fought with him for Deianira.
40   *head*   source.
44   *Fly . . . charged*   commanded his stream to run backward.
47ff.   Ilia, or Rhea Silvia, was made a vestal by her uncle to prevent
     her having children. But she became the mother of Romulus
     and Remus by Mars, and subsequently married the river god
     Tiberinus.
50   *sole*   uninhabited.
54   *Idaean*   from Mount Ida.
     Laomedon   King of Troy, or Ilium, whence her name Ilia.
79   *hoodwinked*   covered.
82   *gave . . . best*   i.e., made love to her.
100   *these others*   these things move others.
101   *this*   stream.
     fondly   foolishly.

ELEGIA VI
He bewails the fact that, in bed with his mistress,
he was unable to perform.

17   *age*   old age.
     shun   ignore.
27   *Thessalian*   magical.
28   *silly*   innocent.
29   *some imbased*   someone impaired.
33   *mast*   acorns.
41   *Pylius*   Nestor, from Pylos.
42   *Tithon*   Tithonus, aged husband of Aurora, the dawn.
46   *lewdly*   vilely.
     forslowed   misused.
50   *Chuff*   miserly fool.

51–2   *in . . . touch*   the punishment of Tantalus, who revealed the
        secrets of the gods.
        thrives   ironic: he suffers intense thirst but cannot drink.
   61   *Phaemius*   a superlative musician (*Odyssey,* I 154).
   62   *Thamyris*   musician blinded by the muses (*Iliad,* II 594).

ELEGIA VII
He mourns that his mistress will not receive him.

    2   *stead*   esteem.
    3   *sometimes*   formerly.
    9   *chuff*   boor.
        whose . . . inferred   whose military exploits brought him great
        wealth.
   15   *gold*   the knight's ring.
   16   *target*   shield.
   25   *we slothful*   poets: ironic.
   26   *trembling*   alarmed.
   28   *Homer . . . worth*   Ovid says, "You could have had this too,
        Homer, had you wished."
   30   *maid*   Danae.
   35   *when . . . possessed*   in the Golden Age, before Jupiter.
   42   *ditcher*   digger.
   51   *affects*   desirest.
   52   *Alcides*   Hercules.
   61   *Sabine-like*   the Sabines were renowned for virtue.
   64   *If . . . forbear*   but if I should arrive with gifts, both keeper
        and husband would make themselves scarce.

ELEGIA VIII
He mourns the death of Tibullus.

    1   *Thetis*   mother of Achilles.
        Morn   Aurora, mother of Memnon, killed by Achilles.
   14   *Iulus*   Ascanius, Aeneas's son.
   16   *Adon*   Adonis.
   18   *we . . . deity*   that god is within us.
   21   *what . . . good*   what good were parents.
23–4   *Where . . . said*   The Latin reads, "and the same father, it is
        said, mourned Linus, singing in the deep woods to his unre-
        sponsive lyre." Linus was a mythical poet, son of Apollo.
   26   *Pierian*   from the spring sacred to the muses.
   27   *Averne*   Avernus, hell.
   29   *lasts*   outlasts.

30 *web ... unframe* Penelope undid at night what she had woven during the day.

31 *Nemesis, Delia* names of Tibullus's mistresses.

35 *forbod* forbidden.

42 *annoy* injure.

45 *Eryx' ... empress* Venus, from her shrine on Mount Eryx.

47 *Corcyra* Corfu, where Tibullus had once been taken ill.

52 *unkembed* unkempt.

54 *thine* your family's.

62 *Calvus* orator and friend of Catullus.

64 *Gallus* poet and friend of Virgil.

66 *godly* blest souls.

ELEGIA IX
To Ceres, complaining that because of her ceremonies he is not allowed to sleep with his mistress.

1 *Ceres* goddess of agriculture.

6 *Nor ... grudge* you begrudge man his prosperity less than any other goddess.

8 *floor* where grain was threshed.

9 *mast* acorns.
    first oracles The ancient oracle of Zeus at Dodona was an oak.

18 *clown* peasant.

19 *Crete* home of Ceres.
    feign Cretans were notorious liars.

20 *Jove* Ceres' brother.

22 *teat-distilling* distilled from the teat.

23 *Faith ... apply* Jove's praise testifies to Crete's truthfulness.

24 *Ceres ... deny* i.e., Ceres would not lie.

25 *Iasion* A Cretan loved by Ceres.
    Candian Ide Mount Ida, in Crete.

27 *marrow ... flame* passion filled her.

30 *corn ... returned* little of what had been planted was harvested.

32 *share* ploughshare.

36 *ear-wrought* made of ears of grain.

39 *did sing* Marlowe misunderstands "canebat," "was white (with corn)."

41 *Minos* king of Crete, renowned lawmaker.

45 *Proserpine* Ceres' daughter, wife of Dis; she reigns for half the year as queen of the underworld.

ELEGIA X

To his mistress, from whose love he cannot free himself.

14 *side*   groin.
21 *What*   why.

ELEGIA XI

He complains that his mistress is so well known through
his poems that she is available to many rival lovers.

1–2 *sad . . . sing*   The general sense is, birds stopped singing to
       lovers as an omen of misfortune, but the translation is both
       inaccurate and confused.

   4 *plain*   complain.

  19 *as . . . hear*   since poets are usually ignored.

21 ff. The disastrous effects of poetry are described through a series
       of mythological examples.

  21 *Scylla . . . steals*   She cut from the head of her father Nisus the
       lock of hair on which his life depended, and was changed into
       a bird (*Metamorphoses*, VIII 6 ff.).

  22 *Scylla's . . . conceals*   She was transformed into a monster by
       Circe, who was jealous of Glaucus's love of her.

  23 *feet fly*   Mercury's feet were winged.

23–4 *hairs . . . takes*   Perseus destroyed Medusa, and rode off on
       the winged horse Pegasus who sprang from her blood.

  25 *Tityus*   a giant seen by Odysseus in Hades.

  26 *dog*   Cerberus, watchdog of Hades.

  27 *Enceladus*   one of the giants who attempted to overthrow the
       gods.

  28 *mermaids*   the sirens.

  29 *east winds*   given to Odysseus by Aeolus.

  30 *Tantalus*   for telling the gods' secrets, condemned to eternal
       thirst and hunger with water and fruit just out of reach.

  31 *flint*   turned to stone.
       Callist   Callisto, loved by Jupiter, was transformed into a bear
       by Juno, and subsequently placed in the heavens as Ursa Major.

  32 *Progne, Itys*   Procne murdered her son Itys in revenge for her
       husband's rape of her sister Philomela. Procne became the
       sparrow.

  33 *Jove . . . gold*   to woo Leda and Danae.

  35 *Proteus*   god of disguise.
       teeth . . . seed   Cadmus sowed dragon's teeth from which his
       army sprang.

36   *Oxen . . . breed*   yoked by Jason in Colchis (*Argonautica*, III 1225 ff.).

37   *Electra . . . sisters*   the Pleiades (but Ovid is referring to the sisters of Phaëthon, whose tears turned to amber [*electra*]).

38   *ships*   Aeneas's ships, transformed to water deities to prevent Turnus from destroying them.

39   *Atreus's . . . table*   Atreus served his brother Thyestes the bodies of his murdered sons.

40   *harp*   Orpheus's lyre.

ELEGIA XII
On the feast of Juno.

1   *Tuscia*   Tuscany

2   *Camillus*   M. Furius Camillus, who freed Rome from the invading Gauls (fourth century B.C.).

17   *their . . . back*   wreathed back over their heads.

19–20   The story Ovid refers to is otherwise unknown.

21   *brought . . . darts*   the goat is the target.

24   *Show . . . ways*   show off: Marlowe translates "praebuerant." Modern editions read "praeverrunt," they sweep the road before her with their garments.

27   *use*   custom.

29   *hollow*   shout.

32   *fact*   crime.
     Halesus   Agamemnon's son and founder of the Falisci, the tribe of the district where the poem takes place.

35   *Hetrurians*   Etrurians, Tuscans.

ELEGIA XIII
To his mistress: if she will be licentious, let her do it discreetly.

13   *walk . . . puritan*   Ovid says, "at least imitate chaste women."

30   *wittol*   foolish cuckold.

31   *lines*   messages.

33   *start up*   jumped up from bed.

34   *new-raced*   newly bruised.

41   *sift*   question.

43   *took*   discovered.

ELEGIA XIV
To Venus, putting an end to his elegies.

3   *Peligny*   Ovid's home was in the Abruzzi, among the Paeligni.

9   *liberty . . . compelled*   in 90 B.C.

10   *careful*   worried.
11   *Sulmo*   Ovid's birthplace.
15   *Both loves*   Venus and Cupid.
17   *Horned Bacchus*   god of wine and ecstatic poetry, sometimes
     depicted with horns.

LUCAN'S FIRST BOOK

There was only one edition of Marlowe's *Lucan*, published in London
in 1600 by Thomas Thorpe, who signed the dedication.

DEDICATION

Edward Blount   one of the most important Elizabethan pub-
lishers.

2   *encounter*   present.
4   *churchyard*   Saint Paul's, where the booksellers had their stalls.
6   *humorously*   irrationally.
9   *old right*   Presumably Blount had once intended to print the
      translation himself.
9-10 *raised . . . circle*   referring to the conjuring of spirits in a
      magic circle.
12   *property*   qualities.
17   *keep state*   remain formal.
21   *marking*   notice.
25   *censure*   criticize.

3   *launched*   wounded.
4   *Armies allied*   relatives fighting each other.
6   *like*   alike.
11   *Crassus*   triumvir with Caesar and Pompey (60 B.C.).
15   *Titan*   the sun god.
20   *Nilus' mouth*   the source of the Nile.
25   *rampires*   ramparts.
28   *lien*   lain.
29   *hinds*   peasants (to work the land).
30   *Pyrrhus*   king of Epirus, who invaded Italy and Sicily
      (280-275 B.C.).
      Hannibal   Carthaginian invader of Rome in the Second Punic
      War (218-201 B.C.).
32   *wreak*   violent destruction.

33-4 *if ... means* i.e., if the Civil War was necessary so that Nero could ultimately ascend the throne.

35 *joyed* enjoyed.

36 *Giants* who attempted to overthrow Jupiter's power.

37 *plain not* do not complain against.

38 *Pharsalia* Thessaly (from Pharsalus, the town where Pompey was defeated by Caesar in 48 B.C.).

40 *Munda* in Spain, where Caesar defeated Pompey's sons (45 B.C.).

41 *Perusian* the town is now Perugia.

42 *Mutin toils* the misery at Mutina (now Modena).
    Leuca Leucas, Leucadia.

43 *Aetna* in Sicily.

44 *is ... bound* owes much.

54 *reeking* hot.

55 *squinting* oblique.

61 *Janus' fane* the temple of Janus, protector of the state during wars, and bringer of peace.

62 *bolt ... gates* The doors of Janus's temple were open during war, shut in peacetime.

68 *garboils* turmoils.

77 *Phoebe's wain* the moon.

78 *Phoebus* the sun.
    affect usurp.

85 *shivered* splintered (during the first triumvirate, 60 B.C.).

90 *Titan* the sun.

91 *Cynthia* the moon.

94 *far-fet* exotic.

95 *Rome's ... blood* when Romulus killed Remus.

97 *one ... church* Romulus set up a sanctuary for fugitives and criminals.

104 *Crassus' ... death* in 53 B.C.
     stayed restrained.

105 *Assyrian Carra* Carrhae, in Syria, where Crassus was defeated and murdered by the Parthians.

109 *share* divide.

111 *Julia* Pompey's wife, Caesar's daughter. She died in 54 B.C.

123 *pirates' wrack* Pompey freed the Mediterranean of pirates.

129 *Cato* M. Porcius Cato, republican and opponent of Caesar.

131 *to* how to.

134 *his theater* Pompey built a theater in Rome.

142 *every blast* at every blast.

156 *overthwarting* hostile.

158   *shivers*   shatters.
169   *butting lands*   boundaries.
170   *Curius*   M. Curius Dentatus (third century B.C.), Roman leader noted for frugality and piety.
       Camillus   M. Furius Camillus freed Rome from the invading Gauls (387 B.C.).
171   *hinds*   country people.
182   *field of Mars*   the Campus Martius, where the Roman assembly met.
199   *Phrygia*   Troy.
       Iulus   Ascanius, son of Aeneas, founder of Rome.
200   *Quirinus*   Romulus.
       advanced   raised high.
201   *Alba hill*   a sacred mountain, site of the first Latin town built by Ascanius.
206   *lets of*   hindrances to.
217   *just*   precisely.
219–20   *wat'ry . . . old*   i.e., it had been raining for three days.
233   *Lucifer*   the morning star.
240   *clange*   clangor.
243   *targets*   shields.
246   *eagles*   insignia of the Roman legions.
254   *Under . . . Bear*   in the far north.
257   *Cimbrians*   German invaders.
       Carthage Moors   Hannibal's troops.
262   *whist*   silent.
268   *Gracchus' deeds*   The Gracchi were popular reformers, overthrown by the senate in 133 and 121 B.C.
290   *Aby*   atone for.
       son   Pompey, Caesar's son-in-law.
294   *Eleius steeds*   racehorses in the Olympic games at Elis.
296   *Souse*   knock.
302   *quit*   requite.
306   *Cornets*   companies.
309   *how . . . bested*   what would our situation be.
311   *quailed*   made soft.
312   *pressed*   i.e., into service.
       of gowns   in togas, civilian dress.
313   *Brabbling*   chattering.
       Marcellus   M. Claudius Marcellus, leading opponent of Caesar.

323   *Milo*   T. Annius Milo Papianus, tribune, who killed his co-
       tribune Clodius, and was defended at his trial by Cicero.

324   *wane*   decrease.

326   *Sulla*   L. Cornelius Sulla, ally of Pompey and dictator of
       Rome, 82–79 B.C.

337   *king . . . Pontus*   Mithridates; Pompey successfully con-
       cluded Rome's war against him.

338   *Must . . . me*   Must I be the last feather in Pompey's cap?

345   *servitors*   veterans.

365   *mainly*   strongly.

366   *purple grooms*   base men wearing aristocratic togas.

370   *hand*   i.e., troop of soldiers, Caesar's "right hand."

372   *Arctic's Rhene*   the northern Rhine.

375   *blest*   victorious.

385   *ram*   battering ram.
       them   the walls.

391   *Boreas*   the north wind.

392   *fets breath*   catches his breath.

397   *Lemannus' nook*   Lake Geneva.

398   *Lingones*   Gallic tribe; the painted spears are theirs. They
       were pacified by the Romans (not, as Marlowe implies, the
       other way around).

399   *Vogesus*   more properly Vosegus, the Vosges mountains.

400   *Isara*   the Isère.

403   *Ruthens*   the Ruteni, in Aquitanian Gaul.

404   *Atax*   the Aude.

405   *Varus*   the Var.

406   *Alcides' port*   Monaco.

408   *Zephyr*   the west wind.

410   *uncertain shore*   of the Netherlands.

416   *Titan*   the sun.

420ff. *They came . . .*   essentially, a brief account of the geography
       and population of Roman Gaul, though Marlowe has a num-
       ber of the names wrong.

421   *Satirus*   An error for Aturus, the Adour.

424   *light . . . pikes*   the people of the Axona, or Aisne, who used
       light spears.

427   *apt . . . cars*   skilled in driving British war-chariots.

428   *Averni*   for Arverni, in the Auvergne.

429   *Ilian*   Trojan.

430   *Cotta*   C. Aurelius Cotta, proconsul in Gaul (d. 73 B.C.).

432 *open slops*   loose trousers.
433 *clange*   clamor.
434 *Cinga*   the Cinca, in Spain.
     Rhodanus   the Rhone.
435 *Araris*   the Saone.
436 *Gebenna*   Marlowe is confused; the passage is about a tribe in the Cevennes.
440 *Hesus*   Esus, the Gallic Mercury.
449 *only . . . you*   you alone.
451 *Erebus*   Hades.
456 *blest*   made happy.
459 *Cayc*   the Cayci, a German tribe.
465 *Vain fame*   rumor.
469 *his*   Caesar's.
470 *Mevania*   Bevagna, in Umbria.
472 *Nar*   the Nera.
474 *not entirely*   not in a single group.
481 *Fame*   rumor.
485 *fathers*   senators.
486 *decreed to*   to be decreed by.
488 *sway of*   headlong.
489 *chained troops*   continuous columns.
492 *inconsiderate*   unthinking.
496 *Auster*   the south wind.
     breach   bay.
508 *easy*   easily.
528 *flattering*   deceptively clear.
532 *climate*   region.
535 *Phoebe*   the moon.
536 *brother*   Phoebus, the sun.
538 *Titan*   the sun god.
541 *as . . . town*   When Atreus served his brother Thyestes the bodies of his murdered sons.
542 *through . . . east*   i.e., backward.
543 *Mulciber*   Vulcan, god of fire.
     Aetna   the volcano in Sicily.
545 *Hespery*   the west coast of Italy.
547 *Fierce mastiffs*   Scylla.
548 *Alba*   Alba Longa, the oldest Latin town, founded by Ascanius.
550 *Theban brothers*   Polynices and Eteocles, inveterate enemies.
551 *hinges*   axis.

553   *Calpe*   Gibraltar.
563   *Bellona*   the war goddess.
564   *Sibyl*   properly, Cybele, goddess of nature and the underworld.
568   *shright*   shrieked.
570   *Erinnys*   a Fury.
573   *Lycurgus*   Thracian king who destroyed the vines of Diony-
      sus, wounding himself in his rage.
574   *Agave*   mother of Pentheus, king of Thebes, who suppressed
      the worship of Dionysus, and was torn to pieces by Bacchantes
      among whom were his mother and sister.
      Megaera   a Fury.
575   *Alcides*   Hercules.
576   *He . . . face*   i.e., although he had already seen hell.
581   *Marius*   Roman general defeated by Sulla.
      Tav'ron   Taverone, the Anio, into which, on Sulla's orders,
      the exhumed body of Marius was thrown.
582   *boors*   peasants.
583   *ostents*   omens.
585   *or Luna*   the city was also called Luna from the crescent
      shape of its harbor.
586   *pyromancy*   interpreting the movements of lightning.
593   *lustration*   ritual purification.
595–6 *vestures . . . manner*   a special way of wearing the toga, with
      one end covering the head and the other wrapped around the
      waist.
599   *saint*   the statue of Cybele.
602   *Salii*   priests of Mars.
603   *flamens*   priests.
605   *what . . . blasted*   something that had been struck by lightning.
607   *bidental*   sacred; places struck by lightning were holy.
609   *salt leaven*   salted flour, used in sacrifices.
625   *pretendeth*   signifies.
635   *Tages*   grandson of Jupiter, who taught the Etruscans sooth-
      saying.
640   *tuneful planeting*   the music of the spheres.
650   *period*   end point.
651   *blue*   "the color of plagues and things hurtful" (OED).
652   *Ganymede*   Aquarius.
      Deucalion's flood   the universal flood.
653   *fleeting*   rushing.
655   *Nemean beast*   the constellation Leo, the Nemean lion de-
      feated by Hercules.

659   *cleyes*   claws.
661   *Hermes*   Mercury.
663   *virtue*   power.
674   *Maenas*   priestess of Dionysus.
       Pindus   a mountain in Thessaly.
677   *Paean*   Apollo (literally, healer).
680   *Philippi*   in Macedonia, where Octavianus and Antony de-
       feated Brutus and Cassius in the crucial battle of the Civil
       War, 42 B.C. But the place was conventionally identified with
       Pharsalus, so that Lucan's reference is in fact to both battles.
683   *Pelusian sea*   Pompey was killed at Pelusium.
684   *headless trunk*   Pompey.
686   *doubtful*   untrustworthy.
687   *Emathian*   Macedonian.
688–9 *mounts Pyrene*   the Pyrenees.

THE PASSIONATE SHEPHERD TO HIS LOVE

The title is first found in the miscellany *England's Helicon* (1600).
There is no reason to consider it authorial.

11   *kirtle*   coat or smock, such as would be worn by a shepherd.
20–1   Thy dishes shall be filled with meat
       Such as the gods do use to eat
       Shall one and every table be
       Prepared each day for thee and me. *Thornborourgh MS.*

SIR WALTER RALEGH: *THE NYMPH'S REPLY*

This poem appeared in *England's Helicon* (1600) following Mar-
lowe's poem.

ANONYMOUS: *ANOTHER OF THE SAME*
NATURE, MADE SINCE

Followed the Ralegh poem in *England's Helicon*.

8   *Phoebus*   the sun.
25   *trimly dight*   nicely adorned.
27   *Flora*   goddess of flowers.

JOHN DONNE: *THE BAIT*

Included in *Songs and Sonnets* (*Poems*, London, 1633); presumably written around 1600.

23 *curious* elaborately made.
   sleave-silk silk divided into very fine strands.

J. PAULIN: *LOVE'S CONTENTMENT*

Love's Contentment appears in MS. Harley 6918 (fol. 92), a miscellaneous collection of poems. Of those in the same hand as *Love's Contentment*, the latest that can be dated were written in the early 1640s. I have been unable to identify J. Paulin. The poem was reprinted by Bullen in *Speculum Amantis* with "letters" (line 31) mysteriously, if elegantly, emended to "numbers."

8 *Utopian commonweal* As in Gonzalo's imaginary ideal kingdom in *The Tempest*, there is "no name of magistrate . . . , No occupation; all men idle, all . . . , No sovereignty" (II i 145 ff.).

24 *homebred schismatic* In Caroline England on the verge of civil war, this had a variety of applications, ranging from political schismatics who refused Charles his ship money to Scottish Presbyterians who resisted the imposition of the new prayer book. Since Charles's "timely force" was, on the whole, singularly ineffective, the following two lines have an ironic force that it is difficult to believe was unintentional.

ON THE DEATH OF SIR ROGER MANWOOD

The literal prose translation is by the editor.

3 *Alcides* Hercules, Jove's son by Alcmena.
7 *Acheron* a river in Hades.
10 *Dis* or Pluto, king of the Underworld.

A Dictionary of Classical Names

Cross-references are indicated by names in boldface

Abydos   A town on the Asian coast of the Hellespont opposite Sestos.
Acanthides   Goldfinches (or, in Chapman's version, thistle-warps), into which Hero and Leander were metamorphosed.
Accius, Lucius   (d. 180 B.C.). Roman tragedian, translator of Sophocles.
Achelous   Son of Oceanus, or alternatively of the sun. He was a rival for the hand of **Deianira**, and fought against **Hercules**, changing himself first into a serpent and then into an ox. Hercules broke off one of his horns, which became the Cornucopia or horn of plenty. Upon his defeat, Achelous was transformed into the river in Epirus that bears his name.
Acheron   A river in Epirus, called by Homer one of the rivers of Hades. The name is also used for Hades itself.
Achilles   Son of Peleus and **Thetis**. In his infancy, his mother attempted to make him immortal by dipping him in the **Styx** (or, alternatively, by holding him in a fire), but the heel by which she held him remained vulnerable and ultimately bore the wound that caused his death. He attempted to avoid the Trojan War by dressing as a woman, but was discovered and conscripted by **Ulysses**. He was the greatest of the Greek heroes and necessary to their victory, but with his glory went a reputation for surliness and dishonorable behavior. He was killed by **Paris**.
Actaeon   A huntsman. He came upon **Diana** and her nymphs bathing, and as a punishment for seeing them naked was transformed into a stag and killed by his own hounds.
Adolesche   The name means "chatterer"; the character is Chapman's invention.
Adon or **Adonis**   Child of Myrrha by an incestuous relationship with her father Cinyras. Adonis was the lover of Venus, who cautioned him against indulging his favorite passion, hunting, lest the wild beasts, who are her inveterate enemies, attempt to make her suffer through wounding him. The advice was ignored, and he was killed by a boar who gored him in the groin.
Aedone   Chapman apparently coined the name from *hedone,* pleasure.

Aeneas   Trojan prince, son of Anchises and Venus. He fled the sack of Troy, was shipwrecked at Carthage, where he loved the queen, **Dido,** but was prevailed upon by divine command to abandon her. She committed suicide, and he sailed to Italy to conquer Latium and found the Roman empire.

Aesope   Asopus, a Thessalian river-god who loved **Thebe.**

Aetolia   A country in central Greece.

Agamemnon   Son of **Atreus,** and commander of the Greek forces during the Trojan War. Upon his return to his kingdom of **Mycenae,** he was murdered by his queen Clytemnestra and her lover Aegisthus, his cousin; they in turn were killed by his son **Orestes.**

Agave   Daughter of Cadmus and **Hermione** and mother of Pentheus, king of Thebes. She was a votary of Bacchus, and when Pentheus undertook to suppress the bacchic cult she joined in the rout of bacchantes that tore him to pieces.

Agneia   The name means "purity."

Ajax   Name of two heroes. 1. Son of Telamon, and after **Achilles** the greatest of the Greek warriors at **Troy.** When the dead Achilles' armor was awarded to **Ulysses,** instead of to him, Ajax went mad and slew a flock of sheep, thinking they were the **Atrides,** who had deprived him of the prize. He then committed suicide. 2. Son of Oïleus. During the sack of Troy he tried to rape **Cassandra,** for which **Minerva** destroyed his ship as he was returning home.

Alba Longa   The oldest Roman city, founded by Ascanius, son of **Aeneas.**

Alcides   Hercules; a matronymic from his mother **Alcmena**'s father Alcaeus.

Alcinous   In the *Odyssey,* king of Phaeacia. He was a patron of agriculture and had fruit that grew all the year.

Alcmane   Chapman takes the name from a Spartan poet of the seventh century B.C.

Alcmena   Wife of Amphitryon. **Jupiter** slept with her and tripled the length of the night to increase his time with her. She bore twin sons, **Hercules,** the child of Jupiter, and Iphicles, the child of Amphitryon.

Alpheus   Arcadian river. The river god loved the nymph Arethusa and pursued her until, in Ortygia, near Syracuse, **Diana** transformed her into a spring.

Amymone   One of the Danaides, daughter of **Danaus** and **Europa.** She married **Enceladus,** but murdered him on their wedding night on the instructions of her father. She was attacked by a satyr, but rescued by **Neptune** (or Poseidon), who loved her and created a fountain bearing her name.

Andromache   Wife of **Hector**.

Andromeda   Ethiopian princess, daughter of **Cepheus** and Cassiopea. Her mother boasted that she was more beautiful than the Nereids. This angered **Neptune**, who sent a sea monster to ravage the land. To appease the god, Andromeda was thrown to the monster, but was rescued by **Perseus**.

Anubis   Egyptian dog-headed god, often identified with **Mercury**; he is ruler of the dead and conducts their spirits to Hades.

Aonian   Pertaining to the muses, from their sacred mountain Helicon, in Aonia.

Apis   Egyptian bull-god associated with the worship of **Isis**.

Apollo   Son of **Jupiter** and Latona (or Leto), god of the sun, patron of rational poetry and song and of the music of strings, bringer of plagues and also their healer, incumbent of numerous oracles, the most famous of which was at Delphi.

Arachne   A superlative weaver. She challenged **Minerva** to a contest, and wove a tapestry depicting the love affairs of the gods. The work was perfect, but the subject offended the goddess, who tore the cloth in shreds. Arachne hanged herself in despair and was transformed into a spider.

Araris   The river Saone.

Aratus   Greek poet of the third century B.C., author of the *Phaenomena*, a poem on astronomy.

Arcadia   In the central Peloponnesus, a mountainous and landlocked country; traditionally the home of Pan and hence of pastoral poetry and music.

Argo or *Argos*   **Jason**'s ship.

Argos   Capital of Argolis in Peloponnesus.

Argus   See **Io**.

Ariadne   Princess of Crete, daughter of **Minos** and Pasiphae. She fell in love with **Theseus**, prince of Athens, whom she rescued from the labyrinth. He later abandoned her on the island of Naxos.

Arruns   A soothsayer in Lucan.

Ascraeus   Hesiod, born in Ascra, in Boeotia.

Atalanta   Arcadian beauty, a superlative runner. Her suitors were required to race with her. Hippomenes prayed to Venus for aid, and she gave him three golden apples, which he threw before Atalanta whenever she took the lead; she stopped to pick them up and he won the race. The lovers subsequently offended Venus by not giving thanks and were transformed into wild beasts. Atalanta was with Meleager at the hunt of the Calydonian boar and was first to wound the animal.

Atax   The river Aude.

Ate   Goddess of discord.

Atreus   King of **Mycenae**, son of **Pelops**, father of **Agamemnon** and Menelaus. His brother Thyestes seduced Atreus's wife, by whom he had two sons. In revenge, Atreus killed the sons and served them up to Thyestes at a banquet. He was eventually assassinated by Aegisthus, Thyestes's son.

Atrides   **Agamemnon** and Menelaus, sons of **Atreus**.

Atthaea   Oreithyia, wife of **Boreas** the north wind. The name is Chapman's coinage, from the fact that she was princess of Attica.

Aurora   The dawn. She married Tithonus, who was granted immortality but not eternal youth. She also loved **Cephalus** and **Orion**.

Auster   The south wind.

Averni   Properly Arverni, a Gallic tribe in the Auvergne.

Avernus, Averne   A lake in Campania (southern Italy) reputed to be the entrance to hell. Also one of the rivers in hell and a poetic name for the underworld.

Axon   The Axones, who lived near the river Axona (now the Aisne) in Gallia Belgica.

Bacchus or **Dionysus**   God of wine, theater, and ecstatic poetry. He is said to have ridden in triumph as far as the Ganges; his chariot was drawn by tigers. See **Semele**.

Bardi   An order of sacred poets in ancient Gaul.

Batavia   Holland.

Bellona   Goddess of war.

Bidental   A place struck by lightning that was afterward consecrated by the sacrifice of a sheep (*bidens*).

Bithynia   A country in Asia Minor.

Bituriges   A tribe of Aquitanian Gaul.

Briseis   **Achilles**' concubine, captured in battle. She was expropriated by **Agamemnon** and this produced the wrath of Achilles that is the subject of the *Iliad*. See **Chryseis**.

Boreas   The north wind. He carried off Oreithyia, daughter of Erechtheus, king of Athens, to be his wife. See **Atthaea**.

Caesar   The title adopted by Roman emperors, after C. Julius Caesar, founder of the empire (d. 44 B.C.).

Callimachus   (third century B.C.) Alexandrian elegiac poet.

Callisto   Princess of **Arcadia** and an attendant of **Diana**. **Jupiter** loved her and seduced her by taking the form of Diana. Their child was called Arcas. **Juno** transformed Callisto into a bear, but Jupiter stellified her as Ursa Major.

Calpe Gibraltar.

Calvus, Cornelius Licinius Famous orator and poet and close friend of Catullus.

Calydon A city in **Aetolia**, capital of King Oeneus, the father of Meleager and **Deianira**. The Calydonian Boar was a monstrous animal sent by **Diana** to ravage the country as punishment for the neglect of her worship. It was hunted and killed by Meleager, accompanied by the greatest heroes of the time. See **Atalanta**.

Calypso In the *Odyssey,* one of the Oceanides, who reigned on the island of Ogygia. She fell in love with **Ulysses**, who was shipwrecked there, and offered him immortality if he would remain with her. He refused, though he stayed for seven years and had two sons by her.

Camillus, M. Furius (d. 365 B.C.) Roman hero who freed Rome from the invading Gauls.

Canopus A city near Alexandria connected with the worship of **Isis**.

Capitol Marlowe uses the term to refer to the capital of Latium, **Alba Longa**.

Cares Caria, in Asia Minor.

Carpathus An island in the Aegean between Crete and Rhodes, from which the sea between Crete and Rhodes is called the Carpathian Sea. See **Proteus**.

Carra Properly Carrae or Carrhae, in Mesopotamia, where **Crassus** was defeated and killed in 53 B.C.

Cassandra Daughter of **Priam**, king of **Troy**. She was reputedly mad, but had the gift of prophecy; her predictions, however, were invariably disregarded. She became the spoil of **Agamemnon**, who took her home to **Argos**, where she was murdered with him.

Cassiopea See **Andromeda**.

Castor and **Pollux** Children of **Leda** by **Jupiter**, and the patrons of navigation. Because they were twins and half-mortal, they spent alternate days in heaven.

Cato, M. Porcius Great-grandson of Cato the Censor, republican and opponent of Caesar. He was besieged by Caesar's forces at Utica in 46 B.C., and committed suicide.

Cayc The Cayci (or Chauci), a German tribe.

Centaurs A race in Thessaly, half man and half horse. They were descended from **Ixion**. See **Lapiths**.

Cephalus A famous hunter, husband of Procris, loved by **Aurora**.

Cepheus King of Ethiopia, father of Andromeda by **Cassiopea**. He was one of the Argonauts. See **Andromeda**.

Cerannia The Ceraunian mountains in Epirus.

Ceremony The goddess is Chapman's invention.

Ceres or **Demeter**   Goddess of agriculture and mother of Proserpine. When her daughter was carried off by Pluto (or **Dis**), god of the underworld, she went into deep mourning, but managed to persuade **Jupiter** to allow Proserpine to spend six months of the year on earth with her. Proserpine's annual return is the beginning of spring. Ceres' home is traditionally said to be in Crete.

Chaos   The oldest of the gods, the original matter from which the universe was formed. His wife was Darkness, his children Nox and **Erebus**.

Charybdis   A dangerous whirlpool on the Sicilian coast opposite the shoals of **Scylla**. Charybdis was a woman who stole the cattle of **Hercules**. and was punished by a metamorphosis embodying her greed.

Chreste   Chapman's coinage from *chrestos*, good, with a pun on Latin *crista*, a bird's crest, hence "Chreste with the tufted crown" (*H and L*, IV 232).

Chryseis   Daughter of Chryses, a priest of **Apollo**. She was captured and held prisoner by **Agamemnon**, but Apollo sent a plague upon the Greeks and Chryseis was returned to her father. It was the loss of Chryseis that prompted Agamemnon to demand **Achilles'** prisoner **Briseis** for himself.

Cilicia   A country in Asia Minor.

Cimbrians   The Cimbri, a German tribe who invaded Rome in 109 B.C. They were defeated by **Marius**.

Cinga   The Cinca River, in Spain.

Circe   An enchantress, queen of the island of Aeaea, the daughter of the sun and the sea nymph Perseis. **Ulysses** visited her on his voyage home, and his shipmates were transformed into swine by her sensual pleasures. The hero himself was protected from this metamorphosis by the magic herb *moly,* which he had received from **Mercury**. He remained with Circe for a year and had a child, or in some versions two children by her. After Ulysses' death either Circe or her daughter Cassiphone became the wife of his son Telemachus.

Cisalpine   The south, or Roman side of the Alps.

Colchis   On the Black Sea, home of Medea. See **Jason**.

Corcyra   Corfu; **Ovid** recalls that **Tibullus** had once been taken ill there.

Corsic   Corsican.

Cotta, G. Aurelius (124–73 B.C.).   Statesman and orator. He was consul in 75 B.C., and in 74 B.C. became pro-consul of Gaul. In 73 he was granted a triumph, but died of an old wound the day before its celebration.

Crassus, M. Licinius (d. 53 B.C.).   Roman general. He put down the rebellion of Spartacus, and was made consul with **Pompey**. He subsequently became censor, and triumvir with Pompey and Caesar. He was betrayed and murdered on an expedition to **Parthia**.

Creusa   1. Daughter of Creon, king of Corinth, Jason's second wife. She was killed by a poisoned robe sent her by Medea. See **Jason**. 2. Daughter of **Priam** and Hecuba, first wife of **Aeneas** and mother of Ascanius. 3. Daughter of Erechtheus, king of Athens, wife of Xuthus (**Xanthus** in Marlowe) and mother of Ion.

Cupid   God of love (literally, "desire"), son of Venus and **Mars**, or in another version, **Mercury**.

Curio, C. Scribonius   Tribune, originally a supporter of **Pompey**, but finally one of Caesar's most devoted followers. He was the son of Q. Curio, who in the Senate had called Caesar "every woman's man and every man's woman."

Curius   M. Curius Dentatus, Roman leader of the third century B.C. famous for his frugality and piety.

Cyclops   A race of giants, sons of Heaven and Earth. They had a single eye in the middle of the forehead. They assisted **Vulcan** at his forge, and made **Jupiter**'s thunderbolts. Their king Polyphemus captured **Ulysses** and twelve of his shipmates, and devoured all but the hero, who succeeded in blinding the Cyclops and escaping.

Cybele   Daughter of Heaven and Earth, and wife of **Saturn**. She is goddess of nature and of the underworld. Marlowe confuses her with Sybil.

Cynthia   The moon, a name of **Diana**, born on Mount Cynthus.

Cyprias   Venus, from Cyprus, her birthplace.

Cyprides   Venus, born on the island of Cyprus.

Cythera   Now Cerigo, an island in the Peloponnesus. It was the favorite home of Venus (and in some versions her birthplace), hence her surname Cytherea.

Danae   Princess of **Argos**. She was locked in a tower by her father, who had been told by an oracle that his grandson would put him to death. But **Jupiter**, who loved her, gained access to her as a shower of gold. Their child was **Perseus**.

Danaus   King of Egypt, and later of **Argos**. He commanded his fifty daughters, the Danaides, to murder their husbands on their wedding night, because an oracle had warned him that he would be destroyed by a son-in-law. All but one daughter complied.

Dapsilis   The name means "abundant"; Chapman's invention.

Deianira   Princess of **Aetolia** and wife of **Hercules** who competed with **Achelous** for her hand. While she was traveling with Hercules the centaur Nessus attempted to carry her off, and Hercules killed him with a poisoned arrow. As he died, Nessus gave Deianira a cloak stained with his infected blood, which he told her would strengthen her husband's love for her. Years later, jealous of Hercules' liaison with Iole, Deianira gave him the cloak, which immediately poisoned and destroyed him.

Delia One of **Tibullus**'s mistresses, to whom he addressed poems.

Delphian Pertaining to the oracle of Apollo at Delphi, hence oracular.

Demophoön Son of **Theseus** and **Phaedra**, and king of Athens. Returning from the Trojan War, he was hospitably received by **Phyllis**, queen of Thrace, and became her lover. He subsequently abandoned her, however, and she hanged herself.

Deucalion Son of **Prometheus** and husband of Pyrrha. He was a Greek Noah, and, after the universal flood, Deucalion repeopled the earth by throwing stones behind him, which became men and women.

Diana In Greek, Artemis, goddess of the hunt. She was devoted to chastity, but as the moon goddess was also known as Lucina, the patroness of childbirth, and Hecate, the goddess of the underworld.

Dido or **Elisa** Founder and queen of Carthage. Her husband, Sichaeus, had been murdered by Pygmalion, king of Tyre, and Dido fled with her followers to found a new colony. She was wooed by Iarbas, a neighboring king, but fell in love with **Aeneas** when he was shipwrecked on her shores. After he abandoned her she had a funeral pyre built and stabbed herself on top of it; it was this action that earned her the name of Dido, or "valiant."

Diomedes Son of Tydeus and king of **Aetolia**, a Greek hero in the Trojan War. He wounded the goddess Venus in battle before **Troy**.

Dipsas An old bawd who corrupts **Ovid**'s Corinna. The name means "thirsty."

Dis Pluto, king of the underworld, son of **Saturn** and **Ops**, and brother of **Jupiter** and **Neptune**, with whom he divided the universe. See **Ceres**.

Doric, Dorian The solemn and heroic mode, apparently confused by Marlowe with the gentle and pathetic **Lydian**.

Ecte The name means "pity"; the figure is invented by Chapman.

Egeria A water nymph. According to **Ovid** she became the wife of **Numa Pompilius**, second king of Rome, and was transformed into a fountain after his death.

Electra 1. Chief of the Pleiades, seven daughters of Pleione and Atlas, who were stellified after their death. 2. The sister of **Orestes**.

Eleius Pertaining to Elis, where the Olympic games were held. The country was famous for its horses.

Eleusina **Ceres**, or Demeter, from Eleusis, where her mysteries were celebrated.

Elisa Dido Elisa was in fact her name, and Dido was an honorific surname meaning "valiant."

Elysium That part of the underworld where the souls of heroes spent the afterlife in eternal bliss.

Emathia Old and poetic name of Macedonia and Thessaly.

Enceladus The most powerful of the giants, son of Earth and **Titan**. He was a leader of the attempt to overthrow the Olympian gods, and was thwarted by **Jupiter**'s thunderbolts. He was imprisoned beneath Mount Etna in Sicily.

Endymion A shepherd loved by the moon. He was granted eternal youth and eternal sleep, so that **Diana** could enjoy his beauty forever.

Enipeus A river in the Peloponnesus. The nymph **Tyro** fell in love with the river god, but she was seduced by **Neptune**, who took the shape of Enipeus.

Ennius (239–169 B.C.). Founder of Roman epic poetry.

Erebus Son of **Chaos** and Darkness, husband of Night; their children were Light and Day. His name is often used to mean the underworld.

Erinnyes The Eumenides, or Furies, the gods' ministers of vengeance and retribution. Their names were **Tisiphone**, **Megaera**, and Alecto, and, according to some writers, **Nemesis**. "Eumenides" is a euphemism, meaning "the kindly ones."

Eronusis Dissimulation; the figure is Chapman's invention.

Eryx A mountain in Sicily where Venus had a shrine, whence her surname Erycina.

Eteocles See **Polynices**.

Etruria Country of the Etruscans, across the Tiber from Rome.

Eucharis The name means "gracious."

Euripus A narrow strait separating the island of Euboea from Greece.

Europa A princess of Phoenicia. **Jupiter** transformed himself into a bull and carried her off. She had three sons by him, **Minos**, king of Crete, Sarpedon, and Rhadamanthus.

Eurus The east wind.

Euxine Sea The modern Black Sea.

Evadne Marlowe's error for Euanthe, daughter of the river god Asopus; she was loved by Nilus, the river Nile.

Figulus A soothsayer in Lucan.

Flamens *flamines*, the fifteen chief priests of Rome, each of whom presided over the worship of a particular god.

Flora Goddess of flowers. She was originally a nymph named Chloris,

and, according to **Ovid**, was transformed into the goddess of flowers after her rape by Zephyrus the west wind.
Furies   See **Erinnyes**.

Gabine   Relating to a particular way of wearing the toga, with one end over the head and the other around the waist.
Galatea   A sea nymph, daughter of **Nereus**. She was loved by the cyclops Polyphemus, but rejected him in favor of the shepherd Acis. Polyphemus killed Acis with a huge rock, and Galatea transformed the dead shepherd into a fountain.
Gallus, Cornelius   (d. A.D. 26). Roman amatory poet. His poems were written to a mistress called Lycoris; he was a friend of Virgil, and is the subject of his tenth *Eclogue*.
Ganymede   A beautiful Phrygian boy carried off by **Jupiter** in the form of an eagle, to be his cupbearer in place of **Hebe**, and to be his lover. In some versions of the myth he became the constellation Aquarius.
Gebenna   The Cevennes mountains, in Gaul.
Gracchus, Tiberius, and **Caius**   Popular reformers overthrown by the Senate in 133 and 121 B.C.
Graces   Or Charites, daughters of Venus and **Bacchus**, or in some versions **Jupiter**. Their names are Aglaia, Thalia, and Euphrosyne, and they are attendants of Venus.
Gyges   Properly Gyes, one of the giants, a son of Uranus.

Haemus   A mountain dividing Thessaly from Thrace. Haemus was the son of **Boreas**, transformed into a mountain for aspiring to divinity.
Halesus   Son of **Agamemnon**, founder of the Falisci, a tribe in Campania.
Hannibal   Carthaginian commander during the Second Punic War, 218–201 B.C. He crossed the Alps with a huge army and elephants, and conquered northern Italy, inflicting great losses on the Romans at Carrae. But he neglected to press his advantage to the gates of Rome, and withdrew to Capua, which became his base of operations for the next thirteen years. He was recalled to Carthage to repel a Roman invasion of North Africa, and was defeated by Scipio.
Hebe   The daughter of **Jupiter** and **Juno**, Jupiter's cupbearer before **Ganymede**. The name means "youth."
Hector   Prince of **Troy**, son of **Priam** and Hecuba, and the greatest of the Trojan heroes. He died at the hands of **Achilles** and his myrmidons, and his body was dragged behind Achilles' chariot around the walls of Troy.
Helen   Daughter of **Leda** and Tyndarus. She married Menelaus, king

of Sparta, but was carried off by **Paris** to **Troy**, thus precipitating the Trojan war. After Paris's death she married his brother Deiphobus; however when Troy fell, she returned to Sparta with Menelaus. See **Leda.**

Helle   Daughter of Athamas, king of Thebes. To avoid the persecution of her stepmother, Ino, she fled on a golden flying ram, but became dizzy and fell into the sea and drowned. The spot where she fell was named for her, the Hellespont.

Hercules   Son of **Jupiter** and **Alcmena.** In his adolescence he chose to follow the goddess of Virtue rather than Pleasure, but this appears to have been his last moral action. His heroism consisted in the exercise of pure power. By Jupiter's command Hercules was subject to the will of Eurystheus, king of **Argos,** and it was at his behest that the famous twelve labors were performed. He married **Deianira,** by whom he was inadvertently killed.

Hermaphroditus   Son of Venus and **Mercury.** When he was bathing in a fountain the local nymph Salmacis fell in love with him. He rejected her, but she embraced him, and at her prayer the gods united them in a single body.

Hermes   See **Mercury.**

Hermione   Leander's sister, an invention of Chapman's. The name is that of the wife of **Orestes,** daughter of Menelaus and **Helen.**

Hesiod   One of the most ancient Greek poets whose work is extant; he himself says he lived at Ascra, near Mount Helicon, and ancient tradition makes him contemporary with Homer.

Hesperides   The three daughters of **Hesperus,** or, in some versions, of his brother Atlas by Hesperus's daughter Hesperis. In their garden were the golden apples of immortality, guarded by a dragon. Obtaining the apples was one of the labors of **Hercules.**

Hesperus   The evening star, brother of Atlas.

Hespery, Hesperia   In Lucan, the west coast of Italy. The name derives from Hesper, the evening star (or the setting sun); hence Hesperia was Italy to the Greeks, Spain to the Romans.

Hesus   Esus, a Gallic god identified with **Mercury.**

Hetrurian   Etrurian, Tuscan.

Hippodamia   1. Wife of **Pelops.** 2. Daughter of Adrastus, king of **Argos,** and wife of Pirithous, king of the **Lapiths.** At her wedding, the **Centaur** Eurytus attacked her, precipitating the great war between the Lapiths and Centaurs.

Hippolytus   Son of **Theseus,** king of Athens. **Phaedra,** his stepmother, fell in love with him, but he refused her, and she denounced him to Theseus. Hippolytus fled, but perished when his horses were terrified by **Neptune**, to whom Theseus had prayed for vengeance. According to some writers, Hippolytus was restored to life by **Diana**, who took pity on his chaste virtue.

Hippomenes   See **Atalanta**.

Hymen   God of marriage.

Hypsipyle   Queen of Lemnos, abandoned by **Jason**, to whom she was betrothed. She is the writer of the sixth of **Ovid**'s *Heroides*.

Hyrcania   A country in Asia on the Caspian Sea.

Iasion   A Cretan youth loved by **Ceres**, by whom she had a son named Plutus.

Iberia   The Spanish peninsula.

Icarius   An Athenian to whom Dionysus gave the secret of his vine. He was murdered by peasants to whom he gave wine. His daughter Erigone was led by his faithful dog Moera to the place where his body was hidden. As a reward, the dog was translated to the heavens as Canicula, or Canis Minor. Icarius became Boötes, and Erigone the constellation Virgo.

Idalium   A town in Cyprus where there was a grove consecrated to Venus.

Ide, Ida   A mountain near **Troy** upon which **Paris**, with a golden apple to award to the goddess of wisdom, **Minerva**; of power, **Juno**; or of beauty, Venus, chose the last. The decision precipitated the Trojan War, and was universally deplored by commentators from antiquity to the Renaissance.

Ilia or **Rhea Silvia**   Daughter of Numitor, king of Alba. Her uncle Amulius was next in line of succession for the crown, and made her a vestal to prevent her having sons who would dispossess him. But she was raped by **Mars**, and bore Romulus and **Remus**. She eventually became the wife of Tiburinus, the god of the river Tiber.

Inachus   A river god in **Argos**, who loved the nymph Melie.

Io   Daughter of **Inachus** and priestess of **Juno** at **Argos**. **Jupiter** fell in love with her, but Juno discovered them together, and to protect Io from Juno's rage, Jupiter transformed her into a cow. Juno detected the metamorphosis, however, and sent the hundred-eyed monster Argus to watch Io. Argus was killed by **Mercury** at Jupiter's command, but Io was then pursued by a gadfly of Juno's. She was restored to her proper form when she reached the Nile. She became the goddess **Isis**.

Ionian   One of the four Greek races; they migrated to Asia Minor and founded Ionia.

Isara   The river Isère.

Isis   The Egyptian moon goddess, controlling fertility. She was identified with Venus, **Minerva**, and **Diana**. She was sister of **Osiris**, whom she also married. See **Io**.

Itys   See **Philomel**.

Iulus   Ascanius, son of **Aeneas**.

Ixion   An ungrateful and treacherous king of Thessaly. When he was ostracized by his countrymen for the murder of his father-in-law, **Jupiter** took pity on him and brought him to Olympus; but Ixion repaid this kindness by trying to seduce **Juno**. Apprised of this attempt, Jupiter created a false Juno out of cloud and sent it to Ixion, and from this union the **Centaurs** were born. Ixion was punished by being bound on a wheel perpetually turning in hell.

Janus   Guardian of doorways, protector of the state during wars, bringer of peace, controller of the seasons and of the beginning and end of the year. The gates of his temple in Rome were open during war, shut in peacetime. He is depicted as having two faces, looking forward and behind.

Jason   The Argonaut, son of Aeson. He formed an expedition to recover the Golden Fleece from Aeëtes, king of Colchis, and was accompanied by the greatest heroes of Greece. In Colchis Jason fulfilled all the conditions Aeëtes set for him, which included taming fire-breathing oxen, sowing dragons' teeth and defeating the soldiers that sprang from them, and killing a dragon. He married Medea, Aeëtes' daughter, and a famous enchantress, and returned in triumph to Greece. He later divorced Medea, who in revenge killed their children and his new wife, **Creusa**.

Jove   See **Jupiter**.

Julia   (d. 54 B.C.). Daughter of Caesar and wife of **Pompey**.

Juno   Sister and wife of **Jupiter** and queen of the Olympian gods. The peacock was sacred to her, as was the lily, originally a purple flower that turned white when a drop of her milk fell on it. She was patroness of marriage and motherhood, as well as of riches and power.

Jupiter   Ruler of the Olympian gods. He was the son of **Saturn**, who attempted to devour him in his infancy, but he was saved by his mother, **Ops**. He overthrew his father, and divided the kingdom of the world with his brothers **Neptune** and **Pluto**. His wife was **Juno**, but his consorts were numerous and his progeny innumerable.

Lachesis   One of the Parcae, or Fates. She spins the thread that determines the length of man's life.

Laelius   Chief centurion under Caesar, credited by Lucan with persuading the army to march on Rome.

Lais   Famous Greek courtesan, daughter of Timandra the mistress of Alcibiades.

Laodamia   Wife of **Protesilaus**.

Laomedon   King of Troy, father of **Priam**. He was the son of Ilus, whence the name Ilium for Troy.

Lapiths   A Thessalian tribe. Their great battle with the **Centaurs** began at the wedding of the Lapith Pirithous and **Hippodamia**.

Latinus   See **Lavinia**

Latium   The Italian district in which Rome is situated.

Lavinia   Daughter of Latinus, king of **Latium**, and wife of **Aeneas**. She had been engaged to her kinsman Turnus, but an oracle said she must marry a foreign prince, and Latinus determined to give her to Aeneas. To prevent the marriage, Turnus attempted to drive the Trojans from Italy, and was killed in the war.

Lemannus   Lake Geneva.

Leda   Daughter of Thespius and queen of Sparta. **Jupiter** loved her, and seduced her in the shape of a swan. She gave birth to an egg, from which hatched **Castor** and **Pollux**. She also gave birth to Clytemnestra and **Helen**.

Leuca   1. Leucas, or Leucadia, an island in the Ionian sea, now Santa Maura. 2. Incorrectly the country of the Leuci, a tribe in Gallia Belgica.

Leucote   Chapman's name for Venus's swan is derived from *leukotas*, whiteness.

Ligurians   The Ligures, a people in modern Piedmont.

Lingones   A Gallic tribe pacified by Julius Caesar.

Linus   Mythical poet, the son of **Apollo**.

Luca   An Etrurian town, now Lucca; also called Luna because of the crescent shape of its harbor.

Lucifer   The morning star, literally "light-bringer."

Lucina   Goddess of childbirth. See **Diana**.

Lucretius Carus, T.T.   Roman poet and philosopher (98-55 B.C.), author of *De Rerum Natura*.

Luna   The moon. Also a name for **Luca**.

Lycoris   See **Gallus**

Lycurgus   King of Thrace. He abolished the worship of **Bacchus**, for which he was blinded by the gods. In some versions of the story, he cut off his own legs, thinking they were vines.

Lydian   Pertaining to Lydia, the country in Asia Minor from which, according to legend, the Etruscans came. It gave its name to one of the three principal modes of Greek music, soft and pathetic, though

Marlowe apparently confused the Lydian with the warlike **Dorian** mode.

Macareus   Son of Aeolus, and brother and husband of Canace. He is the subject of the ninth of **Ovid**'s *Heroides*.

Macer, Aemilius   Epic poet. Friend of **Ovid**'s.

Maenas   A priestess of **Bacchus** or Dionysus.

Malea   Southern tip of the Spartan peninsula.

Marcellus   In Lucan, M. Claudius Marcellus, leading opponent of Caesar.

Marius, Gaius   (157-86 B.C.). Roman general. He waged successful campaigns in Africa, and conquered the Cimbri. He was elected consul seven times, but opposed the dictator Sulla, and in 88 B.C. was defeated by him. He escaped to Africa, but shortly returned to Rome, joined forces with Cinna, captured the city after exceptionally bloodthirsty engagements, and declared himself and Cinna consuls. He died sixteen days later.

Mars   Son of **Jupiter** and **Juno**, god of war, adulterous consort of Venus (wife of **Vulcan**) by whom he was the father of **Cupid** and Harmonia.

Megaera   One of the Furies.

Memnon   Son of **Aurora** and **Tithonus**. He was killed at **Troy** by **Achilles**, but **Jupiter** granted him immortality. A flock of birds rose from his funeral pyre, and fought till half of them fell into the blaze to appease his spirit. The birds were said to return annually to the tomb of Memnon and repeat the battle.

Memphis   Egyptian city connected with the worship of **Isis**.

Menander   (341–291 B.C.). Greek comic dramatist.

Mercury   or in Greek Hermes, son of **Jupiter** and Maia. He is the messenger of the gods, and hence the patron of prose and rhetoric, inventor of the lyre, patron of thieves and lying, but also of philosophy and "hermetic" (from Hermes) knowledge, since he was identified with the Egyptian Thoth, god of wisdom.

Mevania   Bevágna, in Umbria, birthplace of Propertius.

Midas   King of **Phrygia**. When Dionysus offered to grant him any wish, he foolishly asked that whatever he touched might turn to gold, but had to beg for the gift to be rescinded when even his food was transformed. Midas preferred the music of Pan to that of **Apollo**, and as a reward for this further instance of stupidity, Apollo gave him an ass's ears.

Milo   T. Annius Milo Papianus, tribune in 57 B.C. He murdered Publius Clodius, formerly his cotribune, in 52 B.C., and was unsuccessfully defended by Cicero.

Minerva   or Pallas Athene, sprang fully grown from the head of **Jupiter**. She was the goddess of wisdom and the arts, but also of war. The owl and the cock were sacred to her.

Minos   King of Crete, son of **Jupiter** and **Europa**, and a renowned lawmaker. After his death he became the chief judge of the underworld. (His grandson, also named Minos, was the husband of Pasiphaë, father of **Ariadne** and **Phaedra** and builder of the labyrinth.)

Morpheus   Son of Somnus and the god of sleep.

Mulciber   **Vulcan**, god of fire. The name means "melter."

Munda   A town in Spain where in 45 B.C. Caesar defeated the sons of **Pompey**, and thus put an end to the Roman republic.

Musaeus   Fifth-century Alexandrian Greek grammarian, author of the *Hero and Leander* on which Marlowe's and Chapman's poem is based. Until the seventeenth century, however, he was commonly confused with the mythical ur-poet Musaeus, contemporary of **Orpheus**, and by some accounts his son.

Mutina   Roman province in Cisalpine Gaul, now Modena, scene of a battle in the Civil Wars between Mark Antony and Decius Brutus in 43 B.C.

Mya   Chapman takes the name from an ancient Spartan poetess.

Mycenae   In the Peloponnesus. See **Atreus**.

Nar   The river Nera, in Umbria.

Neaera   A nymph loved by the river god **Scamander**.

Nemes   The country of the Nemetes, in Gallia Belgica.

Nemesis   One of **Tibullus**'s mistresses, to whom he addressed poems.

Neptune   God of the sea, creator of the horse, brother of **Jove** and **Pluto**.

Nereus   A sea god, father of the fifty Nereids by the sea goddess Doris.

Nero   Emperor of Rome, A.D. 54–68, notorious for his tyranny and cruelty. Lucan's *Pharsalia* was composed during his reign.

Nervians   The Nervii, a people in Gallia Belgica renowned for their fierceness.

Nilus   The river Nile. See **Evadne**.

Niobe   Daughter of **Tantalus** and wife of Amphion, by whom she had seven sons and seven daughters. She boasted herself happier than Latona, who had only two children, **Apollo** and **Diana**, and ridiculed her cult. As punishment for this *hubris,* Apollo killed all the sons and Diana all but one of the daughters, Niobe, weeping, was turned to stone.

Notus   The south wind.

Numa (Pompilius)   Second king of Rome, renowned philosopher and lawgiver. He established the college of Vestal Virgins, reformed the religion and kept peace. According to **Ovid** he was married to the nymph **Egeria**, though less poetic sources make his wife Tatia, a **Sabine** princess.

Olympus   A mountain on the border of Macedonia and Thessaly, the home of the gods.

Ops or **Rhea**   The daughter of Coelus and Terra, wife of **Saturn** and mother of **Jupiter**.

Orestes   Son of **Agamemnon** and **Clytemnestra**. When his father was murdered by his mother and her lover Aegisthus, he was saved by his sister **Electra**, and was brought up by Strophius, king of Phocis, who had married Agamemnon's sister. With Pylades, Strophius's son, he eventually avenged his father's murder by killing Aegisthus and Clytemnestra. For this he was pursued by the Furies, but ultimately purified by **Apollo**. Orestes and Pylades were considered archetypes of friendship.

Orion   A giant created by **Jupiter, Neptune,** and **Mercury** as a reward for the peasant Hyrieus, who had treated them hospitably and was childless. He was famous as a hunter, and was stellified at his death.

Orpheus   Archetype poet. His music calmed wild beasts and controlled nature. When his wife Eurydice was killed by a serpent, he journeyed to Hades and persuaded **Pluto** to send her back to earth with him, on condition that he did not look at her until the journey was complete. The condition was not met, and Eurydice returned to the underworld. Inconsolable, Orpheus avoided women entirely, and is credited with the introduction of pederasty into Greece. For this he was attacked and torn in pieces by enraged women, the Bacchantes.

Osiris   Egyptian fertility god, brother and husband of **Isis**. He was included in the classical pantheon as the son of **Jupiter** and **Niobe**.

Ossa   A mountain in Thessaly. The giants, in their war against the gods, undertook to storm heaven by piling Mount Pelion on Ossa.

Ovid   P. Ovidius Naso, born at Sulmo, 43 B.C., died in banishment in Tomi, on the **Euxine Sea**, in A.D. 17. In addition to the *Amores,* his *Metamorphoses, Heroides, Fasti, Tristia, Ars Amatoria,* and a few minor poems survive.

Paean   A surname of Apollo, literally "healer."

Pallas   A name of Athena or Minerva.

Pangaeus   A mountain in Macedonia.

Paphos   A city in Cyprus specially favored by Venus. The inhabitants were notorious for lasciviousness.

Parian   From the island of Paros in the Aegean, famous for its white marble.

Paris   Son of **Priam** and Hecuba. He was exposed on Mount Ida as a baby because of a prophetic dream of Hecuba's that he would destroy Troy, but was preserved and raised by shepherds. In his youth he was required to judge among Venus, **Juno**, and **Minerva**, and awarded the prize to Venus. This was universally considered a foolish choice, since it indicated a preference for beauty over power or wisdom. His reward from Venus was **Helen**, the wife of Menelaus, king of Sparta, and his abduction of her brought on the Trojan War.

Parthia   A warlike nation in Asia; Parthia was east of Media.

Pelides   **Achilles**, son of **Peleus**.

Peleus   King of Thessaly, husband of the Nereid **Thetis**, and father of **Achilles**.

Pelion   A mountain in Thessaly. See **Ossa**.

Pelops   Son of **Tantalus**, by whom he was murdered, cut up, and served at a feast of the gods. Only Demeter (or **Ceres**) partook, however, and ate his shoulder. **Hermes** subsequently reconstituted Pelops and supplied a shoulder of ivory. Later, Pelops wooed and won **Hippodamia** by defeating her father, Oenomaus in a chariot race; the victory, however, was gained by bribing Oenomaus's charioteer, whom Pelops killed after the marriage, thus drawing down a curse on his house. He was the father of **Atreus** and **Thyestes**.

Penelope   Queen of Ithaca, wife of **Ulysses**, famous for her fidelity, patience, and ingenuity. During the twenty years of her husband's absence, she kept all suitors at bay by saying she would choose a husband when she finished the tapestry she was weaving. But she undid at night what she had woven during the day.

Peneus   A Thessalian river god who loved **Creusa**, the daughter of Erectheus, king of Athens, and wife of Xuthus (**Xanthus** in Marlowe).

Peristera   The name means "dove"; the figure is Chapman's invention.

Perseus   Child of **Jupiter** and **Danae**, and the prototype of manly virtue for the Renaissance. He killed the gorgon Medusa with the assistance of wings for his feet from **Mercury**, a helmet that made him invisible from **Pluto**, and a highly polished shield from **Minerva**. To look directly at the monster was fatal, but Perseus used the shield as a mirror. He married **Andromeda**, whom he rescued from a sea monster.

Perusia   The ancient Perugia.

Phaedra   Daughter of **Minos** and Pasiphaë and wife of **Theseus**, king of Athens. See **Hippolytus**.

Phaemius   In the *Odyssey,* a superlative musician.

Phaëthon Son of **Apollo**, the sun god. He undertook to drive the chariot of the sun, but lost control of the horses, and was destroyed by **Jupiter** lest he set the world on fire.

Pharos An Egyptian island with a famous lighthouse.

Pharsalia The plain near the town of Pharsalus, in Thessaly, where **Pompey** was defeated by Caesar in 48 B.C. Lucan also uses it as a general name for Thessaly.

Phemenoe Daughter (or priestess) of **Apollo**.

Philippi A Macedonian town where Octavianus and Antony defeated Brutus and Cassius in the crucial battles of the Civil War, 42 B.C. The place was also conventionally identified with **Pharsalia**.

Philomel Daughter of Pandion, king of Athens. Her sister Procne (or Progne) was married to Tereus, king of Thrace. While conducting Philomel from Athens to visit her sister, Tereus fell in love with her and raped her. He cut out her tongue to hide the crime, imprisoned her, and told Procne that her sister had died. But Philomel wove the story in a tapestry and sent it to Procne, who, in revenge, murdered her son Itys and served him up to Tereus at dinner. Tereus's own revenge on the two sisters was forestalled by the metamorphosis of all the figures in the tragedy into birds: Tereus into a hawk, Philomel a nightingale, Procne a swallow, and Itys a sandpiper.

Phoebe A name of Diana, the moon. The word means "bright."

Phoebus Apollo, the sun.

Phrygia The country in Asia Minor in which **Troy** was located. Its chief deity was **Cybele**.

Phthia A town in Thessaly, birthplace of **Achilles**.

Phyllis Queen of Thrace. She was abandoned by **Demophoön**, king of Athens, and hanged herself. She is the writer of the second of **Ovid**'s *Heroides*.

Pierian Relating to the Muses, from Pierus, their sacred mountain, near Mount Olympus.

Pindus A mountain in Thessaly sacred to the Muses.

Plautus, T. Maccius or **M. Accius** (third century B.C.). Roman comic playwright.

Pluto See **Dis**.

Po A large river in northern Italy; its ancient names were Eridanus and Padus. **Phaëthon** was drowned in it when he fell from the chariot of the sun.

Pollux Child of **Leda** and brother of **Castor**.

Polynices Son of Oedipus and Jocasta, and brother of Eteocles. The brothers inherited the throne of Thebes jointly and were to reign in alternate years. But after Eteocles's first year, he refused to resign; and

Polynices fled to **Argos**, married the king's daughter Argia, and raised an army with which he marched on Thebes. The ensuing battle was settled by single combat, in which the two brothers killed each other. They are used as the types of inveterate enemies.

Pompey, Cnaeus (106–48 B.C.). Roman general. He was allied with **Sulla**. He put an end to piracy in the western Mediterranean, and concluded the war with Mithridates. He married Caesar's daughter **Julia**, and was triumvir with Caesar and **Crassus** in 60 B.C. After the death of Julia in 54, he grew increasingly distant from Caesar, and began the Civil War in 49 B.C. He was defeated at Pharsalus in 48 B.C., and though he escaped, he was murdered by one of his centurions.

Pontus   A kingdom in Asia Minor. Under Mithridates IV, it engaged in a long war with Rome, lasting from 88 B.C. until Mithridates's death in 63 B.C. Peace was made with **Sulla** in 84 B.C., but its duration was brief, and he was finally conquered only by **Pompey**, in 66 B.C. Pontus became a Roman province under Julius Caesar.

Priam   King of **Troy** during the Trojan War, husband of Hecuba, and father of **Hector, Paris**, Troilus, **Cassandra**, and thirteen other legitimate children according to Cicero, or fifteen according to Homer. He was killed by **Achilles'** son Neoptolemus.

Progne, Procne   See **Philomel**.

Prometheus   Literally "foresight," son of Iapetus, and brother of Atlas, Menoetius, and Epimetheus ("hindsight"). He was famous for his cunning, and deceived even **Jupiter**, from whom he stole fire to give to men. For this he was bound on a rock in the Caucasus, and his liver endlessly devoured by a vulture. He was released by **Hercules**. He is credited with the creation of mankind out of clay, which he brought to life with divine fire.

Proserpine   See **Ceres**.

Protesilaus   Son of Iphicles and the brother of **Hercules**. He was the first of the Greeks to be killed on the landing at **Troy**. His wife, Laodamia, killed herself when his death was reported to her.

Proteus   A sea god, son of **Neptune**, or according to some, Oceanus. He had the gift of prophecy and lived in the Carpathian Sea, on the shores of which, as he sunned himself, men came to consult him. He answered unwillingly, however, and unless bound, would assume various shapes to escape. He was thus the god of disguise.

Psittacus   A parrot.

Pylades   See **Orestes**.

Pylius   Nestor, from Pylos.

Pyrrhus   King of Epirus, who invaded Italy and Sicily (280-75 B.C.) and suffered heavy defeats at the hands of the Romans. The original

"Pyrrhic victory" in which the victor loses more than the vanquished, was his at the battle of Asculum, 280 B.C.

Quirinus   A surname of **Mars**, also applied to **Romulus**.

Remus   See **Romulus**.

Rhene   Rhenus, the Rhine.

Rhesus   King of Thrace. He marched to the aid of **Priam**, because an oracle had foretold that **Troy** could not be taken so long as the horses of Rhesus were there. But **Diomedes** and **Ulysses** secretly entered Rhesus's camp, slew him, and stole his horses.

Rhodanus   The river Rhone.

Romulus, Remus   Children of **Ilia** and **Mars**. They were ordered to be destroyed by Ilia's uncle, Amulius, but were saved and fed by a she-wolf and raised by shepherds. When they came of age they overthrew their uncle and restored the throne of Alba to their grandfather Numitor. Romulus founded Rome in 753 B.C., and angered by Remus's scorn for the meagerness of the city's defenses, put his brother to death. He populated the city with fugitives, and got wives for them by abducting the **Sabine** women. After forty years' reign Romulus disappeared and became the god **Quirinus**.

Ruthens   The Ruteni, a tribe in Aquitanian Gaul.

Sabines   The aboriginal Italians. The legendary rape of their women took place at a festival to which **Romulus** had deceitfully invited them. Their chastity and high moral character were famous, as were their superstition and skill in magic. They eventually became the allies of Rome, and were granted citizenship in the fourth century B.C.

Sabinus, Aulus   Roman poet, friend of **Ovid**. He composed answers to several of Ovid's *Heroides*.

Salii   Priests of **Mars**, so called from the leaping movements of their dances.

Salmacis   See **Hermaphroditus**.

Santoni   The Santons, a people in Aquitania.

Sappho   Greek lyric poet, born in Lesbos in the seventh century B.C. Though her passions for women were famous, she is said to have thrown herself into the sea for love of Phaon, a young man of Mytilene.

Sarmata   Sarmatia, in modern Poland.

Saturn or **Kronos**   Father of **Jupiter**, whom he attempted to devour in infancy, but who was saved by his mother **Ops**. Saturn's reign was the Golden Age; he was castrated and deposed by **Jupiter**, after which he lived in Latium, reigning jointly with **Janus**, and taught the inhabitants agriculture and the other arts of civilization. He was identified with Time through a late classical confusion of Kronos and Chronos.

Scamander   Trojan river, the god of which loved the nymph **Neaera**.

Scylla   1. Daughter of Nisus, king of Megara. She fell in love with **Minos**, king of Crete, when he was laying siege to her father's city, and she offered to betray Nisus if Minos would marry her. Minos agreed. The prosperity of Megara depended on a single golden hair on the head of its king, and this hair Scylla cut off while her father slept. Minos triumphed, but rejected Scylla, and she killed herself and was transformed into a bird. 2. Daughter to Typhon. The sea god Glaucus loved her, but she scorned him. He asked **Circe**'s aid; she, however, desired Glaucus for herself, and transformed Scylla into a monster. (In some versions of the story the agent of the metamorphosis is Amphitrite). Scylla threw herself into the sea, and was changed again into the particularly dangerous rocks which bear her name, on the Italian coast opposite the whirlpool of **Charybdis** in Sicily. (In some versions, the two figures are identified.)

Scythia   A vast area including northeastern Europe and Asian Russia.

Semele   Daughter of Cadmus and Harmonia. She was loved by **Jupiter**, but **Juno**, in her jealousy, took the shape of Semele's nurse and persuaded her to ask her lover to come to her in his true shape. Jupiter was sworn to grant her whatever she wished, and so complied, but she was consumed by his fire. The child she had conceived, however, was kept for nine months in Jupiter's thigh; it was the god Dionysus, or **Bacchus**.

Semiramis   Queen of Assyria, famous for her beauty.

Sequana   The Seine, and the area around it.

Seres   The Chinese, famous for their silk.

Sestos   A town in Thrace on the Hellespont, opposite **Abydos** on the Asian coast.

Sicilia   Sicily, home of **Vulcan** and the **Cyclops**; its chief gods were **Ceres** and **Proserpine**, and it was from the Sicilian field of Enna that Proserpine was carried off to Hades by **Pluto**.

Simois   A river near **Troy**.

Sisyphus   King of Corinth, famous for his cunning. All authorities agree that he was condemned in Hades to roll a huge rock endlessly up a mountain, but what crime this punishment fits is uncertain.

Sol   The sun.

Stygian   See **Styx**.

Styx   The major river in Hades, whence "Stygian," pertaining to the underworld.

Sulla, L. Cornelius   (138–78 B.C.). Dictator of Rome, 82–79 B.C.

Sybil   See **Cybele**.

Sylvanus   God of the forest. He loved the youth Cyparissus, who was transformed into a cypress tree after killing a favorite deer of **Apollo**'s.

Syrtes   Sandbanks on the coast of North Africa.

Tages   Son of Genius and grandson of **Jupiter**. He first taught the Etrurians soothsaying.

Tagus   A river in Spain said to have golden sands.

Tantalus   King of Lydia, son of **Jupiter** and a nymph, father of **Pelops** and **Niobe**. He was condemned in hell to suffer thirst and hunger in a pond whose waters recede when he tries to drink, and with fruit trees nearby that withdraw when he reaches for them. Various reasons are given for the punishment: that he stole the gods' nectar and ambrosia and gave it to mortals; that he revealed their secrets; that he killed his son Pelops and served the dismembered body at a banquet of the gods.

Tarbel   The country of the Tarbelli, a Gallic tribe in Aquitania.

Tarpeia   Daughter of Tarpeius, governor of Rome. She betrayed the city to the **Sabines** under **Tatius**, and as a reward asked for what they wore on their arms. Instead of giving her their rich bracelets, the Sabines crushed her with their shields as punishment for her treachery.

Tartary   Country of the Tartars, in central Asia, famous for its barbarity.

Tatius   **Sabine** king. He attacked the Romans after the rape of the Sabines, and Rome was betrayed into his hands by **Tarpeia**. He ruled for six years jointly with **Romulus**, but was murdered in 742 B.C.

Taverone   Marlowe's Tav'ron, a river near Rome called Anio in ancient times. By order of **Sulla**, the body of **Marius** was exhumed and thrown into the Anio.

Tellus   Earth.

Tempe   A valley in Thessaly famous for its beauty.

Tenedos   A small island opposite **Troy**, where the Greeks hid to make the Trojans believe the siege had been abandoned.

Teras   The name means "portent"; the figure was invented by Chapman.

Tereus   See **Philomel**.

Thamyris   In the *Odyssey,* a musician blinded by the Muses.

Thebe   Wife of the Thessalian river god Asopus (**Aesope** in Marlowe).

Thersites   In the *Iliad,* the most ignoble and cynical of the Greeks.

Theseus   King of Athens, son of Aegeus. He went to Crete as one of the seven youths whom King **Minos** annually exacted as tribute and threw to the Minotaur to be devoured. Theseus was sent into the

Minotaur's labyrinth, but killed the monster, and returned by means of a thread provided by **Ariadne**, Minos's daughter. They escaped together, but Theseus abandoned Ariadne on the island of Naxos, and returned to Athens. He married **Phaedra**, another daughter of Minos. He was the father of **Hippolytus** by the Amazon Hippolyta.

Thesme   The name is derived from *thesmos,* law. The figure is Chapman's invention.

Thessale, Thessaly   In Greece, reputedly the home of witchcraft.

Thetis   A sea nymph, wife of **Peleus** and mother of **Achilles**, whom she attempted to make immortal by dipping in the **Styx**, or, in another version, by burning away his mortality.

Thyestes   See **Atreus**.

Tibullus   (*c.* 60–19 B.C.). Roman elegiac poet.

Tibur   Tiburinus, god of the river Tiber, and husband of **Ilia** or Rhea Silvia.

Tisiphone   One of the Furies.

Titan   The sun.

Tithon, Tithonus   See **Aurora**.

Tityrus   Traditionally Virgil's name for himself in the *Eclogues*.

Tityus   An enormous giant, son of Earth. He attempted to rape Latona (or Leto), and was killed by her children **Apollo** and **Diana**. In hell, where he was seen by **Ulysses**, his liver was continually devoured by a serpent, or in some versions, by vultures.

Trevier   The country of the Treveri, a German tribe.

Triton   A sea god, son of **Neptune** and Amphitrite.

Troy   **Priam**'s capital, located in Asia Minor near the Hellespont.

Tydides   **Diomedes**, son of Tydeus.

Tyro   A nymph who fell in love with the river god **Enipeus**. She was seduced by **Neptune**, who adopted the form of Enipeus.

Ulysses   The Greek Odysseus, king of Ithaca, shrewdest and wisest of the Greek heroes at the siege of **Troy**. It was he who persuaded **Achilles** to join the expedition, thereby assuring the Greeks of success, and himself carried off the sacred Palladium of Troy. His adventures during the ten years of his return voyage are the subject of the *Odyssey*. His wife, **Penelope**, was renowned for her chastity and fidelity.

Vangions   The Vangiones, a German tribe on the Rhine.

Varro   (116–27 B.C.). Roman poet, lexicographer, and antiquarian.

Varus   The river Var.

Vogesus   Properly Vosegus, the Vosges mountains.

Vulcan   God of fire, the blacksmith of the gods. He created **Achilles'** armor, **Hercules'** shield, **Jove's** thunderbolts, etc.; his forge was in Mount Etna, and his assistants were the **Cyclops**. Though lame and ugly, he was given Venus as his wife, but her adultery with **Mars** was notorious, and Vulcan trapped the lovers in a net and hung them in the great hall of Olympus for all the gods to see.

Xanthus   1. Another name for **Scamander**. 2. In Marlowe's Ovid, an error for Xuthus, husband of **Creusa**, daughter of Erechtheus, king of Athens.

Zephyrus   The west wind.

CLICK ON A CLASSIC
www.penguinclassics.com

The world's greatest literature at your fingertips

Constantly updated information on more than a thousand titles,
from Icelandic sagas to ancient Indian epics, Russian drama to
Italian romance, American greats to African masterpieces

•

The latest news on recent additions to the list, updated
editions, and specially commissioned translations

•

Original essays by leading writers

•

A wealth of background material, including biographies
of every classic author from Aristotle to Zamyatin, plot
synopses, readers' and teachers' guides, useful web links

•

Online desk and examination copy assistance for academics

•

Trivia quizzes, competitions, giveaways, news on
forthcoming screen adaptations

FOR THE BEST IN PAPERBACKS, LOOK FOR THE

In every corner of the world, on every subject under the sun, Penguin represents quality and variety—the very best in publishing today.

For complete information about books available from Penguin—including Penguin Classics and Puffins—and how to order them, write to us at the appropriate address below. Please note that for copyright reasons the selection of books varies from country to country.

In the United States: Please write to *Penguin Group (USA), P.O. Box 12289 Dept. B, Newark, New Jersey 07101-5289* or call 1-800-788-6262.

In the United Kingdom: Please write to *Dept. EP, Penguin Books Ltd, Bath Road, Harmondsworth, West Drayton, Middlesex UB7 0DA.*

In Canada: Please write to *Penguin Books Canada Ltd, 90 Eglinton Avenue East, Suite 700, Toronto, Ontario M4P 2Y3.*

In Australia: Please write to *Penguin Books Australia Ltd, P.O. Box 257, Ringwood, Victoria 3134.*

In New Zealand: Please write to *Penguin Books (NZ) Ltd, Private Bag 102902, North Shore Mail Centre, Auckland 10.*

In India: Please write to *Penguin Books India Pvt Ltd, 11 Panchsheel Shopping Centre, Panchsheel Park, New Delhi 110 017.*

In the Netherlands: Please write to *Penguin Books Netherlands bv, Postbus 3507, NL-1001 AH Amsterdam.*

In Germany: Please write to *Penguin Books Deutschland GmbH, Metzlerstrasse 26, 60594 Frankfurt am Main.*

In Spain: Please write to *Penguin Books S. A., Bravo Murillo 19, 1° B, 28015 Madrid.*

In Italy: Please write to *Penguin Italia s.r.l., Via Benedetto Croce 2, 20094 Corsico, Milano.*

In France: Please write to *Penguin France, Le Carré Wilson, 62 rue Benjamin Baillaud, 31500 Toulouse.*

In Japan: Please write to *Penguin Books Japan Ltd, Kaneko Building, 2-3-25 Koraku, Bunkyo-Ku, Tokyo 112.*

In South Africa: Please write to *Penguin Books South Africa (Pty) Ltd, Private Bag X14, Parkview, 2122 Johannesburg.*

Printed in the United States
by Baker & Taylor Publisher Services